To Pam and Andrew

With Best Wishes

from WARSAW
to WINNIPEG

Stephen A. Cook

Library and Archives Canada Cataloguing in Publication

Carter, Stefan A.
From Warsaw to Winnipeg : a personal tale of two cities / Stefan A. Carter.

ISBN 978-0-88962-937-0

1. Carter, Stefan A. 2. Holocaust, Jewish
(1939-1945)--Poland--Warsaw-- Personal narratives. 3. Holocaust
survivors--Canada--Biography. 4. Physicians-- Manitoba--Biography. I.
Title.

DS134.72.C37A3 2011   940.53'18092   C2011-902126-9

Pubished by Mosaic Press, Oakville, Ontario, Canada, 2011. Distributed in Canada by Mosaic Press. Distributed in the United States by Midpoint Trade Books. Distributed in the U.K. by Gazelle Book Services.

MOSAIC PRESS, Publishers
Copyright ©, Stefan Carter, 2011
ISBN 978-0-88962-937-0

www.mosaic-press.com

We acknowledge the financial support of the Government of Canada through the Canada Book Fund (CBF) for this project.

Nous reconnaissons l'aide financière du gouvernement du Canada par l'entremise du Fonds du livre du Canada (FLC) pour ce projet.

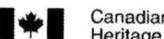

Canadian   Patrimoine
Heritage   canadien

Canadä

And with the support of the Ontario Media Development Corporation.

Mosaic Press in Canada:
1252 Speers Road, Units 1 & 2
Oakville, Ontario
L6L 5N9
Phone/Fax: 905-825-2130
info@mosaic-press.com

Mosaic Press in U.S.A.:
c/o Livingston, 40 Sonwil Dr,
Cheektowaga, NY
14225
Phone/Fax: 905-825-2130
info@mosaic-press.com

I was fortunate in that my family was among a small group, likely no more than ten percent of the Polish-Jews, who were better off and mostly assimilated. My family spoke only Polish. We were deeply immersed in Polish culture and at least some members of the family held strong patriotic sentiments. One of my earliest recollections is being in my bed or crib and looking about a bright room. Painted elephants with colourful harnesses and small boys riding on their trunks surrounded the upper parts of the walls in recurrent patterns. The window opened on the street. We lived in a large apartment on the second floor on Leszno Street 22 in Warsaw. The building was large with three courtyards surrounded by three stories of apartments. My maternal grandfather Jakub Pragier, a short, balding man, owned it. His wife Sara died of diabetes before I was born, but not before giving birth to five children. My grandfather was a gentle man who was loved deeply by his children. He was a lawyer who pled the cases for poor Jewish clients in court, and a member of the Great Synagogue on Tłomackie Street, by which I passed regularly after I started attending school. He was very fond of me when I was a toddler. He might have quit smoking, and as a substitute carried a metal box with small, round, hard candies in his trouser pocket. I knew it, and would touch his pocket and say "Ciu-ciu" to get him to give me a candy. He was also very fond of salt and apparently salted his soup before tasting it. When I was a few years old he developed a stroke and died some months later. Most likely he had high blood pressure, made more severe by his fondness for salt, which led to the stroke.

One of the doors of my room led to a large drawing room that also faced the street. It contained a grand piano on which my mother practiced and played Chopin's waltzes and Beethoven's piano concertos among other music. She studied music and taught piano before I was born and then became a secretary of the school *Spójnia* (Union). She was gentle and loving. I was "the apple of her eye," overprotected and at least somewhat spoiled. She was devoted to her family; she loved deeply her sister Pauline (Pola) and nursed my grandfather during his final illness. After dark, I heard in my room the sounds of music, including that of a piano trio. My father, an amateur violinist, and a friend of my parents Pan (Mister) Józef, who played cello, joined my mother. My music appreciation at the time was not equal to their repertoire and I

Chapter 1
Growing up in Poland

Beginnings

I was born Stefan Andrzej (Andrew) Reicher in Warsaw, the capital of Poland in the late 1920s. The borders of my home country have varied many times over more than a thousand years of its existence. In 1939, the Polish state extended from the shores of the Baltic Sea in the north to the Carpathian Mountains in the south; in the west Poland shared a border with Germany and in the east with the Soviet Union. Poland also boasted the beautiful medieval city of Kraków (Cracow) that was the capital until the seventeenth-century. The eastern parts included Vilnius (Wilno) that is now, and in the more distant past, the capital of Lithuania. Late in the fourteenth-century Poland and Lithuania joined in a union that incorporated large eastern territories that are now parts of Ukraine and Belarus. These eastern territories were lost to Russia as a result of the partitions of the Polish state in the eighteenth-century, and were only partly reacquired by Poland as a result of the war with the Soviet Union in 1920.

Poland is mainly a Slavic nation with the majority of the population being Roman Catholic. Its population was thirty-five million before World War II, of which Jews formed about ten percent. Warsaw was a vibrant city of one and a half million, referred to at times as the "Paris of eastern Europe". About thirty percent of the population of Warsaw was Jewish and the majority of the Jews were not well off. They made a living as craftsmen, many as tailors, traders or small businessmen. They followed a Jewish way of life and spoke Yiddish. Many Jews belonged to orthodox religious groups. Men wore distinctive black clothing and hats. They had beards and sideburns. Their children wore similar dress. Anti-Semitism was rampant and many Jewish children were beaten by the anti-Semitic Polish youth on their way to school.

1

my friends, colleagues, professors, coworkers, and classmates, are mentioned when related to circumstances or events that took place during my life. Many others, whose names do not appear, also played important roles in my experiences.

I wish to thank my wife Emilee and sons Joel and Andrew for their love and support, and for all that they taught me over the years. I greatly appreciate the support and love of my cousin Dr. George Carter of New York. I would not have survived the war if it were not for him and his parents and brother— remarkable people, who play a prominent role in this story. I appreciate the suggestions of Dr. Robert B. Tate, who read parts of the manuscript. I am immensely grateful to Dr. Daniel Stone who read the whole manuscript, suggested many changes and has been of great help by giving me the benefits of his vast knowledge and deep understanding of history. I am very grateful to Mr. Howard Aster and his editorial staff at Mosaic Press, who guided this book to its final version.

I wish to dedicate this book to the memory of the members of my family, who perished in the Holocaust. The world is poorer because they and millions of their brethren were denied the chance to make their full contribution to the society of man.

There appears, therefore, a need to tell more stories of the surviving individuals' experiences from these times. They are all different and there is an urgency to make their stories known, as the number of the survivors dwindles rapidly. Many of the previously published stories from the war-era dealt with the tragic experiences during the war. This account includes my recollections of the rich life we led before war erupted in Poland. It also deals at considerable length with the post-war life in Canada, and illustrates that many of the survivors Hitler failed to destroy were able to establish a new and meaningful life.

In the course of more than seventy years since the 1930s tremendous progress in the sciences and technology has taken place, as well as in my chosen profession—medicine. The medical landscape has changed tremendously in a variety of ways since I began to study medicine and throughout my professional career. The antibacterial drugs sulfonamides first appeared a few years before the war and were followed by the emergence of penicillin and of other antibiotics. Surgical techniques developed during my time make it now possible for the replacement of diseased joints, for bypasses of plugged arteries, and for the transplantation of organs, such as the heart or kidney. The advances resulted in great benefits. Because of unintended consequences, however, new significant issues in medical care have arisen and have not yet been resolved. The new health care systems are accompanied by problems in the delivery of care and in individual physician's ability to spend time with the sick, a factor that is very important because it tends to fragment medical care.

This account is based on my personal recollections, the information provided by members of my family and others, and on the extensive written sources, particularly those concerned with the events of World War II. I am grateful to the Kitzes family, who sponsored me during my emigration to Canada more than half a century ago and opened their home for me; to the University of Manitoba that I had been a part of, first as a student and then as a staff member, for forty-five years; to the St. Boniface General Hospital and the members of its staff, where I was stationed for many decades; to the technologists and other staff of the vascular laboratory at St. Boniface Hospital, with whom I had often spent more of my waking hours with than my own family; and to the granting agencies that supported my research, especially the Manitoba Heart and Stroke Foundation whose grants I held for about three decades. In the story that follows many individuals,

PREFACE

As a youngster in Poland before the Second World War, I was fascinated by geography and studied maps and globes with interest. I drew elaborate, detailed maps before and during the war. I saw the map of the British Dominion of Canada with its provinces that had names, which to a Polish youth sounded exotic—Manitoba, Saskatchewan, and others. I learned that Winnipeg was the centre of the wheat trade in Canada. Little did I know that a decade later Winnipeg would come to mean home, a place where I would the major portion of my life.

This book is my personal "tale of two cities," and of two countries set in the historic context of World War II. I was to travel about forty-five hundred miles west to reach Winnipeg, but I found it surprising that the city, with its much colder climate, lies almost three degrees south of Warsaw. It is also a tale of two epochs extending over about seventy-five years. These two cities and countries differ not only in geography, but also in their social dynamics. Between the pre-war Poland and the post-war Canada, there is a huge difference in the social structure, and the rights, and appreciation of various subgroups of these two societies. Canada is now a multi-ethnic mosaic, and Winnipeg tends to exemplify it best with its multitude of people from all corners of the globe— an antithesis of Hitler's racism. Yet, I also learned that in some respects the two countries were similar before and during World War II. The world of my childhood in Poland was destroyed by the war. The war exacted a huge price on peoples' lives and affected the world profoundly. My family's experiences during the war illustrate some of the horrors of that time. The systematic murder of millions of Jews carried out by the German Nazis was termed "a second original sin" by a Catholic Pole. Yet, large proportions of people from civilized countries tend to remain unaware of the events that occurred during World War II. In 1993 Peter Mansbridge, the anchor of the Canadian Broadcasting Corporation's national news programme, reported that a survey showed that more than a third of Americans believe that the Holocaust might not have happened, and they are not familiar with the names of the death camps, including Auschwitz and Treblinka. The Noble Laureate Elie Wiesel referred to these statistics as frightening.

i

TABLE OF CONTENTS

from WARSAW
to WINNIPEG

A Personal Tale of Two Cities

By
Stefan A. Carter

mosaic press

Figure 1 . My Father Wacław Reicher.

screamed unable to sleep from the noise. My mother had to come quiet me down. The interruptions did not please Pan Józef. Could it be that they played the *Archduke Trio* by Beethoven, which was to become one of my favourite works?

My father was a chemical engineer and worked in a laboratory that was involved in testing related to the sugar beet industry. When I visited him there some years later he performed a miracle. A colourless fluid in a beaker changed to bright crimson when he added a drop of a reagent, then to a pretty blue before returning to its original colourless state. I know that he published a scientific article on the estimation of the temperature of metals from their colour during heating. He loved music and I remember him playing on his violin and whistling the humoresque by Dvorak that apparently was his favourite. He was also very interested in sports, an interest that he shared with me. We attended soccer matches of the club Polonia, of which he was a supporting member, and an international match where Poland played Germany (as I write these words, Poland is playing Germany in Dortmund during the 2006 World Cup about seventy-years later). We followed the fortunes of the Jewish boxers, Shepsl Rotholc from the club Star and Rubinstein from Maccabiah. Rotholc became a national champion in the flyweight division before the war. We watched running races through the streets of Warsaw and during one my father pointed out a welterweight champion boxer Antoni Kolczyński. My father told me that he saw the great Finnish distance runner Paavo Nurmi when he came to Warsaw and ran against a Polish runner Stanisław Petkiewicz. It was a windy day and Petkiewicz stubbornly kept up with the great Finn running just off his shoulder. On the final straightaway he passed Nurmi and raced to the finish line to achieve a remarkable victory. As they fought towards the finish, the crowd very excited, my father heard somebody screaming in his ear. He realized moments later that it was he who was screaming!

Jews in Poland

Growing up I wasn't always aware that my family was Jewish. My realization about our faith took place slowly as my comprehension increased. As a young child my feelings were ambivalent. That was largely related to the fact that we had live-in maids and, when I was toddler, nannies that took care of me when my mother went to work. They were Roman Catholic and talked to me about their religious beliefs. I recall that I felt awkward and uncertain of how I should act when I walked by the numerous Catholic churches on the streets of Warsaw. As I became older I understood more about our Jewish background as a result of talking with the members of my family. I became aware of the existence and importance of Palestine in the aspirations of some of the Jewish people. In a naive way I wondered who should I root for if there were ever a war between Poland and Palestine. At the same time, I was aware that I was Jewish, but it did not affect my life in any practical way, largely because my family was assimilated and not religious. We did not observe Jewish holidays, although one of my aunts fasted on Yom Kippur. I did see little shacks made and decorated by tree branches during the Jewish holiday Sukkoth. I was at first quite unaware of the growing anti-Semitism in the Polish state between the two World Wars and only realized some things about it as the years went by.

The history of the Jews in Poland is interesting. I learned about it mostly only later when I began research on this book. After the collapse of the Jewish state and the destruction of the Temple in Jerusalem, many of the Jewish people who were not slaughtered dispersed westwards over the ancient world, around the shores of the Mediterranean Sea, and into Western Europe. They came to flourish in Spain, but at the same time suffered persecutions in other Western European territories and were slaughtered by the Crusaders. They were expelled from England and France around 1300 and then from Spain at the end of the fifteenth-century. The Jews, who were expelled from Spain and persecuted in Germany and other Western European areas, sought refuge farther east. Those especially affected by the Crusades in Germany began settling in Poland, where Polish kings welcomed them to help with the development of the country. Some Jews were present farther east as early as the eighth-century, likely arriving through Persia and Iraq. Their presence resulted in a Tartar kingdom. The Khazars converted to Judaism in Southern Russia and remained powerful for two centuries.[1]

The first Jewish settlements in Poland probably took hold in the tenth-century when prince Mieszko I became the first ruler of the Polish state in the 900s, and converted to Christianity in 966, which is celebrated as the beginning of the Polish state. Mieszko founded the first Polish royal dynasty of the Piasts. Jews likely lived in Gniezno, at that time the capital of Poland. Protected by the edicts of the kings, the Jewish people flourished in Poland throughout the Piast dynasty. Kazimerz the Great (1333-1370) was the last of the Piast dynasty and one of the most enlightened rulers of the Middle Ages. He was valued by Jews and protected their rights as well as those of the peasants. He was known as "King of serfs and Jews."[2] In 1364 he founded a university in Kraków, which was by then the capital of Poland. King Kazimerz was also said to have a Jewish mistress Esterka.

During the rule of the Piast dynasty an order of the Teutonic Knights, who previously participated in the Crusades, settled in what became Eastern Prussia and started converting the local Prussian population to Christianity. They then began forcing conversion on the Lithuanian people with "fire and sword." The Lithuanians sought protection from their Polish neighbours late in the fourteenth-century that led to a union of the two countries; the Lithuanian Prince Władysław Jagiełło converted to Christianity with the Lithuanian nation, married Polish Queen Jadwiga, and became the King of Poland and Lithuania. A series of wars against the Teutonic Knights followed, but the Polish-Lithuanian forces won their share of the battles and Poland became one of the most powerful countries in Europe. During the rule of the

Jagiellonian kings the Jews fared well. Yet, although Jews found a relatively safe haven in Poland over a few centuries, there were recurrent instances of persecution promoted by some members of the Catholic Church and by the German townspeople who competed with the Jews for urban trade. These persecutions tended to increase in frequency as time went on, especially after the rule of the last of the Jagiellonian kings in the sixteenth-century.

During the seventeenth-century, when Poland was ruled by the kings of the Swedish Vasa dynasty, several disasters occurred. First, the uprising of the Cossacks under Bogdan Chmielnicki massacred thousands of Jews and Poles in the eastern and southern areas. Chmielnicki apparently told his followers that the Poles had sold them as slaves "into the hands of the accursed Jews." The precise number of dead is not known, but the decrease of the Jewish population during that period is estimated to have been at least fifty thousand. Next, Poland was invaded and totally overrun by the Swedish armies under king Charles X. During the resulting "deluge" Jews were massacred by both Swedes and Poles. The Jews returned after the end of the disturbances, but probably lost hundreds of thousands of their citizens. Problems continued during the eighteenth-century under the kings from Saxony. The last Polish king Stanisław August Poniatowski of the Polish nobility inherited a weak state, which became divided among the neighbouring powers of Russia, Prussia, and Austria during three partitions of Poland between 1772 and 1795.

In an attempt to forestall the decline of the state a democratic constitution was proclaimed on the third of May 1791 with considerations of the rights of bourgeoisie and peasants. Legislation aimed at integrating Jews into Polish life was discussed but was not enacted. In 1794 after the second partition, Tadeusz Kościuszko staged an uprising trying to restore Polish independence. A Jewish regiment fought with him. After a fierce struggle that lasted about six months Kościuszko was defeated and the occupying powers ended the existence of the Polish state. After the final partition of Poland, most of the Jews became subjects of the Russian and Austrian states. During the nineteenth-century Polish people staged two major, though unsuccessful, uprisings against the Russian occupier and some Jews participated in them. Although anti-Semitism continued to simmer, liberal trends in Europe during the first half of the century kept it in check. After 1870, however, anti-Semitism increased again.

World War I resulted in the reestablishment of the Polish state. Although Poland promised to protect its ethnic minorities, many of these promises were not kept. The right wing politicians and the Catholic Church promoted anti-Semitism. There were pogroms and mounting restrictions were instituted to limit the educational and commercial opportunities of the Jewish people. Yet, numerous assimilated Jews played prominent roles in the Polish cultural life, including my relatives.

Marshal Jósef Piłsudski governed Poland after staging a coup in 1926 until his death in 1935, and was thought to be relatively friendly towards the Jews. He fought during World War I with Polish brigades under his command on the side of the Central powers, the Austro-Hungarian state, and Prussian-Germany. After his death, however, anti-Semitic policies of the Polish government increased virulently, despite some opposition from moderate factions mostly from the political left. The Polish government actively sought a solution to "the Jewish problem" [3] by looking for places where Polish Jews could emigrate, for example to Palestine and the island of Madagascar, and even discussed the problem with Hitler.

The limitations on the commercial opportunities resulted in severe economic hardships and poverty for the masses of the Jewish people who were not assimilated. [4,5] Those most affected by the poverty were helped to an extent by funds from abroad, especially by the American Joint Distribution Committee, which provided as much as half a million dollars in a year for that purpose.[6] In contrast to the assimilated minority, most Jews lived relatively isolated from the country's Catholic population, used their own Yiddish language, and followed their social and religious ways. Many had a poor ability to speak the Polish language and limited exposure to the Polish culture. At the same time, they often provided a useful service to the Polish population in the form of trade. They made available many items, which Poland needed, in their stores and thus performed a useful function.

Some individual Jewish people were on good terms with their Polish neighbours and willing to help. For example, a Polish veteran of World War II recalled that in his youth a Jew gave him a horse so that he could start farming, without asking for payment except for a wagon of hay as interest. When the Pole saved enough money to repay for the horse the Jew refused the money, saying that the Pole could pay him when he became richer.[7] Although relatively isolated from the Poles, the Jews had several political and youth associations, from communists to conservative right wing parties, and Zionists of several varieties that held conflicting views of whether a Jewish state in Palestine was a theoretical or a realistic concept.

Anti-Semitism was not limited to Poland. It has existed for two millennia and has been referred to as "The Longest Hatred" since it started with Christian Jewish conflicts soon after the beginning of the Christian era. In the late 1930s the virulent anti-Semitic actions of the Nazis in Germany led to the exodus of a rather large number of Jews from that country. The attempts of larger numbers of Jews to avoid the persecutions facing them in Germany were thwarted by the unwillingness of other states to accept them. I was surprised to learn recently that Canada had one of the worst records of allowing Jews to enter its country during this time. From 1933 to 1939 a couple of thousands Jews were admitted to Canada. Great Britain admitted fifty to sixty thousand during that same time.

The ill fate of the ship the SS St. Louis is a notorious example of the difficulties that Jews, who wanted to immigrate, encountered. In 1939, hundreds of German-Jews boarded the St. Louis bound for Cuba, but they were not allowed to disembark. The ship with its Jewish passengers was also refused permission to disembark in the USA and Canada, and was forced to return to Hamburg. Its passengers were thus left to suffer the fate that Hitler planned for them.

Many German- and Austrian-Jews tried to go to the United States. Although a certain number were admitted, larger numbers could not obtain the visas needed to enter. Even though news of the violent pogroms of November 1938 was widely reported, Americans remained reluctant to welcome Jewish refugees. In the midst of the Great Depression, many Americans believed that refugees would compete with them for jobs and overburden social programmes set up to assist the needy. Congress had set up immigration quotas in 1924 that limited the number of immigrants and discriminated against groups considered racially and ethnically undesirable. These quotas remained in place even after President Franklin D. Roosevelt, responding to mounting political pressure, called for an international conference to address the refugee problem.

In the summer of 1938, delegates from thirty-two countries met at the French resort of Evian. Roosevelt chose not to send a high-level official, such as the secretary of state to the conference at Evian. Instead,

Myron C. Taylor, a businessman and close friend of Roosevelt's represented the US at the conference. During the nine-day meeting delegate after delegate rose to express sympathy for the refugees. But most countries, including the United States and Britain, offered excuses for not letting in more Jewish refugees.

Responding to the lack of results of the Evian Conference, the German government was able to state with great pleasure how "astounding" it was that foreign countries criticized Germany for their treatment of the Jews, but none of them wanted to open the doors to them when "the opportunity offer[ed]."

Even efforts by some Americans to rescue children failed. The Wagner-Rogers Bill, an effort to admit twenty thousand endangered Jewish refugee children, failed to win support in the senate in 1939 and 1940. Widespread racial prejudices among Americans—including anti-Semitic attitudes held by the US State Department officials—played a part in the failure to admit more refugees.

Family

My maternal grandfather Jakub Pragier had a brother Stanisław who was a medical doctor and married Józefa Szancer. My mother spoke of their son Adam, her cousin, who became an economist. He must have been a brilliant man. He finished medical studies because of parental pressure but never practiced medicine. He went on to become an economist and obtained a degree of the doctor of law in Zurich in 1912. During World War I he was a member of the Second Polish Legion Brigade that fought with the Austrian and German Armies. He became a socialist and a member of the Polish parliament before World War II. He was a freemason and member of the Kopernik (Copernicus) Lodge in Poland. His political activities lead to a brief imprisonment in 1930. After the outbreak of World War II, he succeeded in escaping to London where he became a minister for the Polish government in exile. During and after the war he published a number of books that dealt with recent historical and political issues. He died in London in 1976 at the age of ninety and was buried at Hampstead. Though married to Eugenia Berke, a lawyer, teacher, and political activist, he had no children. [8]

My mother was the youngest of her siblings. The oldest Heniek (Henryk) died of tuberculosis before age thirty. Next in age was my aunt Pola, a dear sister of my mother who married Dr. Edmund Rosenhauch (Uncle Mundek) from Kraków where she lived with her family. Józio (Józef) the next brother died probably of heart complications of rheumatic fever when he was fifteen. I was told that he would spend evenings teaching young Jewish children of poor families. The second youngest sibling was my aunt Karola, a very beautiful woman. She married Władysław (Władek) Brokman and had two sons. She died before I was born, about a year after giving birth, perhaps of complications of puerperal fever.

Both sisters of my mother had two sons, my older cousins, whom I greatly loved and admired: Zdzich (Zdzisław) Jerzy (George) and Tadzik (Tadeusz Edward), the sons of Aunt Pauline; and Janek (Jan) and Ryś (Ryszard Magnus), the sons of Aunt Karola. Zdzich and Janek, the tallest of all four, were more than twelve years my seniors, and Ryś and Tadzik were younger, though still about seven or eight years older than I. They all visited with us now and then. Their visits were very special occasions and always made me happy. I looked up to my cousins and tremendously enjoyed being with them. My mother tended to serve as a substitute mother to Janek and Ryś when they stayed with us during vacations before World War II. Uncle Władek often sent them to boarding schools abroad. He married a blonde Gentile lady. I remember playing with Ryś with armies of colourful lead soldiers. We set them out on a large table—a 'battle field' and battled for hours. Ryś usually won, but I learned from him and was getting better. I remember Ryś' habit of repeating in whispers to himself what he just said out aloud to me. Though we visited Uncle Władek in his apartment in Warsaw, I did not know him well. I believe that he was quite well off.

I knew Uncle Mundek much better. We visited him and my aunt Pola (Pauline) in Kraków many times. Uncle Mundek was a well-known and a highly respected ophthalmologist and lieutenant colonel in the Polish Army Medical Corps, one of the highest ranks achieved by a Jew. His father fought in the Polish Uprising against the Russian occupation in 1863. Uncle Edmund published many articles in medical journals between 1907 and 1951 in Polish, German, French, and English. He discovered a microorganism in the bacterial flora of the eye, which he told me, was named after him as *Bacterium Rosenhauchii*. Apparently when patients from Poland consulted leading European

Figure 2. Uncle E. Rosenhauch, Białowieska forest, ca.1930.

ophthalmologists in Vienna, they were told that they need not to have bothered because they had Dr. Rosenhauch available at home. He was a jovial man with a short beard, which he was wont to stroke, enjoyed life, and loved to tell jokes. Aunt Pola was more serious, very strict, and highly educated. She expected very high standards of her family and of others. They lived in a large villa, which included a section where my uncle saw patients. There was a large garden in the back with plants and bushes, including berries that my aunt gave to passing children through the back fence. On a ping-pong table in the living room I tried my first strokes against my cousins. Tadzik was left-handed, and he would say jokingly, "Think what I could do if I played with my right hand!" In Warsaw we visited two elderly Aunts Leonka and Gutka, more distant relatives of my mother. They were elderly spinsters,

11

Figure 3. Rosenhauch family, before WWII.

Leonka short, rotund, and jolly and Gutka taller, slimmer, and quieter. They both liked to fuss over me.

From the window of my room I could see abutting our street the short Orla Street that led over cobblestones to Elektoralna Street where my paternal grandparents lived. My grandfather Juliusz Reicher worked in a bank. He was a tall man who prided himself on walking very straight and often admonished me not to slouch. He and my grandmother Dora played cards and counted tricks aloud, though I did not understand the counting because they probably used Yiddish for that purpose. They had four children. My father's siblings included Aunts Stanisława (Stasia) and Maryla, and Uncle Władysław (Władek). Uncle Władek was an engineer who built bridges. He usually wore tall, shiny army boots. Aunt Maryla taught piano. She and other women at the time wore their hair in braids rolled in a bun pinned to the back of the head. Apparently when she let out her hair it reached down to her ankles. Aunt Stasia, born in 1889, was a well-known painter. She married Maksymilian Centnerszwer (Uncle Maks) and had a daughter

Elżbieta. My aunt lived with her family in Warsaw on Hoża Street 49 and we visited them there. Aunt *Stasia* worked in the studio of A.E.Herstein in Warsaw and studied with H.J.C. Martin and E. Renard in Paris. She traveled widely in France, Italy, and Yugoslavia and brought from her travels landscapes and architectural sketches.

Aunt Stasia exhibited her work while in Paris in 1911 and 1912 at the Independent Salon, and in 1912 in the exhibition of a group of Polish artists, which took place in Barcelona. After returning to Warsaw probably in 1912, she participated in exhibitions of various artistic groups, among others in 1913 in the Exhibition of the Societies of Plastic and Young Jewish "Groups" in the Luxemburg Gallery. Her works were exhibited, together with that of other artists, in a huge exhibition organized by the Jewish Society for Promotion of Fine Arts in 1921. She also exhibited the works from her travels in the Salon of C. Garliński between 1924 and 1929.

Figure 4. Aunt S.Centnerszwer, autoportrait.

She was initially interested in portraits, then concentrated on landscapes, but also painted still life and nude models. Her early works included *Night* and *Composition*. Coming under the influence of French post-impressionism, Van Gogh (whom she particularly valued), and formism she used pointillist style and developed a combined approach; characterized by a careful design of the paintings.[9,10] Articles about her appeared in the Jewish newspaper, published in Polish, *Nasz Przegląd* (*Our Review*), one of the leading newspapers of the time. In the November issue 23 of 1929, the interviewer asked her about the situation of the Jewish artists. She stated that the general atmosphere in Poland at the time did affect the Jewish artists, and that they hardly had any contact with the Polish artistic world, while that was not the case in other European capitals. Unbeknown to me, she was approached by Otto Schneid (1900—1974), an artist and art historian, who was gathering materials for a work about Jewish artists before World War II. She wrote a letter in response to his inquiry and enclosed an autobiographical sketch in 1930, which are held in the archives of the University of Toronto, where Schneid spent the last ten years of his life.

Uncle Maks, born in 1889, became a violinist, composer, pedagogue, and music critic. He studied in Paris and Leipzig. He taught singing while in Poland since 1914. His book *Singing* (*Śpiew*) was a required text for high school courses between the two wars. He composed vocal and chamber music works, including "Tristan" and "Ballad" for tenor voice and orchestra. I remember attending a concert of the Warsaw Philharmonic with my parents a few years before the war began at which his composition for a small orchestra was performed. He taught music and was a respected writer. His publications included numerous reviews, as well as essays on a variety of musical topics, including those occasioned by anniversaries of various composers' births and deaths. His writings were thought to merit a collected edition since they provided a prism of the musical life of Warsaw for more than two decades until World War II. His articles appeared in the *Nasz Przegląd* (*Our Review*), in the *Chronicle*, and in other papers. He supported and assisted with the International Society of Contemporary Music, was active in the Jewish Musical Society, and supportive of the Jewish Philharmonic Orchestra. He was asked and became a member of the committee for the 30th Anniversary of the Warsaw Philharmonic in 1931, under the patronage of the President of Poland Ignacy Mościcki, and the honourary chairmanship of the well-known pianist and composer Ignacy Paderewski.[11,12,13,14,15,16]

Early Years

My childhood was happy and carefree. I was an only child and my parents loved me deeply. I think that I was somewhat spoiled being an only child. When my parents went out for the evening I felt insecure and did not fall asleep until I heard the sound of their key opening the front door when they returned. I do not know why but, when I was around six-years-old, while in the master bedroom, I suddenly realized that life was not going to last forever, but that it was finite and that one day even I would die. This realization felt unsettling, but it did not colour my outlook. We obviously were fairly well off and had live-in maids, who cooked, and nannies that looked after me when my mother went to work. We ate well. I recall tasty meals with various soups of which my favourite was borscht with delicious meat filled knishes. The second course would be of meat, potatoes, and vegetables. My favourites were meatloaf that we called *klops* and brisket with browned groats (*zrazy z czarną kaszą*). I always liked potatoes. There were desserts and tea. On one occasion, when I was a little older, my father took me to a winery "U Fukiera" situated at the main square of the Old City district. Colourful houses built in an old architectural style surrounded the square. There he treated me to a small glass of delicious aged Polish mead (honey wine), a drink of the Polish gentry famous for centuries. My health, and that of my family, seemed to be generally quite good.

I was taken to see pediatricians for checkups. The first was Dr. Feliks Sachs, a bald man, who might have been a cousin of my mother. He examined my throat using the handle of a teaspoon as a tongue depressor. I gagged and disliked it thoroughly. He would say, "What kind of a soldier would you make? The enemy would approach with a spoon and you would run away!" Later Dr. Henryk Brokman became my pediatrician. He was a well-known physician who did important work. He survived the war and was honoured with the title of doctor honouris causa at the 25th anniversary of the Warsaw Academy of

15

Medicine. Apart from common childhood illnesses and a mild case of scarlet fever, I had my adenoids taken out under local anesthesia, a very disagreeable experience; and cracked my collarbone when I stumbled and fell while running.

Leszno Street, where we lived in a nice apartment, was a wide and bright street in the central part of Warsaw. From the front balcony off the living room we watched parades occasioned by national holidays and political events, and final stages of the cycling races between Poland and Germany from Berlin to Warsaw. The traffic included horse drawn carriages for hire, *dorożki* and some new taxi cars—the most frequent mode of transportation being red electric streetcars. A smaller balcony off the dining room opened on the first back courtyard where street musicians, violinists or organ grinders, some with a small monkey, would play waiting for small change coins (*groszy*) wrapped in pieces of paper that we and others threw down to them. A block to the west from the gate of our building was Karmelicka Street that originated from Leszno and ran northwards. It was full of crowds of Jewish people dressed in the typical black dress and hats. They spoke Yiddish, which I did not understand. Street vendors offered various wares among which were flat oblong *placki*, a sort of thin baked pancakes. They were salty and deliciously browned. Walking eastwards from where we lived were stores, like butchers, and a store where we would buy a drink *kwas* (different from the Russian *kwas*). It consisted of soda water to which the vendor would add a few drops of a fruit extract that made it into a sort of soft drink. In a bakery we would buy delicious brown rye bread. A few steps further on our side of the street stood an impressive Protestant cathedral in the gothic style. In 1935 a huge solemn ceremony took place there when the British King George V died. Going further east one would pass the Great Synagogue on Tłomackie Street and then reach the Długa (Long) Street. There stood the school *Spójnia*, which I would later attend.

I took piano lessons from my aunt Maryla when I was a youngster. I was very shy and remember playing a simple composition for four hands with her during a recital that she held for her students. She was very kind. Unfortunately my lessons with Aunt Maryla soon stopped and I did not see her again. I was not told at the time that she died, I now think likely because of cancer. I did take piano lessons with other teachers thereafter, but my progress was slow, as I did not seem to have been motivated to practice diligently. I attended concerts of the Warsaw Philharmonic and a Chopin piano competition in 1937 with my parents. A Russian pianist Jakov Zak won the competition; a Russian woman Roza Tamarkina took the second place, and the Polish pianist Witold Małcużynski the third.

We listened to the radio programmes that had comedy revues. The call of the Polish radio was the opening of the *Military Polonaise* by Chopin in A major. We heard and came to know many songs that became popular at the time. Apparently musicologists and musicians of Jewish extraction played a considerable role in the formation of Polish musical culture, including composition of many popular songs during the time between the wars as well as after World War II.[14] Among them was my uncle Maks Centnerszwer. I remember singing "I've a Rendezvous With Her at Nine" ("*Umówiłem się z nią na dziewiątą*") composed by Henry Wars. Artur Schutz was the composer of "Red Poppies on Monte Cassino" ("*Czerwone maki na Monte Cassino*"), one of the songs of World War II most cherished by the Poles.

Warsaw had a number of theatres and an opera house on the *Plac Teatralny* (The Theatre Square), where the City Hall also stood. I recall attending the opera *Straszny Dwór* (*The Bewitched Castle*) by the famous Polish composer Stanisław Moniuszko. In the opera there was a chime clock, which played a catchy tune. Its beginning became a whistled call of a group of youths that included my cousins, which we used during vacations to communicate with one another. Another work that I recall was *Wesele* (*The Wedding*) by a dramaturge, painter, and writer Stanisław Wyspiański. My father often sang a song from *Wesele* "Miałeś chamie złoty róg" ("You had, peasant, a golden horn"). It was meant to be a symbol of the apathy felt by some of the Polish rural populace that contributed to Poland's inability to shake the might of the foreign powers and win its independence before WWI.

We occasionally went to the movies. Originally they were black and white. I saw *Modern Times* with Charlie Chaplin and several films with Shirley Temple. I was particularly impressed with *Hundred Men and a Girl* with Leopold Stokowski and Deanna Durbin. She was a teenager with a pleasant voice and was later nicknamed "The Winnipeg Nightingale" after the city of her birth. I recall another impressive film about Johann Strauss - "The Great Waltz" with a wonderful colouratura soprano Miliza Korjus. Uncle Edmund heard her voice on the radio and then extolled its quality. Later I saw movies in colour, like *The Snow White* and *Tom Sawyer*.

On Sundays I often went with my parents to one of a series of parks abutting on Aleje Ujazdowskie: Ujazdowski Park, the Botanical Garden, or Łazienki (Baths) Park. Close to the entrance of Łazienki stood a monument of Fryderyk Chopin. Large chestnut trees bordered the broad lanes. The chestnuts were not edible, but we used to gather and play with them joyfully. A summer palace of the last Polish king stood on a small island surrounded by an artificial lake with two connecting bridges. At the lake one could rent rowboats and I enjoyed rowing there with my father. Nearby was an outdoor summer theatre, still present nowadays. Not far were grounds where my father took me to see international horse jumping competitions.

We occasionally spent vacation time at a suburban resort, probably Otwock. I recall an incident when I was only a few years old. I picked up a leaf lying on the path in a forest and then dropped it. Later somebody sang a song about a poor leaf that became very sad when a boy discarded it. I was inconsolable and cried bitterly for hours. On another occasion we went gathering mushrooms, a favourite Polish pastime. They were cooked for supper, but my parents decided that I should not have any, probably being concerned that I may not be able to digest them well. I was very upset and, I was later told, cried and screamed for hours.

We frequently spent summer vacations at a resort on the Baltic seaside. We traveled by train, and getting ready always made me feel very excited. In my early years we went to the resort Hel at the tip of the Hel Peninsula, across the bay from the harbour cities of Gdańsk (Danzig), that was made a free city after World War I by the League of Nations, and Gdynia built by Poland after the war so it could have its own port. In Hel lived fishermen and we often stayed with one of their families. They would go out to sea during the night for their catch in small *kuter* boats with a one-cylinder engine. The fresh fish that they brought, such as the flat flounders, were delicious when fried. Also after they were smoked they were used to make sandwiches that we took with us to the beach. A few years before the war, the first bottled soft drinks made their appearance, I particularly enjoyed the orange drinks Al-Or and Or-Si.

The walk to the beach in Hel led through a forest of evergreens. The long and wide beach had beautifully fine and light yellow sand. I built sand castles and played with stones and shells gathered in a small pail. The water was clear and shallow near the shore. Though I could not swim, I would wade a few feet into the water and sit down on the sandy bottom, completely submerged. The rays of the sun played wavy, shimmering patterns on the soft, sandy sea floor around me. It was pleasant to feel cool water in the heat of the sun. The adults talked as they tanned. They used lotions, and women protected their noses from sunburn with green plant leafs. Tall booths made of hard reeds were used to seek shade in and to change into swimming suits. Vendors sold delicious Italian ices and ice cream that was greatly enjoyed. The white lemon ice was my favourite flavour.

At times large passenger ships could be seen on the horizon. We admired the beautiful tall ship, the frigate *Dar Pomorza* (*The Gift of Pomerania*), which served as a training craft for young sailors. We also saw Polish navy ships and were familiar with the destroyers *Wicher* (*Wind*) and *Burza* (*Storm*) each with three stacks, and later the new additions *Grom* (*Thunder*) and *Błyskawica* (*Lightning*) that had one wide stack. At times we found numerous transparent pink jellyfish washed ashore.

A short walk along the beach brought one to a tall lookout tower made of wooden beams called the Stork's Nest. We climbed to the top where the view of the horizon was spectacular. In the evening we would stroll to the small harbour and walked on its piers where passenger ships often docked. There were two smaller twin ships *Wanda* and *Jadwiga* named after the daughters of the Polish President Ignacy Mościcki and two larger ones *Gdańsk* and *Gdynia*.

A bright colleague, Stefan Kraushar, whose mother was a friend of my mother since their school days together, wrote a patriotic letter to President Mościcki, who arrived on one of the ships and handed it to a sailor. No one expected that the letter would be given to the president. It was, therefore, a wonderful surprise when my young friend received a reply several weeks later and as I recall was invited to the palace where the president resided in Warsaw.

Our relatives from Kraków and my cousin Ryś would come as well to where we were vacationing adding to my enjoyment. We carved ships from pieces of bark and used wooden matches for masts and gun turrets. My mother would buy small, painted wooden toy ships for Ryś and me to play with. My cousins played a complex game of states with people—pawns, ships, and imaginary diplomacy. Tadzik had Japan, Ryś Canada, their friend Maryś England, and Zdzich, who was less interested and participated to a limited extent, had Monaco.

I was thrilled to be given an opportunity to join and chose Sweden. In the evenings we would at times go to a nightclub Polonia, where there were refreshments and dancing. My cousin Zdzich was a superb dancer and was followed with envy by the eyes of the crowd as he danced.

A couple of years before the war, we spent a vacation at the seaside resort of Orłowo east of Gdynia. There one day we met on the pier distant relatives of my mother, the Rechthand family (I believe that my mother's family was related to Mrs. Zofia Rechthand). My mother pointed them out as we approached. Feeling very shy, I looked at the parents and their two girls dressed in smart blue suits. The older Genia (Eugenia) was very beautiful with dark hair, whereas the younger Wanda, also pretty, was blonde and had blue eyes. The Rechthands were a rich and influential family in the Jewish community. Mr. Kazimierz Rechthand was a successful businessman. Later in Warsaw we were invited to their spacious apartment where we were served small sandwiches that were eaten with a knife and a fork, a custom I was not familiar with. I followed what everybody else did and that made my mother proud. Despite being ten I did not know yet how to swim and in Orłowo towards the end of the summer I started taking lessons. The weather turned cold and during our lessons we swam in what seemed to be icy cold water.

For winter vacations we went to the Carpathian Mountains including the well-known resort of Zakopane in the Tatra Mountain range. My uncle Edmund co-owned a sanatorium-hotel in the resort of Rabka in the Carpathian Mountains, where we stayed with our family from Kraków. The view of the tall mountain peaks was impressive. In Zakopane, the tall double peak of the Giewont Mountain was the local landmark with its large cross, erected on one of the peaks and easily visible from the valley town. A fairly short drive from the town, up to a higher elevation, was a round lake Morskie Oko (The Eye of the Sea). This glacial lake is somewhat similar in shape to the West Hawk Lake in Manitoba. Steep mountains with snow covered peaks, even in summer, surround it resulting in a breathtaking view. My cousins Zdzich and Tadzik were excellent skiers. I recall Tadzik plotting a strategy for an upcoming twelve-kilometer ski race. I later learned that he used to go on skiing trips from Kraków with a young student Karol Wojtyła, the future Pope John Paul II. I was taking some skiing lessons and tried my skills on easier slopes. In the evenings people skated on an outdoor

Figure 5. Stefan with Aunt Pola, ca. 1936.

rink to music. Uncle Edmund was an excellent skater. When he ice danced with Zdzich or Tadzik people would look with wonder.

One summer we spent our vacation time in Kazimierz on the Vistula River in Central Poland. The Vistula is the largest river in Poland. It flows from the mountainous region in the south through Kraków, northward to Warsaw and into the Baltic Sea. In Kazimierz there are ruins of a castle built by King Kazimierz the Great. It is a picturesque town that has been painted by artists, including my aunt Stanislawa Centnerszwer. I recall that young children of local peasants would sell platefuls of freshly picked wild raspberries to the vacationers for three groszy (equivalent to three cents).

During a couple of summers I was sent to the summer camp of Mrs. Helena Fishaut in the Carpathian Mountains. There, under the supervision of a counselor, we went hiking and played games and sports. I liked wandering in the forest in the shadow of tall evergreens on a soft carpet of brown needles. At times we gathered a variety of mushrooms. After an active day we looked forward to a delicious drink of cold, sour milk, made from unpasteurized milk and similar to yogurt. One game we played was called *serso*. Light wooden rings, made of thin branches, were snapped high and far in the air with a long wooden stick, and the opposing players tried to catch them on their sticks. The word *serso* is derived from the French word *cerceau* that means circle.

21

The game was popular in the nineteenth- and twentieth-centuries and apparently originated in ancient Rome. We had Olympic-style games with different national teams consisting of three members. The sports included running and field events; shot put, discus, and jumps. In the camp I learned to ride a bicycle and shortly before World War II, I was to obtain a bicycle of Tadzik's that he outgrew. At the camp were several of my childhood mates; Mrs. Helena's son Piotr and daughter Ela, Hanka Kon, Alinka Puszett, Piotr Held, Irka, and Stefan ("Wojtek") Minsk who tried to fence with me using the *serso* sticks, which was forbidden.

My early education was in a private group of several children run by Mrs. Helena in her apartment, equivalent to grades one and two. I entered grade three at *Spójnia* School. It was a Jewish school for boys and all of our courses were taught in Polish. We took religion, a class in which, as I recall, we learned the history of the Jews. One could take Hebrew language as an optional course, but my mother thought that it would result in too heavy an academic load for me. My uncle Maks taught music and rehearsed us in singing, particularly of various Polish patriotic songs that we sang at assemblies for national holidays such as November 11th and May 3rd. I came to know many beautiful and stirring soldiers songs such as "We the First Brigade" ("My Pierwsza Brygada"), a song of the Legions of General Piłsudski, who fought for Polish independence during the First World War; and the national anthem "March, March Dombrowski," sung by the Polish Legions who fought with Napoleon. A favourite of mine was "Oh Bloom, My Rosemary" ("O Mój Rozmarynie Rozwijaj Się").

The songs that we learned reflected the strong tradition of glory during the armed struggles over Poland. It began centuries earlier when Poland was involved in many wars and became a major European power, with borders extending far west, east, and north. Polish cavalry was famous and the Polish hussars created havoc in many battles during the sixteenth- and seventeenth-centuries. That tradition continued with the struggles against neighbouring Germany, Austria, and Russia. These countries partitioned a weakened Polish state near the end of the eighteenth-century.

A national hero, Tadeusz Kościuszko, after whom my cousin Tadzik might have been named, fought against the Russians to try and throw off the yoke of the occupation of Poland. The revolt, however, failed. He had become famous because he fought for the independence of the United States from 1776 to 1781. He fought with distinction and attained the rank of general, as did another Polish hero Kazimierz Puławski, who also became a general. The US Post Office issued stamps honouring these Polish warriors.

Polish legions were later formed in France under the command of General Jan Henryk Dombrowski. He was a Polish military leader that fought with Napoleon's armies in various battles hoping his efforts would help to restore Poland's independence. The legions were instrumental in many Napoleonic victories. Furthermore, the common service of tens of thousands of Poles, of all stations and conditions, including Jews, under the banners of French revolution bound together by the slogan "free men are brethren" had produced a deep impression on their modes of thinking, and helped to lessen the social rift which had hitherto separated a nobleman from a peasant and a Catholic from a Jew.

Forever famous in military annals is the Polish charge at Samosierra, the gorge that guarded the road to Madrid from the army of Napoleon. The Spanish batteries of artillery mowed down the French infantry troops one after another as they came within range of their guns. Napoleon ordered a Polish squadron of cavalry to attack. With their usual daring, the light cavalry detachment (szwoleżers-chevaux legers) swept like a tornado through the gorge. Few survived, but Samosierra was taken and the road to Madrid lay open.

Later two unsuccessful uprisings to try and reestablish Polish state took place in 1830 and 1863. My uncle Edmund's father participated in the 1863 uprising. This heroic tradition of fighting for Poland's freedom among its citizens was to continue through World War II. After the defeat of Poland in 1939, a Polish Army of two hundred and eighty-five thousand men was formed within the British forces. The army consisted of Polish soldiers who were taken prisoners by the Soviets, by some that escaped to Britain, and even a few that were originally conscripted into the German Army after they were taken prisoners by the Allied Armies in Europe. They fought with distinction, particularly in Italy, where they took the German stronghold of Monte Cassino after other allied divisions failed. Also, during WWII the heroic Polish tradition endured throughout the occupation in the form of an underground resistance.

The principal of my *Spójnia* School was Mr. Ramberg, whose son Jaś was a friend of mine. I was a good student, but I had trouble with my literary composition. Yet, I read various books including some educational books that my father gave me, like *The Hours of Centuries* about human history and *Brothers from Around the World* about diverse cultures. History was a favourite subject of mine, and I found every period interesting, although I was particularly fascinated by the history of the Greeks. I can still recall verses that we read relating to the Battle of Thermopylae; it was one of several battles fought by the Greeks against the massive, invading Persian armies. A contingent of three hundred Spartan warriors, reinforced by a few hundred of their slaves, led by King Leonidas, heroically resisted a great Persian army in a narrow passage between mountains and the Aegean Sea. Supposedly, after they perished they left a message: "Passerby, go and tell Sparta that here we lie her sons, obedient to her laws to our last moments."

I recall getting a magazine for young people *Płomyk* (*Flame*) or *Płomyczek* (*Little Flame*). These magazines started publication around the time of the First World War and despite some interruptions continued to appear until after 1990. I remember only one puzzle from the magazine and curiously it was this:

$$\frac{K}{A} = ?$$

In Polish, the letter K is pronounced *kah*, the word above is *nad* in Polish, and the letter A is pronounced *ah*, making the answer Kanada, which is how Canada is spelled in Polish! I loved to read from the collected works of the greatest Polish poet Adam Mickiewicz that we had at home among works of other writers. I enjoyed Mickiewicz's ballads and sonnets; among them the *Crimean Sonnets*, "The Ballad of Three Budrys," and "Reduta Ordona," the latter about the fall of a bastion of Polish soldiers during the uprising against Russia in 1830. Mickiewicz was also the best known of the three Polish romantic poets; the others were Słowacki and Kraśinski, thus corresponding to the English trio of Byron, Shelley, and Keats.

Indeed there are some parallels between Mickiewicz and Byron. Mickiewicz, who was born in 1795, grew up in the eastern territory of the Polish-Lithuanian state and considered himself both a Lithuanian and a Polish patriot. He immigrated to France, where he joined

several other prominent Poles including Fryderyk Chopin. In Pari
Mickiewicz became a professor at the Sorbonne. Later he was politi
cally active, and in 1854 participated in the Crimean War where he
contracted cholera and died. Byron also died of disease in Greece in
1824, where he was helping Greece fight for independence against the
Ottoman Empire. While in Paris and homesick for the countryside of
his childhood, Mickiewicz wrote one of the greatest epics of Slavic, if
not world, literature *Pan Tadeusz*, set in 1811 Lithuania. For the Polish
millennium Watson Kirkconnell, a Canadian writer, poet, and professor at United College in Winnipeg from 1922 to 1940, translated it
admirably into English retaining the rhymed verse. [17] I can recite to
this day my favourite passages from *Pan Tadeusz*. It opens with a moving ode to Lithuania [18] (see Appendix 1). Among many excerpts of
great beauty is "The concert of concerts" played by a Jewish innkeeper
Jankiel on a dulcimer, which gives a sense of how Poland's greatest poet
saw a Jewish man as a Polish patriot [19] (see Appendix 2).

One time our school went on a trip to the well-known Białowieski
Forest where a herd of rare bison lived. They were the remains of the
large herds owned by the Russian tsars. We hiked for hours in the forest,
but I do not recall that we came across the animals. Warsaw boasted a
large zoological garden located on the east bank of the Vistula River in
the suburb of Praga (Prague), where my parents took me several times.
There, a few years before the war, a baby elephant was born. A contest
to name it resulted in the choice of the name "Dwunastnica" (Twelfth),
as it was the twelfth elephant born in captivity.

We were interested in collecting single negative film frames from
films with cowboys played by Ken Maynard and Tom Mix. We read
novels; I especially remember the series of books about Indians and
the Wild West of North America by Karl May. The author was a German who was imprisoned during the war, and so he never set foot in
America, but his imagination of that part of the world is truly vivid.
Other books included comedies by P. G. Wodehouse, historic novels
by the Polish winner of the Nobel Prize Henryk Sienkiewicz, a book
about Canada by Arkady Fiedler, and poetry by the Jewish-Polish writer Julian Tuwim. We particularly enjoyed Tuwim's *Market of Rhymes*,
written in a witty style similar to that of Ogden Nash, but perhaps even
better.

After school and on other occasions we went to the large and beautiful Saski (Saxon) Gardens in the centre of Warsaw to play various

games. We played with marbles and used penknives to play a pie cutting game on the earthy ground. One of the games was a variant of hide-and-go-seek, which was almost always won by Peter Held and his girlfriend Irka (Irene). Saski Gardens contained a wooden summer theatre, where I believe that I attended some performances. There was also a pond, with two white swans, that served as an outdoor skating rink during the winters. I skated there with my friends on skates that we attached to our shoes. I recall only one incident in the park when we were attacked with sticks and stones by a youth group, likely an anti-Semitic provocation. The gardens bordered the Piłsudski Square with the Tomb of the Unknown Soldier. During national holidays parades took place there in which battalions of the army and colourful cavalry regiments of Ułans and Szwoleżers took part.

I collected postage stamps, as did several of my peers. Some of them would specialize in collecting stamps of one particular country. I decided to concentrate on collecting Romanian stamps. I maintained my interest in sports, though apart from the summer camps of Mrs. Helena's, it was largely as a fan. There was physical education hour in the gym at school, where at times we played dodge ball, but no organized school sports. At recess we played soccer. We did not have a ball and used an old slipper instead! I had a small book about the 1932 Olympics in Los Angeles by the Polish journalist Kazimierza Muszałówna. It described how Janusz Kusociński of Poland upset the favoured Finnish runners Volmari Iso-Hollo and Lauri Virtanen in the ten thousand-meter race winning the gold medal. He developed blisters on his feet that prevented him from participating in the five thousand-meter race. Stanisława Walasiewicz won the gold medal in the one hundred-meter sprint for Poland. The American fans booed her because she studied in the United States and they thought that she should have run for their country. Another Polish woman Jadwiga Wajsówna won the bronze medal in discus. Muszałówna wrote another booklet about the 1936 winter Olympics in Garmisch-Partenkirchen, the site of Hitler's winter retreat. There the favoured Canadian hockey team was upset 2:1 in the gold medal game by Britain, a team that featured a number of transplanted Canadians. Sweden swept the first four places in the skiing marathon of the fifty-kilometer cross-country race. In various winter competitions Stanisław Marusasz, one of the best ski jumpers in the world, led Polish skiers. He and his brothers competed in various events against the Norwegian brothers Ruud, of whom Birger Ruud was also an excellent ski jumper. In 1938 I listened to a live radio broadcast of the World Cup soccer game that Poland played valiantly against a tough Brazilian side in Strasbourg, France. Poland took Brazil into extra time before losing 6:5.

At one time we took a boarder, a Mr. Waldemar Trenkler, in our apartment on Leszno Street in the far off room where my grandfather had lived until his death. Mr. Trenkler was friendly and showed me various stars and constellations in the night sky. How he made his livelihood we did not know, as he did not go out to work, but apparently spent considerable time going over the Warsaw telephone book. Later in 1938 we moved, without the boarder, to a smaller but very

Figure 6. Cousin Tadeusz
Rosenhauch ca.1938.

nice apartment on Smolna Street 36, close to the broad Nowy Świat (New World Street) and Aleje Jerozolimskie (Jerusalem Avenue) where there were national art and military museums. Aleje Jerozolimskie led through a bridge on the Vistula River to the suburb of Praga on the east bank.

As the 1930s were drawing to a close, important international events were taking place. Germany annexed Austria and entered Czechoslovakia. Shamefully Poland obtained small parcels of land from the Czechoslovakian territory as well as from Lithuania. Meanwhile, I learned about certain manifestations of anti-Semitism. My uncle Edmund was told that he would be made the head of the Department of Ophthalmology if he converted to Christianity, which he refused to do. My cousin Tadzik, a medical student at the time, was subjected to the "Ghetto bench," which meant that Jewish students were assigned specific banks of seats in the lecture theatres. They refused to sit there and in protest stood during lectures together with some Polish students who supported them. Anti-Semitic Poles gave their Polish colleagues who supported Jewish students a hard time, including beatings.

Figure 7. Stefan with Mother (standing) and Aunt Pola, 1939.

I was not aware that the international tensions mounted in the summer of 1939. Poland signed a common defense act with Great Britain. As part of the act, in accordance with the so-called Peking Plan, three of the four Polish destroyer ships, all except *Wicher*, sailed on August 30 to England to avoid destruction by the much stronger German naval forces in the Baltic Sea during the imminent outbreak of the hostilities. These Polish ships were to distinguish themselves in sea battles alongside the British Navy during World War II. The destroyer *Błyskawica* was the only ship of the Polish Navy awarded the medal of Virtuti Militari, the highest Polish military honour. Among other engagements *Błyskawica* participated in the evacuation of the Allied Forces from Dunkirk, and defended the Isle of Wight against a German air strike.

In August 1939 we were spending vacations in the Tatra Mountains in the resort of Zakopane and my aunt from Kraków came there to join us. We went for walks and I played some table tennis outdoors with a colleague from Warsaw, who was also vacationing there. My mother and aunt were very close, and I can remember when we were saying goodbye before going back to Warsaw, that they cried as they always did whenever they parted. This time they were never to see each other again.

Chapter II
The War Years

"Blitzkrieg" and Early Occupation 1939 - 1940

Germany invaded Poland on September 1, 1939. On September 3, Great Britain declared war on Germany. The British Embassy was on Nowy Świat, close to where we lived on Smolna Street. We walked to the embassy building where Polish Foreign Minister Joseph Beck arrived and appeared to the gathered crowd on the balcony with the British ambassador. France followed Britain's suit. In a couple of days, while Warsaw was bombed and many buildings destroyed, special editions of newspapers appeared reporting that French armies broke through the German fortifications of the Siegfried Line— probably pure propaganda.

Polish authorities called on the population to leave the city and to proceed east away from the advancing German Army. Apparently men were going to be mobilized in the east to help fight back. Among crowds clogging the traffic, I walked along a dusty road with my parents. I was eleven then and remember being really scared for the first time in my life, as German fighter planes came low over the road with their machine guns blazing. We were told by the passing Polish soldiers to lie in the ditches by the side of the road. As the gunfire from the planes sounded near, my heart pounded heavily. In the town of Falenica, which we reached in a few hours, the thirsty throngs descended on the general store, but all there was left were bottles of vinegar, which some people drank. We got to about thirty-kilometers from Warsaw and stayed in a small town of Otwock. There was a shortage of food and tobacco. My father who smoked was most uncomfortable and tried to satisfy his craving by smoking rolled up wood shavings.

Polish armies were no match for the might of Germany. They resisted heroically but to no avail. There is a legend, though not well documented, that Polish cavalry supposedly tried to attack German infantry and tanks. A Polish garrison on a small peninsula Wester-platte in the free city of Danzig was decimated. The only available Polish destroyer *Wicher* tried to support the garrison but in vain. In a couple of weeks, German troops arrived in the village where we were staying. We were made to go outside and stand. My mother pushed me to stand near my father hoping that that would make it less likely that he would be taken away. I do not think that Germans took anybody. Warsaw soon fell, however, and we returned to our apartment in the city with some vegetables obtained from local farmers.

Germans carried out acts of terror, killing Jewish people during the 1939 campaign and some members of the Polish intelligentsia. We learned that a German bomb killed our previous boarder Mr. Walde-mar Trenkler. I heard it said that when he lived with us previously, he was likely preparing for the German authorities lists of Jewish people and their addresses from the telephone book. German authorities soon issued orders against the Jews. Signs marked Jews Forbidden, in German and Polish, appeared at entrances to parks and at other sites. Already at the beginning of December 1939 Jews had to wear a band with the Star of David on their right arm that made them obvious targets for attacks by the Germans and anti-Semitic Poles. I was not aware until much later that the Germans brutally started murdering Jews in a haphazard manner already during the 1939 war campaign and continued anti-Jewish measures by carrying out individual acts of humiliation, such as shaving their beards, beatings, and murders on an ongoing basis. They also confiscated Jewish property. At first my family's life seemed to proceed on a fairly even keel, though the atmosphere was uneasy. I would go by streetcar to play with a friend Staś Kopel, but my mother would be anxious when she let me go to my friend's place, as he lived in another part of the city. I took private lessons at home to continue my education at the grade eight level.

Meanwhile, we wondered what happened to our relatives when the war broke out. I did not learn until after the war that Uncle Maks and Aunt Stanisława went to the city of Białystok, which was in the territories occupied by the Soviet Union. My uncle and cousins in Kraków tried to enlist with the Polish Army authorities, but were told to proceed eastward away from the advancing German offensive. They drove toward the city of Lublin. They stopped in the town of Cyców, where many wounded Polish soldiers were trickling in from a battle that took place at Chełmno. My uncle and cousins attended to the wounded in a makeshift hospital. Uncle Edmund and Zdzich dressed wounds and did some surgery, while Tadzik organized the facility and triaged the victims. Then, as the Germans continued to advance, the family proceeded farther east to Lwów, where they came under the occupation of the Soviets. There they met with my cousin Ryś. When the war began he was studying in Switzerland. Ryś was very patriotic and set out for Poland through the Balkans to help fight the enemies of Poland and arrived in Lwów, where he participated in the defense of that city. The Soviet troops overcame the Polish forces and Ryś was taken prisoner. He escaped and was able to make his way through the border to Hungary and then on to France. He left for Great Britain on the last ship from France as the German Army overran the country.

During the winter of 1939—1940 our relatives from Kraków contacted us somehow. My aunt Pauline wanted us to come and join them in Lwów. We did set out east by train to near the border between the German and Soviet occupied areas. There we waited during the night in a barn for many hours to be taken across the border by a guide. Unfortunately, the border was guarded too closely and regretfully we had to return to Warsaw. Had we succeeded in getting through, who knows how things would have turned out for us.

In April 1940 Germans ordered the Jewish Council, which they constituted, to built brick walls across streets to enclose a section of Warsaw where most of the population was Jewish. They issued an order that all Jews move under the penalty of death into the part of the city within the brick walls by November 15, and that Poles living there move out. Approximately eighty thousand Poles moved out and some one hundred and forty thousand Jews moved into the Ghetto, where there were already slums even before the war. That resulted in a terrible overcrowding. A large proportion of the Ghetto population was forced to live with one or more families to a room. We did move into the Ghetto and stayed for a brief spell in the apartment of my mother's friend Mrs. Kon on Pawia (Peacock) Street, which overlooked the notorious Pawiak Prison. Before the deadline we did not know whether we would be able to move freely, leave the Ghetto and come back. The day after, we found that the Ghetto was closed. We could not leave; we were trapped. I remember a very heavy feeling in my chest, a foreboding feeling. Only later did it become apparent what was to come.

Warsaw Ghetto 1940 - 1942

The population in the Ghetto was close to half a million and would increase whenever Germans brought in more Jews from numerous nearby towns, as well as from other countries especially Germany. This further increased the unbelievably overcrowded quarters and left many homeless. The Ghetto was under the jurisdiction of the Jewish Council (Judenrat), which was established on German orders and was responsible to the German Occupation Authorities. The chairman was Adam Czerniaków and Mr. Rechthand was one of the members. A Jewish police force with sticks as their only weapon was formed to help keep order. The members of the Ghetto police came from various backgrounds. Among them were the boxing champion Rotholc and my colleague Piotr Held, who became a junior policeman. The conditions in the Ghetto were extremely harsh. The lack of coal led to extreme cold in the winter and some people froze to death. Germans oppressed the population of the Ghetto in many ways—killed some, took others to camps for heavy labour, but mainly starved them. The food rations were about one hundred and sixty calories per day. Nobody could survive on that.

These realities immediately affected the majority of the population that was in abject poverty. Many turned to begging which was widely prevalent on the streets of the Ghetto. To try and prevent widespread starvation, smuggling of food and of other items was necessary and indeed very active. It took place either through the guarded gates into the Ghetto, with German soldiers and Polish police being bribed or through the holes in the brick walls. The latter was usually carried out by Jewish urchins seven- to fifteen-years-old, many of whom when caught paid with their life. Some pre-war criminals and other unscrupulous entrepreneurs made fortunes from smuggling, wallowed in luxuries, and frequented a cabaret restaurant in the Ghetto. A minority of people had savings or valuables that could be sold to buy food, and others carried on business. Also German businessmen set up factories to make items such as uniforms and munitions for the German war effort that employed Jewish labourers who made a meager living. With the means available to Judenrat and various organizations, social assistance was set up to try and help the majority who were poor. There were soup kitchens and other social agencies. These efforts, however, were insufficient.

Tremendous overcrowding contributed to extreme hardships and poor hygienic conditions. Starvation and disease, with an epidemic of typhus transmitted by lice, claimed many thousands of lives. Corpses lying on the streets were a common occurrence. I remember seeing them being carted away for burial. The starvation, disease, deaths, and an underground medical school which operated in the Ghetto, are thoroughly documented in a book written by Charles Roland, who graduated from the University of Manitoba, Faculty of Medicine in Winnipeg a couple of years after I did.[1] He became a professor of history of medicine and the editor of the prestigious *Journal of the American Medical Association*. Roland was interested in the subject of the prisoners of war and studied the inhumane experiments that the Japanese carried out on their prisoners. One man that he interviewed was formerly in the Warsaw Ghetto. That led Dr. Roland to pursue the subject further. His book documents that over the eighteen months, from December 1, 1940 to August 1, 1942, there were more than seventy thousand deaths, meaning that approximately fifteen percent of the Ghetto population died.

While these horrific events were taking place, a certain proportion of people were better off and other aspects of life did go on. One hoped that the war would end. My parents did have savings, including bonds that my grandfather willed to my mother. My father was working in the supply department of the Jewish Council, participating in the manufacturing of artificial honey from sugar, which was supplied on occasion as an added item to the food rations in the Ghetto. At times he brought home some of the honey for us. We were among those with some means and better off than a large majority of the Ghetto population.

After our initial brief stay in the apartment of Mrs. Kon, we moved into a room of an apartment of a dentist on Elektoralna Street, in a well-to-do section of the Ghetto. We were not starving, although there were some hardships. There were shortages of coal used for heating in the winter. We piled many layers of clothing and blankets on our beds, and would even put a weighty object such as a small chair on top to try and keep warm. Electricity was not available, at least at times. We used carbide lamps that emitted a pungent smell. My paternal grandparents lived nearby. Though they seemed reasonably well at first, my grandfather broke a hip and shortly thereafter died of complications, and my grieving grandmother who became ill with swollen legs followed him before long.

The Rechthand family also lived in a nearby building and we often visited them. They were active in many ways; the daughters were taking English lessons. The Germans authorities altered the borders of the Ghetto from time to time reducing the available living space, which every time added to the difficulties under which the population of the Ghetto struggled. In the autumn of 1941, the buildings on Elektoralna Street where the Rechthands and we lived were excluded from the Ghetto. We obtained, I believe with the help from Mr. Rechthand, a small apartment on Chłodna (Cool) Street.

I spent time playing various games with my friends including Piotr Held, who became a junior Jewish policeman. Although Germans forbade and closed all schools, there were secret schools, and, as I mentioned before, even a medical school associated with the University of Warsaw. It is estimated that at least ten thousand students participated, though no accurate numbers are available. There were also vocational schools that German authorities allowed. The faculty of the medical school researched the biological effects of starvation in the Ghetto. The results were published after the war providing important information.

Teaching in secret schools at various levels took place in small groups of students in students' apartments. I was in such a group taught by the professors of the *Spójnia* School. Professor Zdzisław Libin taught Polish literature, Miss Ewa Tom, who was a friend of my mother taught biology, Professor Kojrański taught physics, and Professor Arnold Kirschbaum taught history. I recall being taught in history that the ideals of Liberty and Equality were mutually limiting, a tenet I came to believe as being very true. The girls and boys were in separate groups. I met new classmates Jerzyk Duński and Stefan Halpern. I was to cross pathways with Stefan more than once in the future. Another classmate became ill with appendicitis. His appendix burst before he could be operated on and he probably developed peritonitis. Unfortunately his treatment failed and he died. His death affected me deeply. Here was a boy just like me who was no more, it was a very difficult and personal experience. Seeing the anonymous corpses lying on the sidewalks was difficult but less personal.

I spent some time with Toporol (the Society for Supporting Agriculture), an agricultural youth agency that made use of small plots of land within the Ghetto to cultivate vegetables in an effort to add to the meager foodstuffs that were available. It even made use of areas of ruins of bombed buildings, where the ground was covered with bricks and mortar that had to be cleared away before planting tomatoes and other crops in mulched earth. Participation in the activities of Toporol was thought to provide youth with training for the future, perhaps for some in Palestine, and led to positive feelings and an optimistic spirit among us. These and other activities were a form of resistance against the oppression.

Underground newspapers were issued, literary works were produced and other cultural events took place under difficult conditions. These included lectures, theatre, and music. More than thirty concerts of the Jewish Symphony Orchestra and more than twenty recitals took place.[2] An eleven-year-old girl played one of Mozart's piano concertos during a concert in 1941. The singer Marysia Ajzensztadt, nicknamed "the nightingale of the Ghetto," participated a number of times. I remember going to a concert of the symphony orchestra with Wanda Rechthand in 1941; one of the works played was the Unfinished Symphony no.8 by Schubert. Our professor of history in the secret school played in the violin section. There were new songs about the realities that faced the Ghetto population, some with new words to the pre-war tunes. Jokes, often of the black humour type, made rounds. One was as follows: "The last two Jews left in the Ghetto meet on the street. The first asks: 'What is new?' He is told: 'Good news! The German offensive was repulsed from the gates of Washington, D.C."

Thus, although thousands were starving, the majority was still alive and the conditions tended to stabilize somewhat by the summer of 1942 as the epidemic of typhus appeared to subside. But at that very time rumours started circulating that Jews from the Warsaw Ghetto were going to be transferred eastwards. The anxiety mounted. Some Jews decided to leave the Ghetto and hide in the Aryan part of Warsaw. One of them was the teacher Miss Ewa Tom. She stayed overnight in our apartment on Chłodna Street before leaving the Ghetto the next morning. At that time the Nazis were well into their "Final Solution," intended to systemically kill all Jews in Europe. After they attacked the Soviet Union in June 1941, and occupied large Soviet territories, special German Einsatzgruppen were dispatched to slaughter thousands of Jews behind advancing German Army. Thus almost 1.5 million people, mostly Jews but also Roma (Gypsies) and non-Jewish Communists, were murdered by the end of 1942.

In occupied Poland, the Germans also began Operation Rheinhard in which Jews were murdered in the gas chambers of death camps, beginning in December 1941 in Chełmno. Beginning on July 22, 1942, they ordered transports out of the Warsaw Ghetto with Jewish people loaded in cattle cars at a railway siding in the northern part of the Ghetto, which became known as the Umschlagplatz (literally—distribution place). We were told that people were being moved to work in camps, but there were rumours that the truth might be worse. People employed in the German factories and by the Jewish Council were at first exempted from the deportations. Panic gripped the Ghetto as crowds ran around trying to find a place of employment. I recall meeting briefly a very disturbed friend Andrew Lubelczyk. He was running to try and find a place that would spare him from a transport. He was a son of a medical doctor. Before the war he was unusually afraid of thunderstorms and would run to hide under a bed when he would hear thunder rumble. I recall another scene, probably from that period of time. I was helping in an office, perhaps on Leszno Street, likely at the behest of Mr. Rechthand. It might have been an office related to the Judenrat or a German factory, where the vital certificates of employment were being issued. Crowds of people pushed against the entrance doors. It was my function to let them in a few at a time. It was most difficult to stem the pressing mass of people. I recall a professor from my secret school among the throng.

The chairman of the Jewish Council, Adam Czerniaków committed suicide when Germans demanded that he sign an order for the transports of thousands of children and other inhabitants from the Ghetto. Yet transports proceeded. First the poor and homeless were taken, then the sick from hospitals, and people who could not find a valid work certificate. The poor and hungry were enticed to volunteer for the transports by offers of bread and marmalade. Dr. Janusz Korczak, born Henryk Goldschmidt, a world famous writer and pedagogue, led his whole orphanage, of which he was in charge, to the trains. Offered a safe sanctuary outside the Ghetto, he refused and stayed with the children. He led them with his coworkers, some of whom were also offered a refuge, in an orderly way keeping up the children's spirit. Germans conscripted Jewish police to bring fellow Jews to Umschlagplatz, resulting in tragic situations and scenes hard to imagine.

My father, attached to the Jewish Council's supply department, had to live near his workstation in another part of the Ghetto than my mother and me. Mr. Rechthand again helped by arranging that my mother and I become attached to a German factory in the area of the

Smocza and Nowolipki Streets. I believe that it was a textile enterprise owned by a German businessman Schultz. The Rechthand family was there too with Mr. Rechthand's sister and her husband. My function was that of an office gopher. We lived in an apartment on Smocza Street close to the factory. Since a large proportion of the population of the Ghetto was by then taken away, the apartments were more readily available. Also, by then apparently the horrible fate of the people taken away in the transports began to be slowly recognized, though some would not believe it.

The trains from the Warsaw Ghetto with three hundred thousand to four hundred thousand Jews went to the gas chambers of the death camp of *Treblinka* northeast from Warsaw, leaving perhaps sixty thousand alive in the Warsaw Ghetto for another few months. Jews died in gas chambers between July 22 and late September of 1942. Though I was very scared, I was not aware of the truth at the time. While we were at the German factory my mother became very ill probably with dysentery. She lost a tremendous amount of weight and was just skin and bones. I tried to take care of her; the doctor who saw her recommended treatment with intravenous glucose injections. I ran through then deserted Ghetto streets to a pharmacy and bought ampoules of glucose, which the doctor then administered to my mother.

In the first week of September an order came that everybody from ours, and other factories, was to go under the penalty of death to Umschlagplatz. The day was Sunday September 6, 1942, and that day's German action was referred to as "the cauldron." My mother was very weak and emaciated, but she bravely summoned all her strength, got dressed and put on lipstick in an attempt to look as well as possible in order to try and avoid deportation. The sun was shining. It was a warm day. We walked together among crowds along Smocza Street toward Umschlagplatz supervised by German SS men and Jewish Ghetto policemen. I remember a Jewish policeman reporting to a German SS man repeating "Jawohl Herr Commandant!" (Yes Mister Commander!) as the German repeatedly slapped his face. We arrived at the entrance to the Umschlagplatz, which, from the entrance, appeared to me like a large green field. At the entrance stood an SS man who motioned people individually to the left, to the area of the trains or to the right, from where one would return to one's work place. My mother was motioned to the left and me to the right. We looked at each other and then had to move on. I never saw my mother again.

The action of "the cauldron" resulted in over fifty thousand people going to their deaths in Treblinka or in a number of cases dying on the way to the camp, suffering horribly dehumanizing conditions without food, water or basic hygienic facilities such as toilets.[3]. By the end of September only about sixty thousand of the original half a million population remained in the Ghetto, about half "legally" working for the German factories or for the Jewish Council and the other half stayed illegally in hiding. Among the victims were many fine musicians. Tragically, the vast majority perished in the ovens of the Treblinka death camp. What remains of their lives is their music—folk melodies, classical and popular music, and recordings that bear witness to the Jewish musical culture, and the Jewish and Polish music, which they had created with a sense of belonging to the people among whom they had lived for centuries.[4]

I returned to where we lived near the factory. Mr. Rechthand was there but his wife and sister-in-law were detained at Umschlagplatz with my mother. It was possible at times to get people back from Umschlagplatz by bribes, using American dollars. Mr. Rechthand succeeded in getting his wife and sister-in-law out, but not my mother. I am sure it was not for lack of trying; my mother looking feeble from illness might have made the task impossible. I was devastated and depressed. I felt hopeless, sick, and unable to go to work. I begged Mr. Rechthand to issue me a certificate that I was sick and thus could stay off work. He likely had limited authority, but reluctantly complied with my request. After a day or so I resumed my work duties. I struggled over the next few weeks and tried to carry on.

During October I received a telephone call at work from the Aryan side of Warsaw. Thinking about it now it may seem surprising that telephones were operating in the Ghetto at such time. They did operate because there had to be communication between the German and Ghetto authorities and certainly with the German factories. Mr. Rechthand might have aided my receipt of the call. On the other end of the line I was surprised to hear the voice of my cousin Tadzik Rosenhauch, who before the war lived in Kraków with his family that included my mother's sister, Aunt Pauline (Pola). I had no idea that he was in Warsaw. How he was able to track me down I do not know.

When the war broke out my uncle with his wife Pola and sons Zdzich and Tadzik had proceeded eastward to Lwów, controlled under the Soviet occupation. Zdzich worked in an eye clinic as an ophthalmologist. They were there when Germany attacked Russia and overran Lwów and Ukraine in 1941. Soon they set out northward toward the Baltic Sea intending to get to neutral Sweden and then on to Great Britain. They got as far as the vicinity of Vilnius and found that it was too dangerous to proceed further and returned to Lwów.

The dangers to Jews were mounting. A grateful patient of cousin Zdzich gave him her husband's original documents, as her husband was deported to Siberia. Tadzik obtained false Aryan documents and they both went to Warsaw where they contacted friends they knew from before the war that helped them find a safe place to live and work. Meanwhile, my aunt and uncle decided to go to the Ghetto in Wieliczka, a town near the famous salt mines, close to Kraków. In 1942 the Germans imprisoned my uncle, a well-known eye doctor, in the notorious Montelupich Prison in Kraków for close to two months. He told me after the war that while in prison he was ordered to take care of an eye problem of a high-ranking German official. His sons, already in Warsaw, heard that he was in prison. They asked a friend Ms. Zofia Mroszczak to go to Kraków with a fine diamond they gave her to bribe the German officials to let my uncle go. He was released and then was in the Ghetto in Kraków. He escaped by jumping from a slowly moving streetcar going around a turn near the outskirts of the Ghetto. Thereafter he and my aunt went to Warsaw and remained there and in its vicinity hidden through the rest of the war, including a period of time in a cloister. They had close calls, were blackmailed by unscrupulous Poles, but also greatly helped by other Righteous Poles.

On the telephone my cousin asked me about my mother and I told him the sad news. My cousin and Mr. Rechthand were able to arrange for me to leave the Ghetto and to meet Tadzik on the Aryan side on a specific day. My father, still in the Ghetto, did not want to leave for the Aryan side. He was apprehensive since he had a very Semitic appearance. Before leaving, I went through the empty streets to say goodbye to him in another part of the Ghetto where he was staying. He told me that a friend of his committed suicide by taking cyanide before being taken by the Germans. That apparently was common among Jews at that time, if they were able to obtain the poison. My father and I parted never to see each other again.

I left the Ghetto early one morning with a party of workers, several of which left the Ghetto daily to work on the Polish side and returned to the Ghetto after work. We marched in formation through the

Ghetto gate and then through the streets outside the Ghetto, which I saw for the first time in two years. We arrived at a carpentry workshop on Królewska (King's) Street across the street from the Saski Gardens where I played often before the war. There appeared to be no guards and nobody was paying any attention to me. I walked out carrying my winter coat wrapped in a package under my arm and walked slowly along Królewska Street toward the Square of Marshal Pilsudski. There I entered a small café, the arranged meeting place. I saw my cousin Tadzik at a table with another young man whom I did not know. I walked up to them. After a casual matter-of-fact greeting I had a cup of tea and then we left. I learned later that the other man was a member of the Polish Underground Army and had a revolver, in case I was followed.

In Hiding 1942-1945

My cousin first took me to a movie, where it was dark so that my Semitic face could not be seen. It was dangerous for Jews with Semitic facial features to be seen in daylight because anti-Semitic Poles were good at recognizing them. They would blackmail Jews or turn them over to the German authorities. Then we went to the apartment on Łęczycka Street in the Ochota district of the city where he and his older brother, Zdzich, lived with a Polish family, Mrs. Zofia Herfurt and her daughter Hanka who was nearly finished with her medical studies. They were extremely helpful to us and I stayed there overnight. The next evening, Zdzich took me to another place in the suburb of Praga, on the other side of the Vistula River. We walked through the streets and over the bridge in darkness on purpose, because of my curved Semitic nose that was potentially dangerous, as I might have been noticed by anti-Semitic blackmailers.

I stayed with a Polish family at the apartment in Praga for some weeks. I think that there were other places to which I was then transferred for relatively brief periods of time. The reasons why the transfers were necessary I do not recall or might not have been told. The arrangements, which my cousins made for me, took a lot of doing and money and undoubtedly saved my life. The funds, I believe, came in part from the earnings of my cousins and in part from the savings, which their parents, my aunt Pola and uncle Edmund, had from before the war. During my time of hiding in the Aryan Warsaw I had false documents, a Kennkarte and an assumed name. My cousins obtained the false Aryan papers for me. I do not recall the official story of my assumed life. My cousins told me to learn Polish Catholic prayers, how to cross oneself and I did so. That was very important in case officials should question me.

Among the places where I stayed between 1942 and 1944, my longest and best was at the apartment of Miss Zofia Różycka who lived with her elderly mother in one of the Warsaw's suburbs. I stayed with her for more than a year. Her brother, whom I met when he visited, served as a Polish Consul in New York before the war. He told us of being exposed to the comic strips in the New York newspapers. Initially he felt they were childish, but with time came to read them regularly.

I had a nice room where I spent most of my time. In my room was a bookcase filled with complete works of Moliére translated into Polish by the talented Polish physician and poet Tadeusz Boy-Żelenski, who was murdered in Lwów in 1941 by a Ukrainian military group together with other Polish intellectuals after Germans overran that city. I read all the Moliére's works to fill the time. Because of my Semitic appearance I could not go out and stayed throughout my sojourn with Miss Różycka at her apartment.

Miss Różycka was a very kind, intelligent, and understanding lady. She brought books from a lending library for me to read. She returned them and brought me others and continued doing this throughout my stay. I also spent many good hours discussing all kind of subjects with her and her friend Mr. Witold who was a very bright and intelligent man. He was about sixty but seemed to be in great shape and looked more like a forty-year-old person. During that time, through my discussions with them and extensive reading, I became aware of various issues and realized that for the first time in my life I was thinking. I stopped being a child. I recall that I started taking stock of what transpired and what I was able to achieve over the previous years on my birthdays. During the time when I was in hiding, I corresponded with my aunt who was also in hiding. My cousin Tadzik served as a messenger, as he was blonde and had a better non-Jewish appearance than his brother Zdzich. My aunt saved some of my letters and I was surprised to read them more than sixty years later as I forgot largely their content. The following excerpts in my English translation provide an insight into the way I lived and felt at that time.

Dear Auntie,

Many thanks for your letter. You are right that the most important thing now is to fill one's time and I cope as well as I can. Recently I finished going through my material in biology and physics and to take its place I started reading *Chemistry in Daily Life* by Lassar-Cohn, which is a set of interesting lectures, as well as *The Mechanism of Human Life* by Dorsey, which deals with biology. I tend to think that I would like to become a chemist; i.e. if one could not be a general or an officer in the navy. Chemistry, apart from being quite interesting, tends to overlap and branch into two very interesting fields, namely physics and biology. Yet my interests tend to change, and are at present wide and flexible. Among the prescribed curriculum I worked through the works of Kochanowski (*Jan K. – Polish poet of the 16th century*) including *Satyr, Trifles, Laments,* and *The Dismissal of the Greek Messengers.**

As I am bored, I intend to write an essay "English Society in the Light of Modern Literature". I am gathering material reading Chesterton, Smith, Huxley, and Galsworthy among others. I finished reading Dickens in French and now am reading *La craiserie du hachich*. It is a description of adventures in Africa and the Mediterranean Basin. Since I find it pretty hard with many new words, my progress is slow. I found the book by Lati biased as he made Germans seem diabolical and the French people saintly. I read works by Fiedler, but my favourite book was *The School of Eaglets* by Janusz Meissner about Polish air force training.

---

* I still know by heart Kochanowski's poignant poem about health:

Szlachetne zdrowie,	Bo dobre mienie,	Dobre są,
Nikt się nie dowie,	Perły, kamienie,	Ale,
Jako smakujesz,	Także wiek młody,	Gdy zdrowie wcale.
Aż się zepsujesz.	I dar urody,	

Author's translation:

Noble health,	For good fortune,	Are fine,
None will know,	Pearls, precious stones,	But only,
How you taste,	Likewise young age,	If health is whole.
Until you fail.	And personal beauty,	

I recently read a book I can heartily recommend. It is one of the best books I read—Alfred Neumann's *New Cesar* and the second part *The Second Cesar State* (*Kaiserreich*)—an account of Napoleon III, from his birth to his death. It is excellently written and presents well the epoch of that time. The histories of the French Revolution and of the Napoleonic era are the times that I know and like the best. Yet studying and reading cannot fill the time completely, so I have to think of other endeavours. I play various war games; imaginary sport matches, and now began making ships from tree bark, which I paint. A ship for you is ready, but I have not sent it, because of fear that it might get damaged in transit. It is a sort of model of *Hood* made from wooden matches. *Hood* was a super-cruiser and the pride of the British fleet, which was sunk by a shot from the German battleship *Bismarck* early during the war. The British fleet then chased and sank *Bismarck*. One of the new Polish destroyers participated in the chase. I do some simple calisthenics as I think that one needs to do something to make up for the general lack of exercise. If weather permits I try to take some sunbaths, because of what I read in De Kruif's *The Struggle of Science with Death*. Studying Latin is quite possible, but only if one does it systematically. In the seventh grade, when our principal taught me, I knew the subject as well as my own pocket and I was one of the best students in our class. However, afterwards I developed gaps, which I am unable to overcome. Many kisses for Uncle. Does he remember our joke?

> Many hearty kisses to you,
> Your nephew

* * * *

A painful event took place during my stay with Miss Różycka. The uprising in the Ghetto erupted in April 1943. The smoke from the burning Ghetto spread over Warsaw. I sadly knew that my father likely was still there, but I could not do anything about it. I never found out what happened to my father. About five hundred to one thousand mostly young

Jewish fighters decided to fight and die rather than go passively to their deaths. They fought heroically against overwhelming odds. They had few weapons, mostly pistols, some Molotov homemade grenades, and a few rifles. These were procured by purchases on the Aryan side and a meager number of small firearms reluctantly provided by the Polish underground forces that refused to get involved in any practically effective way in the Jewish struggle.

The Polish underground was not sympathetic and did not want to commit to a major intervention, which they felt would weaken their future military actions. There is a report of one failed attempt at breaching the Ghetto wall by a detachment of the Polish underground.[5] Indeed, when I visited Poland in 1988, I met a Gentile lady who told me about such an action and lent me a book that I read in which an incident consistent with the above report was described. In it two Polish fighters ran up to the wall of the Ghetto and placed a mine on it in an attempt to blow a hole in it, while other members of the unit were covering them. A superior German force, however, repelled the attempt and wounded some of the Polish fighters. The lady's husband, whose code name, I believe, was Kret participated in the skirmish.

Despite few arms, the Jewish Ghetto fighters exacted on the Germans unexpected setbacks and casualties. The Germans then started burning the Ghetto building by building and the battle ended with the Ghetto left completely in ruins. Sporadic fighting continued for several weeks. Most of the fighters perished, including their Commander Mordechai Anielewicz. A small number escaped mostly through the sewers to the Aryan side and some survived the war in hiding or in the partisan units in the forests. Among the survivors was the second in command in the Ghetto, Marek Edelman, who became a cardiologist after the war. The Warsaw Ghetto Uprising was the first organized urban resistance in Nazi occupied Europe and other outbreaks of resistance followed. These included outbreaks in the Białystok Ghetto and in the death camps of Treblinka, Sobibor, and Auschwitz. There were also many Jews in partisan units in the forests of Poland, Lithuania, and Belarus who participated in resistance and sabotaged German war efforts by blowing up railway lines and in other activities. The significance of the Warsaw Ghetto Uprising can be gleamed from the words printed in a New York leaflet on occasion of the 50th anniversary of the uprising in 1993:

Half a century ago the world stood mute during the most unspeakable event in history—the cruel and systematic murder of six million innocent men, women and children. While the German Nazi Holocaust consumed its victims, while Jews were herded into Ghettos and concentration camps and brutally starved, gassed and burned, the nations of the world remained silent.

Then, in April 1943, came an outcry from the Warsaw Ghetto as the Jews rose up against their German oppressors.

In the weeks and months that followed this first organized civilian resistance in Nazi Europe, courageous Jewish men and women, boys and girls, gave new meaning to heroism and self-sacrifice. Facing certain death, they repelled wave after wave of Nazi attack. The walls crumbled, food and water and ammunition ran out, flames turned the Ghetto into an inferno. Still they fought. And the words Warsaw Ghetto Uprising were inscribed with blood onto the pages of Jewish history.

In the end, nothing remained of the Ghetto but smoke and rubble. But the courage and daring of those Jews who fought the Germans fifty years ago echo down the years. They demand that we living, the generation that lived through the horrors of the Holocaust—and all the generations to come—remember, record and teach its lessons.

So that the world will not forget the suffering and martyrdom of those who perished in those tragic days. And, as we gather to remember, so that mankind will never know another Holocaust.

Thus, the Warsaw Ghetto was no more. Perhaps two thousand to three thousand Jews remained hiding in the ruins and some might have survived. Also, it is often not realized that a minute "official" Jewish presence continued after the destruction of the Ghetto. It consisted of a hundred to a hundred and fifty Jewish workers in the Pawiak Prison, which stood within the Ghetto borders and was used by the Germans.[6] The Germans used the prison to bring Jews there who were caught hiding on the Aryan side of the city, and large numbers of Polish people. The prisoners were executed in the nearby ruins of the Ghetto. An estimated eight thousand Jews, including the visionary historian Emmanuel Ringelblum, lost their life there. Ringelblum headed the underground Jewish Archives in the Ghetto. Important documents on the life and events in the Warsaw Ghetto, which they compiled, were hidden in sealed milk cans, two of which were recovered from the ruins after the war. The Germans destroyed the infamous prison together with most of the city of Warsaw after the collapse of the Polish Warsaw Uprising in 1944. Another small group of Jews survived with many Polish inmates after the destruction of the Ghetto within its borders in the so-called Warsaw concentration camp established by the Germans in October 1943 on Gęsia Street at the site of a former prison.[7] About a hundred and twenty Jews regained their freedom there, liberated by the fighters of the Warsaw Polish Uprising in August 1944. Some joined the struggle against the Germans and fought with distinction.

* * * *

One or two neighbours, who lived in the same apartment block, visited Miss Różycka on occasion and met me. One day in 1944, two Polish policemen arrived, came into my room early in the morning, and said that I should get dressed and go with them to the police precinct. When, terribly scared, I pleaded being sick they told me to drop my pajama trousers. I murmured with a reassuring tenor something to the effect, "Oh, is that what this is all about?" and lowered my pants. They looked and without saying much left! Undoubtedly my life was saved because my father in a prescient moment refused to allow me to be circumcised when I was born, perhaps because of concern for my pain or esthetic feelings. It became obvious that one of Miss Różycka's neighbours informed the police and thus it was not safe for me to stay with her any longer.

She notified my cousin Tadzik. He and his family made arrangements and he soon arrived and took me to a clinic. There, a specialist operated, under local anesthetic, on my curved nose and made it straight. I learned after the war that facial surgery and plastic surgery to create foreskin on the penis were performed during these times to improve the chances of survival in Jewish people who were in hiding as Aryans. After a few days, when the bruising about my nose subsided, I left the clinic. My cousins found a room for me to live with a Polish family, who did not know that I was Jewish. For the first time since leaving the Ghetto, I was able to move freely, went out and seemed to live the life of a Polish youth in Warsaw. I always felt some anxiety that I might get caught or exposed, but I was able to deal with it and maintained a relaxed, matter-of-fact air about me that was essential.

One day while walking on a broad street I saw walking towards me a young girl who was one of my peers from the pre-school years before the war, Ela Fishaut. We stopped, at first awkwardly, and said hello and talked for a few minutes. She told me where she lived with her mother, Mrs. Helen Fishaut, who ran the private group school and summer camps before the war, and invited me to visit. I did and we talked, particularly about people we knew.

I believe it was there that I learned that Wanda Rechthand the bright young daughter of Mr. Rechthand, who was of so much help to my family and me, did leave the Ghetto and lived on the Polish side. Another of the young girls we knew, who might have lost her parents, also wanted to leave the Ghetto and the Rechthands helped her leave. Unfortunately she was caught after she was on the Aryan side for some time. The Germans undoubtedly threatened or tortured her. She apparently was with them when they came and took Wanda and both were not heard from since; most likely they were executed near the Pawiak Prison in the Ghetto. Mr. Rechthand and his beautiful older daughter Genia were also caught and killed, just a few days before Warsaw was liberated in 1945. Only Mrs. Rechthand was to survive the war. I learned that there is a symbolic grave of Mr. Rechthand and his two daughters in the Jewish Cemetery in Warsaw. When I mentioned to my cousins my encounter and visit with the Fishauts, they said that it was potentially dangerous and that I was not to contact them again. Indeed I did not see even my cousins often for that reason.

By the summer of 1944 the tide of war had already turned. The German Army that in 1941 and 1942 reached deep into the Soviet territory was retreating and the advancing Soviet Army arrived not far from Warsaw. Late in the afternoon of August 1, I was walking home and met by chance my cousin Zdzich. He was still living in the same apartment in which I stayed the first night after leaving the Ghetto. I lived in the same district not far from the Narutowicz Square. There seemed to be some excitement in the air. We parted and I went home. Soon the news spread that the Polish Underground Home Army (Armia Krajowa or AK) started uprising and was taking control of Warsaw from the German Army.

The uprising lasted until October 2 when the Polish command surrendered after approximately eighty-five percent of Warsaw was completely destroyed and after more than two hundred thousand Poles including some Jews died in the uprising. The uprising failed as the Soviet Army offered little or no help. A detachment of the Polish soldiers, who fought with the Soviet Army temporarily crossed the Vistula River and connected briefly with the insurgents, but could not hold their positions. Politics were involved in the power play between the Soviets and the Polish Underground Army loyal to the Polish government in exile in London. Attempts to help the overmatched Polish forces were also made by dropping of weapons and supplies from Allied airplanes, which flew over Warsaw from far away fields in Western Europe. Their task was made very difficult, because the Soviets refused to allow them to land in the territories that they controlled nearby. Among them were Canadian pilots, some apparently were shot down and their sacrifice is acknowledged. The uprising in 1944 resulted in nearly complete destruction of the beautiful city. The political situation, likely fed by the historic Polish fighting tradition, led to the decision of the Polish Underground Army to stage the uprising. Unfortunately the destruction of the city and the loss of large number of lives seemed to have been in vain.

During the first few days of the uprising the family I was staying with and I were holed up indoors while the noise of gunfire and explosions were raging outside. Soon the German Army took control of the outlying parts of Warsaw including the area where we were. They ordered everybody out, set each building on fire, and had us walk over fields out of the city. As I walked among crowds through the fields out of Warsaw, members of Lithuanian or other Baltic and Ukrainian armies units fighting with the Germans were guarding us. They stopped people and took away any valuables they might have had. One young soldier stopped and searched me. He found a gold watch given to me by my mother that had belonged to my grandfather and a ring with a small diamond. He took the watch and to my surprise gave the ring back saying, "This for me, and this for you."

We eventually arrived in the maintenance yards for locomotives in the village of Pruszków. There a camp was formed for thousands of the Warsaw population. From there a majority, except probably those who were not suitable for work, were sent by trains to Germany to work in various jobs and factories to assist in the German war effort. I learned after the war that among them was my cousin Zdzich. I did meet Miss Różycka and her friend Witold briefly in the Pruszków camp. I almost went on a train with them, but the guards stopped me before I was able to follow presumably because the train was full. In the camp there were Polish medics and doctors from a nearby hospital in the village of Tworki. They took people out of the camp that had, or said that they had, dysentery. They tried to get young Polish men out. I was among them and after a few days in the hospital I was released to go free.

Soon after my release, however, while on a local train I was caught when the train was stopped and all passengers were told to get out and stand in line. An officer in a German Army uniform inspected us. He spoke fluent Polish; he was likely a volksdeutsch, an ethnic German who lived in Poland before the war. He said to me, "You look Jewish!" Amazingly, thinking about it now, I answered flippantly to the effect that perhaps my great-grandmother had a soft spot in her heart for a Jew. He then just passed on down the line and I was brought back to the Pruszków camp. My matter of fact response likely saved me from a potentially serious danger. How was it that I, an inexperienced teenager, who tended to be overprotected at home and did not have street smarts, acted so coolly? Malcolm Gladwell in his book *Blink: The Power of Thinking without Thinking* suggests that a subconscious part of our brain may spring instantaneously into action in certain situations.

Knowing the ropes in the camp, I "got dysentery," was admitted to the Tworki hospital and released again. This time I was assigned to a Polish farmer in the countryside, in a village probably in the area of Łowicz. I stayed there and lived with a family of local farmers. I used my mother's ring to buy a warm coat for the winter. I slept on a bunk in a stable that I shared with a horse. I attended church on Sundays with the whole community. This was the obligatory social highlight of life in the rural areas. The villagers were simple poor people; somewhat unsure and reluctant to have to share their limited resources with the strangers from Warsaw. They had no choice, however, since the official head of the area issued specific orders. During the meals everybody ate together from one big bowl using individual spoons. I felt awkward among these country people. I also felt very isolated and alone. I wondered what happened to my cousins, aunt, and uncle. I recalled that my mother spoke, probably when we were in the Ghetto, that her cousin Adam Pragier escaped to London where he was a member of the Polish Government in exile. I thought that if I somehow managed to get to Western Europe I could contact him. It was just a pipe dream, however, as there was no practical way that I could accomplish it. I just continued to hang on and eventually the Russian offensive reached and passed the area in 1945.

Finally the war was coming to its end. The Allied Armies landed in Europe and opened western fronts, first in Italy and then in France. The German forces were unable to resist the offensives from the west and the Soviet armies were advancing from the east. The American and British Air Forces' planes were bombing German cities and factories. Liberation of Europe from Hitler's hordes was taking place and in May 1945 Germany surrendered. Unfortunately, for the majority of the European Jewry the end came too late. Hitler nearly succeeded in killing all the Jews in the territories held by the Germans and in most countries that were allied with Germany, like Hungary for instance.

Between 1941 and the end of the war about six million of the Jewish people from the German occupied Europe were gassed in the death camps of Treblinka, Chełmno, Bełżec, Sobibor, Majdanek, and Auschwitz–Birkenau. Jews were killed with machine guns by the hundreds of thousands by the German Einsatz groups in the Ukraine and Russia, died in concentration camps, were individually shot when caught in hiding, and were killed during death marches—when thousands of camp prisoners were mercilessly driven by their German tormentors westwards as the Soviet armies were approaching the camps.

Germans succeeded in destroying some camps such as Treblinka, but most of Auschwitz-Birkenau was not destroyed because Germans had to abandon it in a hurry as the Soviet Army threatened to encircle them. Yet, a small fraction of the Jewish people in Europe survived despite the Nazis' attempts to destroy them. Some survived in hiding often helped by the Righteous Gentiles, some managed to stay alive hiding in the forests or fighting as partisans, and others survived after fleeing or being taken east by the Soviets and returned after the war ended.

CHAPTER III
EARLY POST-WAR YEARS

Aftermath and Spring in Kraków 1945 –1946

After the Soviet Army liberated Poland, most Jews finally came out of hiding. Various organizations - Polish, Jewish and others set up by the Red Cross, appeared over the weeks and months that followed the liberation in larger centres so family members and friends could establish contact. One year after the end of the war, close to two hundred and fifty thousand Jews were registered with Jewish committees in the major cities in Poland. The largest proportions of these were those who returned from the Soviet Union. Many Jews felt elated that they survived! Others, however, felt differently. Most grieved the deaths of their families; others did not know what happened to their dear ones and kept wandering in search for them. Many were apprehensive and uncertain of what the future held, since the communities where they lived before the war were completely destroyed. Their insecurity was reinforced to a considerable degree by the rise of virulent anti-Semitism and the outbreak of anti-Jewish violence in the country. This arose because some Poles perceived Jews to be aiding the Soviet take-over of Poland; others, supported by the Catholic Church, continued traditional anti-Semitic beliefs; and still others simply wanted to keep Jewish property that they had acquired during the war.[1] Amazingly, if that is an appropriate word, Poles murdered one thousand Jews between liberation and the beginning of 1947. That included pogroms on a large scale in villages, in cities, and in forests by the armed Polish detachments of the Narodowe Siły Zbrojne (National Armed Forces). The pogrom in the city of Kielce was an example of the anti-Semitic backlash.[2]

There were many Jewish partisans who fought valiantly in the forests against the Germans, sabotaging their operations by derailing trains on the main lines among other tactics. Some fought in Jewish groups, but many were members of the partisan groups of the Polish, Lithuanian or Russian units, some very well organized. Survivors were also frequently witnesses to the murder of Jews by the armed Polish, Russian or Lithuanian collaborators. Yitzak Arad, who was a Jewish partisan in the forests of Lithuania and Belarus commented: "The prime lesson we had learned was that we must not permit ourselves to be weak and at the mercy of the people among whom we lived."[3] He became an emissary of the Jewish Zionist movement in the post-war Poland and stated: "I traveled through many parts of Poland and the ruins of Jewish life confronted me everywhere. Empty synagogues, demolished schools, desolate cultural institutions. Only the cemeteries bore witness to Jewish communities that had flourished for generations."[4]

After the Soviet armies moved westwards towards Berlin and life tended to quiet down, crowds of displaced people from Warsaw and other cities started to trek on foot, by bicycles, or in overcrowded irregularly running trains, from where the end of the hostilities found them. They tried either to return home, although their homes often did not exist, to find members of families or at least register with various aid organizations. Although it was known that Warsaw was almost completely destroyed, many set out towards it and so did I. I knew that I lost my parents and did not know what happened to my relatives. I was hoping that I might at least be able to find out about my cousins Tadzik and Zdzich and their parents, who were in Warsaw until the uprising in the autumn of 1944.

I first stopped at the hospital in Tworki, where I was before being sent to the countryside. I met some nurses who knew me. They said that the new chief physician wanted to see me. When I entered his office he said that he knew my aunt Pauline and uncle Edmund and that they were looking for me. He gave me their address in Kraków. I found that a train to the city of Katowice in southern Poland, about seventy-kilometers west from Kraków, would be stopping in a field near the hospital. When the train arrived I got on it and traveled to Katowice, and from there I boarded a train destined for Kraków.

After arriving at the station, I walked through the street of that beautiful city with its medieval architecture and many churches. It looked the way I remembered it from our visits there before the war, untouched by the ravages of Hitler's army. I made my way to the address

I was given and arrived at the apartment building on Dunajewskiego Street no.3. I walked up the stairs, located the apartment number, and rang the bell. The door opened and there was my aunt Pola in a black dress. She opened her arms with an exclamation of relief and joy and we embraced. Then my uncle appeared. I was with my family again. The reunion, however, was not joyous. I learned that my wonderful cousin Tadzik was killed during the Warsaw Uprising in 1944.

He volunteered as a medic to a hospital of the Polish Underground Army that staged the uprising, together with his Gentile girlfriend Danuta Krzeszewska. The hospital, run by the Order of the Maltese Knights, was an underground military hospital active throughout the war, but its activities were especially important during the uprising in 1944. Its commander was Lieutenant-Colonel Dr. Stanisław Korwin Milewski-Lipkowski (1881—1966). He was a wise and kind man, who served as beloved and wise commander to those he worked with. A letter that he wrote to my aunt Pauline, Tadzik's mother, provided insights into the horrific events that the insurgents lived through and of my cousin's experiences and fate.

The hospital was located originally on Senatorska Street near the centre of the city held by the Polish Army. Dr. Milewski-Lipkowski's letter stated that he immediately developed "a sympathetic and mutually trusting relationship" with my cousin. The amount of work was tremendous and my cousin "went to work with enthusiasm and continued effort, which within a couple of hours won the appreciation of all the personnel." Germans started an offensive on August 7 that forced the hospital to move. They burned buildings on Elektoralna Street, where my grandparents lived before and during the war and where I stayed for a period of time in the Ghetto, and then the army attacked from the Saski Gardens where I played often before the war. Dr. Milewski-Lipkowski was severely wounded. The hospital was overtaken a number of times by the Germans. On August 14 a group of a hundred and fifty vicious and drunken SS men took the hospital and forced all to leave within an hour. By a quirk of fate the hospital moved down the Marszałkowska Street, a main artery, to a nearby part of the city centre still held by the Polish insurgents. The Doctor's letter continues:

The state of my health was quite precarious and I had surgery. During that time I saw doctor Graszewski (my cousin's alias), as I always thought of him, only a few times when he visited me. At the same time, I heard many praises and words of appreciation and sympathy from people who worked with him. On the 4th of September there began a steady barrage of artillery, together with aerial bombing, which within a number of hours destroyed the city centre. In the morning around nine or ten o'clock the building at *Jasna* Streeet 11 was hit badly. Dr. Graszewski was wounded lightly in the head. He dressed the wound and with Sister Krzeszewska they began to move the wounded and other patients from the bombed building to the neighbouring house of Gebetner. At the time Dr. Lewandowski, who was wounded lightly in the head, came to me at Górski Street 7, where I was situated. As soon as Dr. Lewandowski's wound was dressed, a second wave of bombing of the *Jasna* Street building began. Dr. Graszewski and Sister Krzeszewska were carrying a wounded woman [Janina Sarnecka, a sister of Hanka Herfurt, another Gentile friend of my cousins]. All three were killed by a single missile. At the same time my quarters were bombed. Dr. Lewandowski, who was sitting opposite me at the table, sustained the fracture of the base of his skull. Only some hours later, during a lull in the attacks, I was informed that the Maltean hospital was completely disorganized because of the heavy losses. During these two hours, nine members of our staff perished and I do not know how many patients. Taking advantage of another lull in the attacks I managed to get to the building of Gebetner, where the remains of our hospital [staff and patients] were camped out on the staircase. Those that were not wounded or injured were in shock. In the courtyard, covered with blankets, lay the remains of Dr. Graszewski. I took leave of him with a short prayer. I said goodbye to a young patriot, a noble man, who perished at his post while rescuing a compatriot. Virtually I envied him then that the fate let him perish nobly and spared him living through the indignity of defeat and ill treatment. He died as a free man while performing the most admirable Samaritan mission of love of his fellow being.

Perhaps my depiction above is somewhat too brutal. Yet, it is difficult to relate the events of the uprising without a modicum of reality, which was nightmarish. That is why one cannot assess human character within hours, days or weeks. A few moments encompassed whole epochs and revealed the true value of the human character. One saw people without masks and that is why, although our collaboration was brief, I do not hesitate to declare that I came to know Dr. Graszewski the way he was to the core—a shining spirit. I am certain that if he were to survive the uprising, we would be bound by a lasting friendship. Alas Fate ordained otherwise.

My cousins and their parents knew Danuta Krzeszewska and her mother Florentyna; they met before the war while skiing during winter vacations. These two women were also Righteous Gentiles who helped my relatives to survive while in Warsaw and its vicinity. Dr. Milewski-Lipkowski wrote that he was going to inform my cousin's high school in Kraków, because they should be proud of its graduate. I am not sure that I ever met Danuta, but I feel that I was quite familiar with that bright young woman. She knew four languages and studied philosophy before the war and then in secret during the war. During the siege of Warsaw in 1939 she was helping to move archives of the University of Warsaw from a burning building. She was wounded and was awarded the Cross of Valour. Today, Tadzik's and Danuta's names are inscribed on the memorial wall of the Museum of the Warsaw Uprising.

I was very sad and obviously my aunt and uncle were affected very deeply. I might have felt somewhat guilty that I survived, while Tadzik, whom I loved so much and without whose care I would not have survived, did not. My aunt and uncle welcomed me, however, with love and it was clear that I was now a bona fide member of their family. Still, I tended at times to think that perhaps it was all a mistake and that Tadzik might one day appear. It was not known what happened to cousin Zdzich, but it seemed very likely that he was taken from Warsaw in 1944 for labour in Germany. We were concerned and hoped to hear from him as time went on.

In a neighbouring apartment lived Mrs. Bonhard with whom my aunt and uncle were friendly. She lost her husband during the war and was crestfallen. She played piano well and I often visited her and listened to her play Beethoven's piano sonatas. The music had a soothing effect. Perhaps I felt a connection to the past and my mother's music making. Sometime later my aunt, a very determined lady, set out for Warsaw to bring to Kraków Tadzik's remains. She was accompanied by Mr. Józef, a faithful driver of my uncle and aunt before and during the war. She returned with the remains and my cousin was buried at a brief funeral ceremony at the Jewish cemetery in a suburb of Kraków.

I believe that it was from my aunt that I acquired some family photographs from before the war. How she managed to keep them after the family had to flee hurriedly from their home in 1939, and all the various cities and places that she and my uncle had to move through during the war years, I am not sure, but one story I was told suggests how the photos might have been saved. Apparently when my aunt and uncle returned to Kraków shortly after the war, they went to the villa in which they lived prior to the outbreak of the hostilities in 1939. The building was now in the hands of the Russian Army officials, who allowed my relatives to take their belongings that were still there. Among those belongings might have been the family photographs. In addition, the officials told them to take a set of the famous Rosenthal China; they said that it must obviously be theirs as it is marked with their name! Apparently the difference from their name of Rosenhauch was not noticed.

I did not know what happened to other members of my family: the Centnerszwers, my cousins Janek and Ryś. I never found out what happened to my uncle Władek Reicher or aunts Leonka and Gutka, presumably they perished. In the case of other members of my family I did not find out about their fate until much later. Somehow, perhaps through some agencies, I learned that some of my peers from before the war did survive including Alinka Puszet, with whom I corresponded. She lived in Katowice and then got married and moved to Warsaw and lived on Elektoralna Street. She later immigrated to Israel. Ela Fishaut apparently settled in Australia after getting married and Hanka Kon married a Gentile and remained in Poland. My bright friend Stefan Kraushar, who wrote to the president of Poland before the war, survived the war and settled in the USA. Among those that did not survive was Staś (Stanislaw) Kopel with whom I played in Warsaw during the early period of occupation before the formation of the Warsaw Ghetto. Jaś Ramberg, my colleague and son of the principal of our school *Spójnia*, immigrated to Israel where he became a brilliant scientist. Unfortunately, he died at a relatively young age.

I slowly settled into our life in the beautiful city of Kraków with its many medieval buildings and the magnificent Wawel castle of the Polish kings, who resided there until the capital was moved to Warsaw early in the seventeenth-century. The Germans did not destroy the city because they had to withdraw in a hurry as the Soviet armies were threatening to encircle them completely. A ribbon of parkland, "Planty", with trees and benches encircles the central part of the city. It replaced the defensive walls and moat that used to defend the city in the remote past. In the centre of the city is a square with the Church of St. Mary, which has two towers of unequal height. The legend has it that two brothers were building the towers in a competition to see which one would finish first. One of them, jealous and desperately wanting to win murdered his brother. Overnight the tower of the murdered brother miraculously rose to full height. Near the top of the taller tower are four windows. From there a watchman would survey the city surroundings during the Middle Ages to look for approaching Tatars, who attacked the city from time to time. When he spotted them he would sound alarm by playing a tune "Hejnał" on a trumpet. At one time, according to legend, an arrow shot by a Tartar hit him in the throat while he was playing and the tune stopped. To commemorate that event the trumpeter plays the melody daily on the hour, but breaks it off abruptly for a moment in the middle. He plays consecutively from each of the four windows facing in four directions.

I enrolled in an accelerated high school course intended to allow students to complete two years in one, in order to make up for the time lost during the war. I was taking the last two high school years in 1945—1946 and enjoyed biology and other subjects. I found that I was able to write compositions better than before the war, perhaps as a result of the extensive reading that I did while hiding in the apartment of Miss Różycka in Warsaw.

I made some friends in school. My uncle practiced ophthalmology in an office attached to the apartment where we lived. He allowed me to watch him and at times to assist in a minor way. He explained his findings and the treatments that he used. As a result of this experience I became gradually interested in medicine and decided that I would like to study it after finishing high school. Hanna Herfurt, who with her mother helped my cousins during the war in Warsaw, was also in Kraków. She at times assisted my uncle during surgery. I remember one incident when my uncle operated on a patient for a detached retina in a clinic downtown with Hanka and me in attendance. For this surgery he needed diathermy equipment, which he did not have. He reluctantly had to ask a Polish ophthalmologist to lend it to him. When we returned home, he found that a pair of small electrodes from the borrowed equipment was missing. He understandably became very upset and angry. He told me to go and not come back until I found the missing electrodes. I left the apartment dazed and unsure what I could do. I went back to the clinic where the surgery was done. I talked to the personnel and asked where were the sterile dressings and linen used during the surgery. They directed me to the laundry, where I found the bundle and meticulously went through it shaking each sheet and piece of the linen. To my great relief I found the two small electrodes and brought them home.

Figure 8. My school certificate, Kraków 1945.

During the ensuing period of time, we officially changed our last names to Carter. We felt that we did not want to bear names of German derivation. Carter was a name of a favourite book character of my deceased cousin Tadzik, detective Nick Carter, and so we adopted it. Late in 1945 or early in 1946 we still heard nothing about Zdzich. My aunt, a very determined person, set out courageously on her own to Germany to look for him. Meanwhile, my uncle and I enjoyed our time together. I continued to observe his office practice and we enjoyed meals of tasty food that was not available during the war years. One patient of my uncle was a late-teenage girl whose eyes were badly damaged by debris during the Warsaw Uprising in 1944. By the time she saw my uncle she was essentially blind because of a detached retina in one eye that was not attended to previously and had severe scarring in the other eye. My uncle decided to cut through the scar tissue hoping that it may restore her some sight. I attended the surgery. Unfortunately the surgery did not help and she remained essentially completely blind. She and I became friendly and went out together. I recall that once while walking in the Main Square of Kraków I asked her to wait briefly and went to buy her a small bouquet of flowers as a little surprise. We remained in contact for a period of time after she moved to Wrocław, where she became a lawyer and married. I still marvel at her courage and determination and a letter from her, hand-written despite her blindness. Meanwhile we heard that my cousin Janek, the older son of my aunt Karola, died shortly after the war, perhaps from complications of tuberculosis.

Then finally we did hear that my aunt found my cousin Zdzich, who at the time worked as a physician in the displaced persons (DP) camp in Landsberg, Germany. My aunt and cousin soon moved to Munich. We planned to join them, but before leaving, I hoped to pass a hastily arranged examination to get my final high school diploma in the spring of 1946. This was done with very kind cooperation of the Polish school authorities, since the final school year was not yet completed. I had to cram for the examination, including material for the course Introduction to Philosophy that I had not yet began. Fortunately I was able to pass and obtain the certificate.

Soon my uncle made arrangements to leave. My uncle had official permission to travel abroad and went from Kraków to Prague, the capital of Czechoslovakia. I did not have permission, so he arranged for me to travel by train to a town near the border with Czechoslovakia and to proceed to a house, where I gave a password and was let in. Then during the night the guides took me, and actually carried me on their back, across a river at the border to a town where I waited for a couple of days for a document that allowed me to take a train to Prague where I met my uncle. We spent three days in that beautiful city and then proceeded by train to Germany and arrived in Munich.

Munich 1946 – 1948

My cousin Zdzich was a physician at the UNRRA (United Nations Relief and Rehabilitation Administration) University for displaced persons in Munich. It occupied the building complex of the German Museum on an island on the Isaar River in the centre of the city, where the displaced students and staff lived and teaching took place. I shared a room with Zdzich. The university was bustling with activity and people from virtually all countries of Eastern and Central Europe. There were recreational activities. I enrolled in a pre-medical course consisting of various biological sciences and remember well the lectures of Professor Novikow, who used to be the Rector of the university in Moscow and was an impressive lecturer. I interacted with students of many nations and detected only occasionally anti-Semitic attitudes. Since the end of the war, because of the horrific experiences that we had to go through due to intolerance and hatred, I reasoned idealistically and perhaps naively, that I must be different, and decided to base my relationship with others on what they were like as individuals and not on their ethnic origin. Among various extracurricular activities I enjoyed playing table tennis. I also watched table tennis matches between elite players. One of them was Bernie Bukiet, a Jewish man from Poland, who played and I believe defeated top German players. He later became a legend in the United States and was inducted into the US Table Tennis Hall of Fame in 1981. Many years later in Winnipeg I saw Bukiet play at the Winnipeg Arena during a Harlem Globetrotters show against another top ranking player.

Displaced people in Germany realized the temporary nature of their situation and tried to make plans for emigration. At one time Zdzich and I took a few Spanish lessons, as there was a possibility of emigration to South America. Meanwhile my uncle and aunt established contact with his sister who lived in New York City since

Figure 9. With cousin Zdzich (George),
Munich, 1947.

before the war and eventually it was possible for her to make arrangements for my uncle, aunt, and Zdzich to go to the USA. Unfortunately, I could not be included because of the restrictive immigration laws of the USA, as I was not a member of the immediate family. That caused my family considerable worry until a solution presented itself. When Zdzich was liberated, he became attached to a US Air Force unit as an interpreter. Subsequently he worked as a physician in a DP (Displaced People) camp. In a camp in Landsberg he met Etta Brenner, a Jewish nurse from Canada, who worked for UNRRA. She was originally from Warsaw, but immigrated to join her uncle and aunt, Volodia and Mary Kitzes, many years before the war. They lived then in Innwood, a town in the Interlake region of the province of Manitoba for many years. Subsequently they moved to Winnipeg where they ran a grocery store on St. Matthews Avenue. Etta contacted her family and they agreed to sponsor me to come to join them in Winnipeg, as part of a new programme to allow some immigration of the displaced youth. I learned much later that it was a part of a brand new Canadian policy on

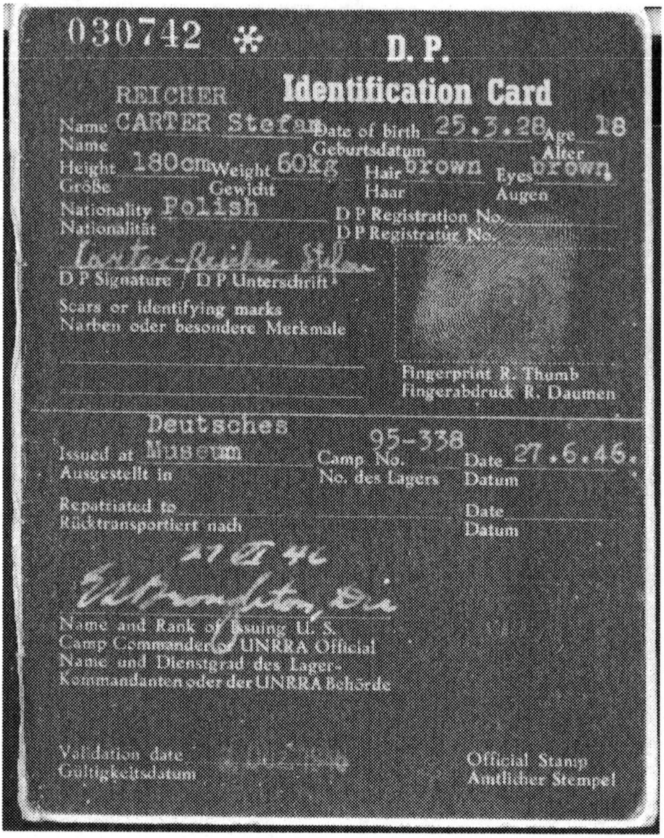
030742 *

D. P.
Identification Card

REICHER
Name CARTER Stefan Date of birth 25.3.28 Age 18
Name Geburtsdatum Alter
Height 180cm Weight 60kg Hair brown Eyes brown
Größe Gewicht Haar Augen
Nationality Polish D P Registration No.
Nationalität D P Registratur No.

D P Signature / D P Unterschrift
Scars or identifying marks
Narben oder besondere Merkmale

Fingerprint R. Thumb
Fingerabdruck R. Daumen

Deutsches
Issued at Museum Camp No. 95-338 Date 27.6.46.
Ausgestellt in No. des Lagers Datum
Repatriated to Date
Rücktransportiert nach Datum

Name and Rank of Issuing U.S. Camp Commander or UNRRA Official
Name und Dienstgrad des Lager-Kommandanten oder der UNRRA Behörde

Validation date
Gültigkeitsdatum
Official Stamp
Amtlicher Stempel

Figure 10. My displaced person I.D. card. Munich, 1946.

immigration and that previously Canada had a very restrictive policy that prevented most Jewish and many other immigrants from entering the country.

The immigration process was very, very slow. Meanwhile my uncle became a physician-in-chief of a DP camp in Feldafing, a town on the beautiful lake Starnbergersee a short train ride from Munich. Years later in Winnipeg, I met a man whose parents met in Feldafing. I often took a train to visit my uncle and aunt there and spent pleasant times swimming and boating. One day I saw my friend Stefan from the secret school in the Warsaw Ghetto walk up the steps of the German Museum in Munich. We renewed our friendship and he would come to visit me in Feldafing at times. He later enrolled at the university in Frankfurt am Main. I visited him once in Frankfurt where we went to see the opera *Martha* by Gounod. Stefan later immigrated to the USA, and settled in Los Angeles where he worked as a psychologist. It was in Feldafing that I had my appendix taken out under local anesthetic by a German surgeon who worked in the camp.

In Munich, besides studying, I took swimming lessons at an indoor pool, watched famous marionettes at the City Hall building do their regular daily dance to music, and attended concerts. One of the concerts was most remarkable. The young Yehudi Menuhin performed with a German orchestra. Some Jewish people were shocked. He played consecutively the violin concertos by Bach, Mendelssohn, and Beethoven, and for encore played a Chaconne for solo violin by Bach. Some German students in the audience, who sat near me, were beside themselves marveling at his playing. I felt a reawakening of my interest in music and took a few lessons in music theory from a German teacher for which I paid with cans of sardines. Whatever I learned, however, was not applied to any practical endeavour and was soon forgotten. I saw a few operas in Munich and went to many concerts. The price of tickets was quite affordable, compared to high prices and difficulties in obtaining many food items. There was a Jewish Students' Union where I met many colleagues, some of whom I was to become reacquainted with in Winnipeg.

Among the students I met was Adam Rosenblum. We were both studying medicine and attended lectures together. Adam was a short man with graying hair, older than my peers and me. He told me that he was a pharmacist in Warsaw before the war, was in the Polish Army in 1939, and was taken by the Germans as a prisoner of war. What I remember most is that we shared an interest in music and attended concerts frequently. After a year or so in Munich the UNRRA and its university were dissolved and other students and I transferred to Munich's German university. I continued with my studies that included courses in anatomy and physiology. I became friendly with a girl Mała ("little one") who played the violin. She immigrated later to Israel. I also recall talking to a German student who told me that they spent many evening hours playing Mozart's string quartets. I attended a special meeting called by a Jewish student who was in the Zionist movement that endeavoured to bring as many Jews as possible to Palestine. He wanted us all to commit then and there and sign up for immigration to Palestine. I had my plans with my family and so did other students. He failed to persuade most. He went towards Palestine but, as many others, was caught by the British and was interned in Cyprus.

My family left for the USA. I continued studying in Munich and going through the unending immigration process. I was slowly studying English. After going through a book of English grammar, I started reading the novel *Earth and High Heaven* by Gwethalyn Graham. It was the first Canadian novel to reach number one on the *New York Times* bestseller list in 1944. I wrote down innumerable new words and memorized their meaning regularly. Also, I was able to establish contact with my cousin Ryś who was in England. I mentioned earlier that when the war began in 1939 Ryś quickly returned from Switzerland to participate in the defense of Lwów and escaped, ending up in England. There in July 1940 he joined the 1st Polish Armored Division. He was sent to Normandy on July 11, 1944 and saw action there, in Belgium, and in Holland. After the war he settled in Great Britain, as did a number of Polish soldiers. He married a young English woman named Doris. I exchanged letters with them and Doris gracefully referred to my newly learned English as "charming."

Figure 11. Ryszard and Doris Brokman soon
after the war.

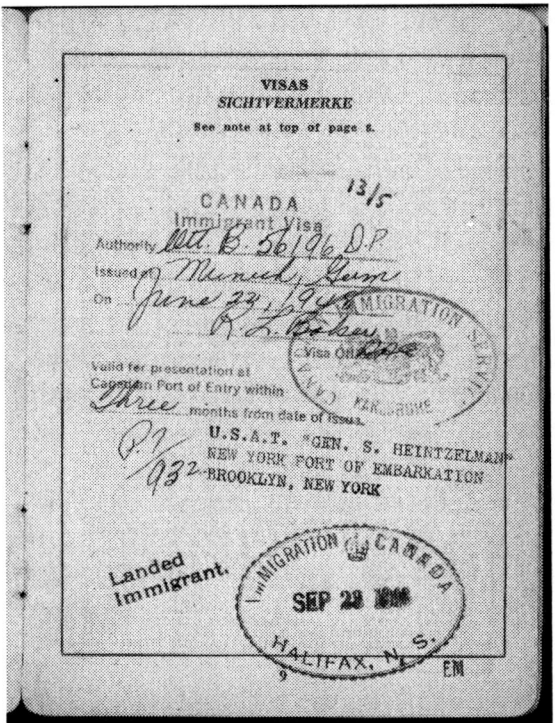

Figure 12. My immigration document - arrival in Canada.

The immigration offices were situated some distance from the city of Munich, which required the prospective immigrants to take lengthy train rides to the Funk Caserne, previously the military barracks, where immigration and health officials filled many forms and performed medical examinations. Finally towards the end of the summer of 1948 all the formalities were completed and I was cleared to proceed to Bremerhaven from where ships were taking immigrants to North America. Before I left, Adam Rosenblum gave me a musical composition of his, under the pen name E. Leves, to take with me for safekeeping, as he was remaining to continue his studies in Munich. The officials in Bremerhaven were looking for people who could help perform various tasks on the ship. I tried out for an interpreter and was accepted. Our ship was an army transport, the *General Heintzelman*. The journey was very pleasant except for the first day; when in choppy waters of the English Channel, many of us became seasick and were "feeding the fish." Then we settled down. Our English group put out a daily newsletter with news items that the crew provided for us. The weather was fine. We saw flying fish from the deck of the ship. After some eight days at sea we arrived at Pier 21 in Halifax and went through the Canadian immigration in September 1948.

Soon we boarded a train and traveled for a couple of days. Early on the train went through Quebec. When it stopped we tried to buy food and did, although there appeared to be a great difficulty in communicating with the locals. Although I knew French well enough to communicate, they either did not understand my pronunciation or pretended not to understand. The train then sped for hours through a beautiful world of lakes and forests. I looked at it with wonder and thought that I would love to explore such a land in the future. Eventually we arrived at Winnipeg, and disembarked at the Union Station. In the crowd of the railway station building I recognized Etta, who introduced me to her uncle and aunt.

CHAPTER IV
WINNIPEG AND MEDICAL TRAINING

Early Years in Winnipeg 1948 – 1956

We drove to my new home at no. 657 St. Mathew Avenue, where the family lived in a house, which incorporated a grocery store that Volodia and Mary Kitzes ran. I shared a room with their son Ben. Ben was a young man who worked as a pharmacist. During the war he served in the Canadian Air Force. He soon introduced me to the Canadian Football League. He was an avid fan of the Winnipeg Blue Bombers and took me to a game at the old Osborne Stadium. I sat and watched—considerably confused. Two teams in colourful uniforms lined up against each other. After the whistle of the referee a pile up of players immediately resulted, and so it went, apart from an occasional kick of the funny-shaped ball down the field. This was very different from the European football, called soccer in North America.

The Kitzes family made me feel at home and essentially became my adopted family. I helped Volodia in the evenings to square his daily store accounts. He was a gentle, easygoing man. He was interested in the opera and was probably singing in his younger days. He originally came from Odessa and met Mary in France. They married and came to Canada before World War I. After the war began they remained and became Canadian citizens. Mary was born in Puławy a town in Poland, where a mighty family of Polish magnates named Radziwiłł resided at one time and the Czartoryski family at another. She was a lady with a strong personality and usually played the leading role in the family. I heard that she played a prominent role in the social life in the town of Innwood, when the family had a general store there prior to coming to Winnipeg. She held strong opinions and did not hesitate to express them. Etta started taking courses to become a public health care nurse, perhaps as a result of her experience with refugees in the

DP camps in Germany. Ben worked in a drugstore that he co-owned at Corydon Avenue and Wilton Street, which during my early years in Winnipeg was at the end of a bus line. Ben had a car. I learned how to drive and worked at times delivering for the drugstore in what is now the Crescentwood area. The streets south of Corydon were not paved, and if it started raining I had to hurry so I could get out before the streets became muddy and impassable to vehicular traffic. Ben was a good baseball player, a centre outfielder. He organized a Crescentwood Community Club baseball team and became its player-manager. The team was quite good and participated in tournaments. I remember going with the team to a tournament in Teulon in the Interlake region. Ben was an active member of the Crescentwood Community Club for many years. His mother, whom I referred to as Auntie Mary, later would go there to play bingo. Now a painting contributed by Ben hangs in the Crescentwood Clubhouse where it commemorates his contributions to the community.

I corresponded with a few friends in Europe and visited with a family that I came to Canada with on the transport ship from Germany. I became primarily absorbed in my new environment and life in Winnipeg. The Kitzes family had friends. Among them probably the closest was the Werier family with their matriarch Mania. I believe that there were three sisters and three brothers. Val was a journalist working then for the *Winnipeg Tribune*. Soon after arriving in Winnipeg I met him and his very charming fiancée Eva. I attended their wedding and for the first time in my life saw a *chuppah*. Val's brother George was an actor, Harry a social worker, and their sister Ruth was a good pianist. The younger sister of Ben, Juliette was married to Marcel Goldenberg and lived in New York where they were friendly with my family there. Also, other relatives of Volodia lived in New York and its vicinity. A few months after my arrival Juliette and Marcel came for a visit with their baby daughter Diane. I attended a concert of the Winnipeg Symphony Orchestra directed by its first conductor Walter Kaufman. It was held in the Winnipeg Auditorium, now The Archives Building. They performed Handel's *Messiah*, which I have not previously heard. I was enchanted with the beauty of the music and the wonderful aria-like solos.

Prior to coming to Canada I corresponded with Rabbi Louis Milgrom of the Hillel Foundation in Winnipeg concerning the continuation of my studies. Soon after I arrived in September 1948, Rabbi

Milgrom drove me down Pembina highway to the campus of the University of Manitoba in the suburb of Fort Garry. There I registered for the second year of the pre-medical course, which was held at the downtown campus on Memorial Boulevard. I met many colleagues—Jewish and Gentile Canadians from Winnipeg, from rural Manitoba and Saskatchewan, and some Canadian and British war veterans who were older than I. The courses that we took included a number that I was familiar with from my studies in Munich: physics, chemistry, botany, and zoology. I also took introductory French that was easy for me because of my experience with French in Poland, and English that was probably the biggest hurdle. I studied hard. In the English course we took Chaucer, Milton, Johnson, and Woodworth. At the end of the year my lowest mark of sixty-seven percent in English was also the mark I was most proud of. I had high marks in other subjects and won an Isbister Scholarship for one of the highest standings that would be helpful when I applied for admission into medicine the following year.

My family in New York knew a prominent Jewish family in Montreal, who contacted their friends the Aronovitches in Winnipeg. Mrs. Aronovitch called me and took me to the beautiful Assiniboine Park. Through her, I got work during the Christmas vacations at the firm of her husband helping with the Christmas season mail. There I met and worked together with another young boy from Europe. His name was John Hirsch. He was a Holocaust survivor from Hungary and came to Winnipeg with a group of Jewish orphans a year before I did. John found a home with Sybil Schack, a Winnipeg school principal and educator. John was a brilliant student. He studied English literature and was interested in theatre. He went on to found the Manitoba Theatre Centre and became a world famous theatre director. Our paths were to cross again a few years later.

I spent the summers of 1949 and 1950 working as a member of a traveling X-ray unit that did chest X-rays throughout the province of Manitoba. This was a part of the tuberculosis prevention programme. The units were big trucks with X-ray machines under the direction of an X-ray technician-driver and two student assistants. We X-rayed hundreds of people in towns all over the province, from north of Winnipeg to the towns in the south near the border with the USA, and from the western towns such as Melita and St. Lazare, which was situated in a beautiful valley, to the eastern regions near western Ontario. There were towns with French speaking population like St. Rose, those with people of Icelandic origins and others. My nondescript accent made it difficult for people to tell my origins and I was taken for a European from many different countries. We stayed in the local hotels during the weekdays and usually returned to Winnipeg for weekends. I got to know the province well.

During an early trip I became acquainted with the North American dish that was new to me. We stopped at a roadside food stand and ordered a "nip"—a Canadian hamburger. In the town of Virden we went bowling in the evening after work. We bowled one game of five-pins. The next morning I could hardly walk due to severe pain in the muscles of my right leg. I thought that I had poliomyelitis. The pain, however, was due to strain that my muscles were not accustomed to and improved over a couple of days. One of my fellow students was Hal, who was of German extraction and that put my resolve to be tolerant to the test. We got along well. My other fellow student was Maurice, a young French-Canadian, who later did announcing on the local French radio station CKSB.

During one of the summers an unusual incident occurred. One evening our X-ray technician suddenly started running around wildly. He indicated that an insect got into his ear, buzzed loudly, and was driving him crazy. I obtained small tweezers from somebody, and

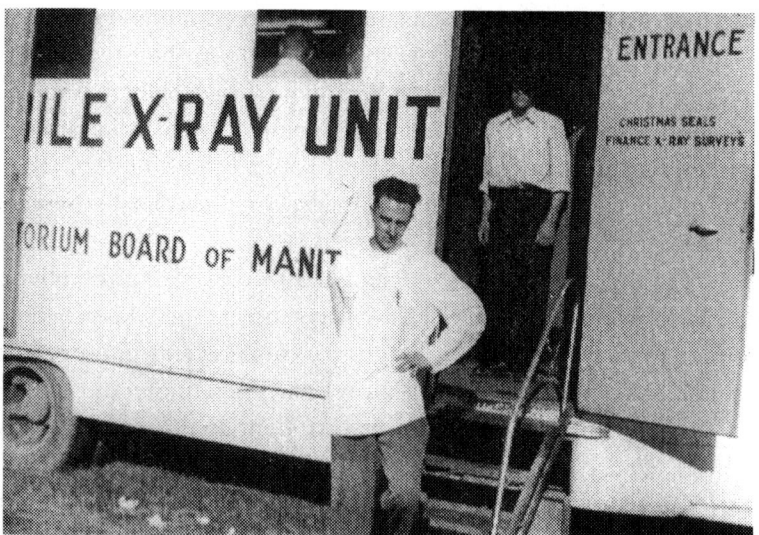

Figure 13. In front of an X-ray survey truck, 1950.

using my knowledge of the anatomy of the ear canal, I was able to remove the bee. The technician reminded me more than fifty years later that he was my first patient.

* * * *

To be admitted into the faculty of medicine one had to have references. Here, Etta proved most helpful. I believe that she worked at one time for a Dr. Bowman, a public health physician, highly respected in the community. He agreed to interview me and then provided the reference. Dr Ruvin Lyons, a highly respected obstetrician, provided another reference. His niece Becky was a public health nurse, a colleague of Etta's when they were in Germany and where I met Becky. Dr. Kaminetsky, a general practitioner provided the third reference. I vaguely recall having a brief interview with the Dean of Medicine Dr. Mathers. I think that he had a reputation of being a tough man. The interview, however, was not a problem. With the references and my Isbister Scholarship my chances for admission were good and I gained the admission into first year medicine in the fall of 1949. By then Dr. Mathers was not the dean anymore. He was replaced by Dr. Lennox Bell, known as "Buzz". Miss Cousens, a secretary from the downtown university campus, moved to the Faculty of Medicine as did my classmates and I.

I walked to the medical school on the Bannatyne campus from my home base at St. Mathew's Avenue. I felt awe when I first walked the hallowed halls of the medical faculty buildings. Our class of 1954 totaled about seventy students, six of them females. We had a great group with varied backgrounds. I was the only student from Continental Europe. I knew most of my classmates from the previous year at the university. They were mostly Canadians from Manitoba or Saskatchewan. Among them was Hiro Nishioka of Japanese heritage. His family, which resided in British Columbia, was dispossessed and forcibly relocated during World War II because they were unjustly considered as potentially dangerous "foreign aliens" after Japan attacked the USA. Hiro took lecture notes in so small a handwriting that he could fit a whole course content on the back of a postcard. Not surprisingly, he became a neurosurgeon. We had two British veterans Bill Doughty and Ron Bennet, and Canadian veterans: Bob Nixon, who served in the Pacific theatre and was a prisoner of war, and Sam Steinberg. Among my Canadian colleagues were a large number of Jewish-Canadians. That,

I recall being told, was a huge change from the previously prevailing pattern in which there were small admission quotas for students of Jewish origin and others.

I did not learn the details of what actually transpired to bring that change about until more than half a century later, when my classmate Dr. Morris Loffman gave a talk at the 50th reunion of our class in 2004. The matter was also dealt with in the essay on anti-Semitism in Manitoba in the 1930s and 40s by Jonathan Fine of Kelvin High School, which won the Manitoba Historical Society's 1995 Dr. Edward C. Shaw Young Historians Award[1] and by the journalist Terrence Moore[2]. The story is of considerable interest and especially meaningful to me because of my previous experiences in Poland.

There was anti-Semitism in Manitoba, as in other parts of Canada. Jews were not welcomed at some recreational clubs. In 1948 the Puffin Ski Club made its policy official—Jews were simply not welcome. In that same year the press revealed that the middle class residential development, Wildwood Park, as well as the upper class exclusive neighbourhood of Tuxedo, excluded Jews. Wealthy Anglo-Saxons mainly populated these areas. Jews were "personae non gratae" at Victoria Beach, a popular summer retreat for "WASPs." Some of the Jewish orphans, who came to Winnipeg during the same period as I did, encountered prejudice when they were not accepted for jobs after putting Jewish as their cultural origin on applications. A focal point of anti-Semitism, however, was the School of Medicine at the University of Manitoba. Originally, entry was based upon academic performance and "the moral, social, and physical qualities" of the student, without apparent discrimination. This principle did not remain.

In the 1920s the resources of the Medical College became insufficient to effectively teach large numbers of students. This led to attempts to limit entries into medicine.[3] After the appointment of Dr. Alvin T. Mathers as Dean of Medicine in 1932, a quota system was instituted, unknown to the general public. In 1943 a group of non-medical Jewish students from the Avukah Jewish Student Organization began researching the issue and information on each of the one thousand and five hundred students who had applied since 1926. The person who did the lion's share of work was Solomon (Shlomo) Mitchell, at the time a lecturer in Actuarial Science in the Department of Mathematics at the university. He obtained his B.A. from the University of Manitoba and M.A. from the University of Toronto. He came from a family in

Winkler. He and his brother Leon, who became a prominent member of the Winnipeg Jewish community, had keen minds and loved playing with numbers, quoting Shakespeare, and playing chess.[4]

Shlomo compiled a card index based on information from various directories, data on applications for admission to medicine, and on students and their academic records; including students that were accepted and rejected.[5] It was discovered that the basis of admission was not scholarship, or any other objective standard, but race and gender. Application forms for admission required information about student's racial origin. All applications were classified into four lists: one for Jews, another for women, and the third for Slavs, Mennonites, and students of other origin. A fourth list, for Anglo-Saxon, French-Canadian, and Icelandic students was the preferred list. Students on the non-preferred list with an average of seventy percent were refused admittance while "preferred" students were accepted even though they might have failed the required courses. The student who failed was then allowed to write a special exam in the summer and admitted. A pre-determined number of applicants from the preferred list were admitted despite their poor showing. These facts were similar to the situation in Poland before the outbreak of World War II, reminding me of the quotas limiting admission of Jewish students there, and of the "Ghetto Benches," which my cousin Tadzik experienced in Kraków.

In the 1920s an average of twenty-four Jews a year were admitted to the University of Manitoba School of Medicine. This dwindled to five Jews in 1938.[6] The Avukah students obtained the documentary evidence from the Office of the Dean of Medicine by a covert operation referred to as "worthy of a CIA's best" by my classmate Dr. Loffman. The matter was raised in the Manitoba Legislature by Morris Gray, Member of the Legislative Assembly (MLA) on behalf of the Jewish population and by other members on behalf of the Ukrainian citizens of Manitoba.

Hyman Sokolov, a well-known Jewish lawyer, presented the findings to the Select Committee of the Manitoba Legislature on March 16, 1944. The president of the University and Dean Mathers were in attendance. Sokolov exposed the injustice of the "preferred" and non-preferred lists for Jews and other minorities: "It is nauseating to contemplate a system which weeds out the fit and the capable," he said, "while it permits incompetent and unqualified students to obtain a preference." The committee was shocked. Judge A. K. Dysart, the chairman of the Board of Governors of the university and Dr. Sidney Smith, the president of the university, said that it could not be true, but if it were, it would be changed. In their view the regulations for the class entering in 1944—1945 were entirely satisfactory. The class included five Jews and seven women. Thus at the time nothing has changed. Yet, some university professors were opposed to the discriminatory admission system. Among them was Professor of Zoology R.A. Wardle, who lectured to my class when we were taking pre-medical courses in 1948—49. He gave a list of students who were applying for admission to medicine to a member of a Jewish organization.[7] A Dr. Dwight L. Johnson, a graduate of the Manitoba Medical College, a practicing physician in Brandon, a MLA, and a member of the Select Committee wrote a remarkable and forceful letter to the committee's chairman. Referring to the matter he stated in part:

> As a doctor and graduate of the Medical College, I am jealous of its good name, its contribution to the welfare of the society, and advancement of science. I am personally confident that discrimination of the type that has existed is detrimental to both of these worthy objects. High scholastic standards cannot be achieved or guaranteed if competition is limited to certain preferred groups. It follows that the standard of the school is threatened at the same time. Discrimination, if allowed, might be used to eliminate some of the keenest of the competition and thus permit the reward of mediocrity and the maintenance of low standards. This is not calculated to safeguard and improve the good name of the College, and I for one, as a citizen of this province, a graduate of the school, and an elected representative of the people, most strongly object.

> I would like to point out that at this particular time in the history of our country, citizens of both sexes, all religions, and every ethnic group represented in our land are giving of their blood and their lives to destroy an international system based on prejudice, intolerance, and racial discrimination. Are they coming back to find that we have allowed intolerance, prejudice, and racial discrimination to become recognized principles in our national life? The answer is in

our hands. I cannot find it in my mind to believe that we will allow such a catastrophe."[8]

Dr. Mathers, however, argued that, "certain nationalities and groups" would never be accepted as doctors and, therefore, should not be admitted to medicine, warning that the university would become "Jewish." His view was that the number of Jewish students should reflect the proportion of Jews in the general population, and not be based on their abilities to pass examinations. It is interesting that in 1943 an excellent Jewish student Morley Cohen was initially refused admission, but then accepted because of the intervention of a professor of zoology, presumably R.A. Wardle. Had he not been admitted, the open-heart surgery that he was to institute in Manitoba in 1959, likely would not have been available until a later date.

Despite Dean Mather's claims and initial resistance of the Board of Governors an investigation was launched. The accusations were verified and the university was forced to change its policy. The following December the Board of the Governors of the university instituted regulations that selection of the students for admission to the Faculty of Medicine be made without regard to the racial origin or religion. The class admitted the following year included twenty-three Jews and eleven women, among them a sister of Dr. Loffman.

Dr. Loffman stated:

> The winners in this struggle were not the Jews or the Ukrainians, but all the citizens of Manitoba. The enlightened policies of the Medical College created a level playing field for every student seeking admission to medicine. The reputation of the University of Manitoba Medical College advanced. In terms of abolishing racial, ethnic, and religious discrimination, our medical school was ten to fifteen years ahead of most Canadian and American Medical schools.

This indeed must have been the case. In answer to Dean Mathers' letter to deans of other Canadian medical schools asking about their admission criteria, the majority did not state that they did not discriminate against Jews.

There was strong anti-Semitism in Quebec shown for example by the unprecedented strike of interns in Montreal hospitals in 1934 because of the appointment of a Jewish intern. There is also evidence of quotas limiting Jewish students' admission to the University of Toronto[9] and to other medical schools in the USA and Canada. The Manitoba Medical School went on to become a progressive and successful institution despite Dr. Mathers' dire predictions. Graduates of diverse ethnic origins achieved a large degree of success: Anglo-Saxons, Jews, Slavs, Mennonites, and others. Two prominent examples were Dr. Arnold Naimark who became Head of the Department of Physiology, Dean of Medicine, and President of the University of Manitoba and Dr. Henry Friesen, a leading researcher, who became Head of the Department of Physiology and then Director of Canada's Medical Research Council in Ottawa; a Jew and a Mennonite who might not have been admitted had the quota remained in place.

* * * *

During my time at the medical school I did not experience anti-Semitic attitudes among students or staff except for one minor incident. In our first year we spent seven hundred hours studying anatomy. We spent many hours in the dissection laboratory in groups of eight students to a dissecting table. We also studied physiology and biochemistry. The Professor of Anatomy was Dr. Ian Maclaren Thompson, who besides teaching us anatomy gave us lectures on statistical methods. He was an excellent lecturer. I studied hard, did well, and was awarded a medal for the highest standing in anatomy. We had four tests during the year. I obtained the highest mark in one of them. One of the technicians working in the department said to me that he was glad that I was first and *not one of those Jews*! There were two Isbister Scholarships awarded for the highest two places in the standing at the end of the year. I received one after our first year tied with Manny Shore (*one of those Jews*). Although I remained a good student, there were many other excellent students in our class and my standings slowly slipped down by one place during each of the following three years.

There were various extracurricular activities, in which I participated to some extent. They included playing table tennis in an old gym at the medical school. We had a great match against the third year students with six single players and three double teams each. Our British veteran Bill Doughty, also an excellent soccer player, was the best player overall. I was the second best in our class. I think that our class won a very close competition. I played soccer on the second tier medical team. One day we played a team of another faculty at the Fort Garry campus, but we had only five players. Then our classmate Jack Faiman, who played goal for one of the Winnipeg city league teams, arrived to register at the university offices, and agreed to play. With him in goal the match ended in a 0:0 tie despite our opposition having a full complement of eleven players.

During the match I experienced a very fulfilling moment. As I ran step for step with an opposing player for the ball that was rolling toward our goal, I gave him a slight hip check and suddenly became aware that he was no longer there and I was alone in possession of the ball. I watched our medical hockey team play hard against medicine's archrivals the engineers and saw my classmate Al Downs work hard and poke-check the opposition. The game played at the old arena at the Exhibition Grounds was very exciting. I also watched female members of our class compete in swimming at the Sherbrooke Street pool. I was a member of our five-pin bowling team. I visited the Hillel House, a Jewish students' facility, a few times where I played table tennis and bridge.

One of our classmates Jim MacPherson was a professional football player and played for the Winnipeg Blue Bombers of the Canadian Football League. I listened with interest to the radio broadcasts of the Bombers' games, during which I repeatedly heard the announcer say "MacPherson over the ball"; that was because Jim was playing centre and it was his task to snap the ball to the quarterback behind him on every offensive play. There was a six-man football intramural competition at the university and our medical faculty team, that included some of my first year colleagues, excelled often winning the overall competition. Our varsity soccer team with Bill Doughty as a leading player was also very successful.

I corresponded with my family in New York where they settled in an apartment on the west side of Manhattan. My uncle was allowed to practice ophthalmology after passing only an English language test. He was not required to take medical examinations because of his renown. My cousin Zdzich, who started using his middle name George (Jerzy), also pursued his medical career in ophthalmology. I could not visit my family, however, until I became a Canadian citizen, which required a period of five years to attain. Otherwise there was some risk that I would not be let back into Canada. I also corresponded with my

THE DAILY COM...

THIS REUNION MEANS a bright future for partially-blind Sig-
mund Eisenberg, 9, who arrived yesterday with 1,166 other DPs on
the Gen. McRae. Waiting for him at the Hotel Marseilles reception
center of the United Service for New Americans was Dr. Edmund
Carter Rosenhauch, himself a DP. Dr. Rosenhauch, an eye specialist,
gave the lad successful treatments when they were in an AMG hospital. Now that they are reunited, he will complete the cure.
Staff Photos by De Biase

Figure 14. Uncle Edmund with a patient, New York, ca. 1950.

cousin Ryś in London where he settled and ran a business; with one or
two of my friends in Poland and with my friend Adam Rosenblum in
Munich. He remained there and finished his medical studies. In 1951
he came to Canada and wrote to me from Montreal. He indicated that
he was urged to immigrate because of a danger of an armed conflict
and came on a contract to work as a chemist in a chemical factory. This
turned out to be a spurious formality. In reality, he was given work in a
hospital, which was for hopeless cases. His work was that of an orderly,
and he also worked in the kitchen. After a few weeks he was given work
as a laboratory assistant. His low pay did not change. His predecessor
at the new job reached age seventy and was terminated. Adam's letters

to me in 1952 made it clear that he was extremely unhappy with the conditions in which he found himself in Montreal. He had to work for low wages doing chores, which were not related to his qualifications, and he did not see any realistic prospects for improvement. He felt that he could not stand the situation much longer and wrote that he was saving in order to return to Germany or perhaps even to Poland. Then I had never heard from him again. I continued to be busy with my studies.

A man who was to figure prominently in my professional life was Dr. Joseph Doupe, who headed the Department of Physiology and also lectured. The faculty of medicine had a special summer research programme for students available after their second and third years of studies. Later on it was shifted to the summers after the first and second year. Students did a research project with a faculty member, wrote it up as a thesis, and presented their findings at a session run like a medical scientific meeting. If they completed the requirements they were eligible to obtain an additional degree of Bachelor of Science in Medicine when they graduated later.

I approached Professor Thompson and told him that I would like to do a project with him, and that I was particularly interested in the relation of neurology to psychology. He had a project on the regeneration of cut nerves in experimental animals and we agreed that I would proceed with it during the summer after the second year. As the time was approaching for me to begin, Professor Thompson informed me that he did not obtain funding for the project necessary to provide a payment to students for the summer's work. I was given a choice of working with him on a growth factor; otherwise he suggested that I approach Professor Doupe who might have a project more in my line of interest. I chose the latter.

Dr. Doupe explained to me that any research question becomes interesting as one delves into it, but he suggested a project related to the sympathetic nerves in diabetes, which I eagerly accepted. My project was under the direct supervision of Professor Doupe himself and arose from his own research in England during the war concerning the changes in the circulation in limbs affected with peripheral nerve injuries. Some of the cut nerves included sympathetic (involuntary) nerve pathways that controlled blood flow to the limbs. Since diabetes could adversely affect nerve function in some patients, Dr. Doupe thought that the sympathetic nerve function might be compromised in them.

I embarked on my project with enthusiasm. My studies consisted of measuring skin temperature changes in response to body heating and cooling, a function governed by the sympathetic nerves, and some studies of changes in blood flow using a plethysmographic (volumetric) method. The patients for the study were recruited at the Winnipeg General Hospital. The then chief-resident-doctor in medicine Dr. John Maclean put me in touch with them. Dr. Maclean was a wonderful human being and an excellent physician. He became my close and cherished colleague some years later.

My research with Dr. Doupe showed that indeed diabetic patients often exhibited abnormal responses that were indicative of impaired function of their sympathetic nerves to the blood vessels of the lower extremities. I completed my thesis and was granted the degree of B. Sc. (Med.) upon graduation. The results of that research, however, were not published until about twelve years later when additional experiments of Dr. John Moorhouse who later worked with Dr. Doupe were added. When John and I returned from our graduate studies, we wrote up the study. It was published in the *British Medical Journal* in 1966. As it turned out that was the last publication of which Dr. Doupe was a co-author. Unfortunately he died soon after the paper was published.

My research experience with Dr. Doupe was invaluable. Importantly, it was his imparting the notion that it was essential to be able to think critically that was vital in shaping the acumen of the students in the B. Sc. (Med.) programme that he administered. One day I was showing Dr. Doupe a roll of plethysmographic record from one of my studies. It was a long record of pulse waves obtained from a finger. Unfortunately I forgot to mark where the beginning of the record was and where was the end. I looked at the record confused. Dr. Doupe in essence told me to figure out which was which. What seemed an interminably long silence followed, during which Dr. Doupe continued to smoke his cigarette and I squirmed unable to come up with a solution, a situation that was also experienced at times by many of my colleagues. I gradually overcame my feeling of paralysis, realized that there must be a way and finally came upon the solution. It was based on the fact that the first part of each pulse related to the *contraction* of the heart was quicker than the second part, related to the *relaxation* of the heart.

We honed our skills in critical thinking during weekly seminars with Dr. Doupe. We took turns presenting articles from scientific medical journals that dealt with our research areas. After the presentation we tried to criticize it. Practically every time, however, Dr. Doupe would ask further critical questions that brought the methods or conclusions of the paper into question and in essence he tore the work apart. The sessions with Dr. Doupe and his penetrating and critical remarks felt at times uncomfortable, but the large majority of students realized that the remarks were not personal, but were intended to instill in us the ability to assess data critically. We appreciated his interest in our development. Indeed many of his students went on to illustrious careers and made important contributions to their chosen disciplines.

Some other classmates spent their summers working with the Manitoba Follow-Up Study, which followed about four thousand Canadian airmen from the war. The study continues to this day. It resulted in a large number of important publications on various medical subjects and factors related to heart disease and aging. My classmate Ted Cuddy was among those that participated during those summers. He became a prominent cardiologist and directed the study for many years.

Other classmates worked in various jobs during the summer vacations to help finance their studies, like working on the railroad lines or took training as reservists, an arrangement that included support of their studies in exchange for an obligation to stay in the Armed Forces for a period of time after graduation. Those of us who remained in Winnipeg could take opportunity to spend some time in St. Joseph's hospital where we learned how to tie surgical knots and picked up some other clinical experience from the attending doctors.

During the second year of our medical studies we took physiology, pharmacology, pathology, and bacteriology. In physiology we did class projects that in some of which we were the subjects. One of the projects involved nerve study in cats under the direction of Dr. Michael Saunders. In another we were measuring one another's blood pressure. One day while I was measuring blood pressure of a classmate, Bill Doughty put an ice cube down my back. Though shocked, I calmly proceeded with the measurement. Bill was most surprised at my "stiff upper lip." One colleague fainted when given an intramuscular injection of a hypertonic solution to experience the feeling of "visceral pain"—he obviously did. Another went into insulin shock, not uncommon in patients with diabetes, when injected with this drug.

The final examination in physiology was a shocker. All the questions were in the form of research hypotheses that we were to formulate on various problems. Having studied the subject was by itself not sufficient. Challenged, we sweated in the underground gym where the exam took place, the more so because it was a very hot day. Professor Doupe had boxes of cool soft drinks brought for us during the examination. We did not do well. I am not sure that anybody received a mark as high as seventy percent. The class obtained higher marks in other subjects. Dr Doupe's unorthodox approach to challenging students, which was legendary, was also invaluable in our education and development of critical thinking. Dr. Doupe was a multifaceted and complex human being. He held lively parties at his home for students and staff. He held interviews at the school with individual students that were a part of the course and counted toward the final mark. He asked one of my classmates: "What is the capacity of the human bladder?" and the student answered: "Two." Dr. Doupe asked, "Two what?" The answer was "Two beers!" That seemed to be good enough for Dr. Doupe.

Dr. Doupe brought in several promising researchers, interested in a variety of body organ systems, to the department to teach and do research. They included Dr J.A. Hildes who was interested in gastrointestinal problems and body acclimatization to extremes of temperature; Dr. Mike Saunders specializing in neural pathways; Dr. Marcel Blanchaer a biochemist; Dr. Jack Armstrong a heart specialist and others. They formed a multidisciplinary team that taught the students and led them in research projects in the B.Sc. (Med.) programme. Dr. Doupe also arranged hospital positions for them, where they developed diagnostic, treatment, and research programmes that started Winnipeg on the road to excellence in medical research and health care. Terrence Moore, a Winnipeg writer and journalist, wrote a book about the life of Dr. Doupe in 1989.[10] At the end of the second year I received a medal for the highest standing in bacteriology. As we studied various pathological disease states and saw gross specimens of the diseased organs from the faculty's collection of pathological exhibits, several of us experienced symptoms of the illnesses that we studied.

Students continued to engage in various extracurricular activities. My dormant love of music again came to the fore. I organized musical lunch sessions during which I played records of classic music in the physiology lecture theatre. Dr. Doupe grudgingly allowed them and they were well attended. Though Dr. Doupe did not seem to be a fan of music, others organized a "Joe Doupe" string quartet that played some concerts with a movement from Schubert's "Trout Quintet," with an added pianist, as their signature music. That musical group was resurrected at the celebrations of the 100th year anniversary of the Manitoba Medical College in 1983.

The University of Manitoba put out a newspaper the *Manitoban*, which contained information and news about the events within the university. In the early 1950s individual faculties were given a chance to put out an issue of the paper. In 1951 the ongoing rivalry between the engineers and the medics gave rise to a highlight of the university life that spilled onto the pages of the paper. The Engineers' issue of January 23 hailed the upcoming Power Prom during which the queen of the evening was to be crowned. My medical colleagues decided to put a wrench into the Engineers' plan and came up with a bold plot. Posing as the *Manitoban's* advertising manager one of my classmates arranged to have the candidates for the queen abducted under the guise of taking them to a photo session for the newspaper. The girls were then told the truth and had little choice but to cooperate, which they did willingly as good sports. They were taken for evening celebrations to a café where one of them was crowned the Queen. Dr. Doupe, I think, participated in judging the contest. The next issue of the *Manitoban* by the medical students was named "Medicoban" and contained an article about the event entitled "*Snatch Plot Laid Bare*" and among poetry "*The Engineer's Lament*":

> We are, We are, We are, We are,
> We are the Engineers,
> We had some girls for the Power Prom,
> But we lost the pretty dears,
> Drink soda pop and ginger ale
> And cry along with us
> We don't give a *darn* for any *darn* man
> Who won't share a queen with us.

There followed other editions of the paper. After another medical issue that contained an abundance of off-colour items and scatological humour, the university suspended the practice of issues by individual faculties.

During the third and fourth years we started seeing patients in hospital clinics, usually in groups of about eight students assigned to a clinic led by a faculty member of a clinical department such as medicine, surgery, obstetrics etc. These many able doctors taught us well, and I believe without financial compensation. We traveled to a number of Winnipeg hospitals. We became well acquainted with the local winter climate. One day while I was waiting for a bus at the notorious intersection at Portage Avenue and Main Street, my ear lobes became solidly frozen in a matter of minutes; they were as hard as blocks of wood. Luckily, there was no permanent damage. We had a break of a few weeks after the third year. I decided to spend it in the Sanatorium for patients with tuberculosis in the village of Ninette in western Manitoba. I interviewed and examined patients, which gave me additional experience. In my free time I worked on my data from the studies that I conducted with Dr. Doupe previously and prepared my dissertation for the degree of B. Sc. (Med.).

* * * *

In the summer of 1953 we started our internship. We were the last class required to do their internship before graduating with our degrees; subsequent classes received their degrees after the fourth year of the medical school before doing their internship. A few of our classmates opted for doing the internship elsewhere, mainly in British Columbia. The large majority of the class lived during the internship in the old intern's residence near the Winnipeg General Hospital, which is now a part of the Health Sciences Centre complex. We were assigned two to a room in the residence. My roommate was Don Besant, who was a good colleague. He had an unusual way of dealing with excessive heat during hot weather. Our quarters were not air-conditioned. He would wrap himself up in bed with thick blankets "to keep the heat away." We received board and room, but I believe no pay for our year of work and education. There was food a plenty served in our quarters, although one tended to get tired of poached eggs for breakfast every day. Cold cuts were available in the kitchen for the hungry twenty hours a day.

We worked at the General Hospital taking monthly rotations in various specialties such as internal medicine, general surgery, urology, neurosurgery, and others. Every few nights we were on call for the emergency department that required taking care of patients who showed up in the emergency room for a variety of health problems. It was in the emergency room that I performed my first and one of overall few surgical procedures, such as sowing up cuts and lacerations, some quite extensive, and taking out a superficial cyst. The emergency shifts, especially at the beginning of the internship year were very trying for me and likely for my colleagues since we were inexperienced. Also, if the night shift was a busy one, we had to go on the next day's work with little sleep.

In our daily work we took histories and examined patients who were admitted to the hospital in our service and followed their progress under the supervision of the more experienced resident doctors, further advanced in their training, and of the attending medical staff doctors, who were overall in charge of the patients. On some rotations we were also expected to perform blood and urine tests; and in all cases, if immediately needed, during the night shifts. We spent considerable time doing these and peering through the microscope on blood and urine samples and on the fluid taken from the spinal canal, that we obtained by inserting a needle into it. I found that it was often helpful to obtain a patient's chart from a previous admission and go over it. There was frequently information that was helpful in dealing with a new problem and we would obtain the charts from the hospital records office in the case of admissions during the night and pored over them.

There were trials and tribulations, but we gained valuable experience. We were paired in our services, so that we would check out to our partner on a night off and he would be called for any problems that might have arisen with our patients. My partner was Bob Nixon, the veteran of the Pacific Campaign. We were called when needed during the night by the central telephone operator through the speakers in our rooms in the intern's residence when a problem would a rise with one of our patients or if our presence was required for emergency surgery or some other reason. If one did not answer right away, the operator became insistent repeating his message louder and louder. That did not sit well with the reluctant colleague's roommate and those sleeping in neighbouring rooms. During the day in the hospital we were paged, when needed, by a loudspeaker system manned by the telephone operators. One day it seemed that the great icon of Canadian medicine Dr. William Osler (1849—1919) came to life at the Winnipeg General Hospital. Over the loudspeaker the voice of the operator sounded:

"Paging Dr. Osler, Dr William Osler!" One of our classmates asked the telephone operator to page the Great Dr. Osler.

I recall assisting at an emergency appendectomy of a young boy. The surgeon Dr. Ken Trueman called me "Sidney Cooper" after a character from a novel. Dr. Trueman was a tall man and wore glasses. He calmly "explained" to the young patient that to get his appendix out we used "appendix seekers" and some of them were "tall and wore glasses." We saw and cared for a large numbers of patients. Some I still remember more than fifty years later. There was a young man with severe diabetes, who though bright, would not take care of his condition and repeatedly wound up in the hospital with recurrent complications. While on call for the emergency room, I saw a man with symptoms that led me to diagnose a fresh case of diabetes. I admitted a beautiful, healthy looking young woman who was diagnosed with a malignant cancer. Some months later she was readmitted near death with her body ravaged by disease. In the meantime we learned that her family spent a large fortune by taking her to a "clinic" in Mexico or southern United States that claimed to cure patients with cancer. I admitted a man who was one of Winnipeg's leading sport personalities, who came for a routine checkup. An elderly, obese woman came for surgery to remove her gall bladder. As part of my routine physical examination, I thought that there might have been a lump in her breast. A biopsy showed that she indeed had a malignant lump. This led to surgery, which had a chance of curing her, though I did not find out what eventually happened as I was transferred to another service.

There were recreational facilities in our quarters that included a pool table and table tennis. They were used extensively. Occasionally parties, some quite wild, were held. We made day excursions to a beach on Lake Manitoba near St. Laurent in the Interlake region, one of many beaches in the province. Some of my classmates, among them Don Besant and Ross Campbell, got married and I attended their wedding ceremonies. I did go out on some dates, but did not form any close relationships. I was shy and I concentrated on my studies. We followed sporting events, especially the exploits of the Winnipeg Blue Bombers. I attended an occasional game with Ben Kitzes. My classmate Jim MacPherson played for the Bombers while in medical school as did Tom Casey, who entered the medical faculty a couple of years later. Tom, a black American, was born in Ohio in 1924 and served in the US Navy in 1944 and 1945. In 1949 he joined the Hamilton Wildcats to play football, and in 1950 came to Manitoba because of prospects of admission to the medical faculty and opportunity to play football for the Blue Bombers.

When Tom arrived, the great flood of the Red River was in full swing and he quickly volunteered to man the crews that sandbagged the riverbanks. It was an auspicious year for the Bombers. Tom and other talented players, including the quarterback "Indian" Jack Jacobs, joined the Bombers, leading to a great improvement in the team's performance and ultimately a Grey Cup appearance. Tom was the leading rusher in the Western Conference that year and soon became the prevailing choice for the All Star Team in 1950, '51, and '52 and for the All Star Defensive back in 1953, '54, and '55. He set a record with a run of a hundred yards for a touchdown in 1952 in addition to setting a record of sixteen touchdowns in one season. Sports writers gave Tom the nickname "Citation" as his speed resembled that of the famous race horse Citation. Jim also continued his stellar play on the line, blocking and protecting his quarterbacks. A third Bomber from our faculty was Norm Hill, a couple of years my senior. As tough end he effectively rushed the opposing quarterbacks. Among the Blue Bombers' exploits particularly memorable was the amazing comeback victory in the last two minutes of the final Western play-off game against the Edmonton Eskimos. With the score tied late in the game, Dave Skrien intercepted a pass by Edmonton's quarterback Claude Arnold. Dave lateralled the ball to Tom Casey. Tom took off and ran until he reached the end zone to score to the winning touchdown. The play covered ninety-five yards and resulted in a 30: 24 victory for Winnipeg. Tom was inducted into the Canadian Football Hall of Fame in 1964. While we followed our colleagues' experiences on the field, we took their calls in the hospital while they were away with the team. When the football season was over all of us checked out to them for a night shift and they had to work extremely hard to keep the matters under control.

During 1953—1954, the year of our internship, there was a great epidemic of poliomyelitis in Manitoba. The stricken patients were admitted to the municipal hospitals. Many had not only paralysis that affected their limbs, but had to be in respirators because of the paralysis of the respiratory muscles. Dr. John (Jack) Hildes, an associate of Dr. Doupe, was in charge and directed the operations tirelessly going with little or no sleep for weeks on end. Respirators were flown to Winnipeg. Members of our class were assigned to help and I was among them. I was asked by Dr. Hildes to drive to Morden to fetch a small chest res-pirator. I spent many shifts among the rows of respirators tending to the sick. It was difficult to see these unfortunate victims; among them I recall a swimming champion and a pregnant woman. The efforts of Dr. Hildes were recognized. He was named Manitoba Citizen of the Year for battling the world's worst polio epidemic, by a board named by the *Winnipeg Tribune*. The award was inaugurated that year as a matter of public interest.

At the end of the year we had to pass oral and written examina-tions before graduating. Although my colleagues and I passed them without difficulties, I did not get very high marks. I was surprised to be awarded a Dr. Charlotte W. Ross gold medal and prize for the highest standing in Obstetrics. Dr. Ross was a female pioneer physician and community leader in eastern Manitoba in the late nineteenth-century. Finally, the internship was over and we graduated with the graduation ceremony taking place at the University's Fort Garry campus.

Some of my classmates went into general practice. Others includ-ing myself continued our education with little or no break. I went on to do a year of study in internal medicine at the Winnipeg General Hos-pital. There I broadened my clinical experience and honed my clinical skills across a wide spectrum of disease states. Among various cases I spent most of one night treating a patient with severe diabetic coma in the emergency room. During that year "the senior" staff were able to stay in an apartment across the street from the medical school and were paid a "princely" sum of fifty dollars a month. As a part of our studies we did reviews. I reviewed the current state of atherosclerosis (harden-ing of the arteries) research, which I presented to my colleagues. It was published in a local medical journal of the university. I also helped a noted Winnipeg cardiologist Dr. Robert Beamish to analyze the effects of a new anticoagulant drug. The results were published in the *Journal of the Canadian Medical Association* in 1956.

The following year I completed a research study that led to my degree of Master of Science. Dr. Doupe arranged for me to work with Dr. Mark Nickerson, who arrived from the USA to become the chair-man of the Department of Pharmacology. I learned that Dr. Nickerson came to Winnipeg because of a problem with the US Un-American Activities Subcommittee of Joseph McCarthy, who conducted witch-hunt hearings to find communist sympathizers during the cold war era. The USA's loss was Canada's gain. Dr. Nickerson was a world authority

Figure 15. My graduation photo, 1954.

on sympathetic nervous system and a contributor to a classic text of pharmacology. He brought with him two graduate students Bill Yard and Irv Shemano with whom I soon became friends. Dr. Nickerson quickly built a large department active in research and teaching.

My thesis dealt with shock provoked by physical injury or blood loss in experimental animals. Because my project was related to that of Bill Yard's we worked closely together during that year. Although my major subject was pharmacology, physiology was my minor subject. This allowed me to continue to work on my critical reasoning by participating in seminars with Dr. Doupe.

In 1954 I became a Canadian citizen. This allowed me to visit my uncle, aunt and cousin in New York. For the first time in my life I boarded an airplane and before long saw my family for the first time in seven years. I looked in wonder on the mass of skyscrapers of New York and various sites of that unique city. My aunt and uncle lived in an apartment on the upper west side of Manhattan. My uncle was busy practicing ophthalmology and my cousin Zdzich, now known as Dr. George Carter, pursued his specialization in ophthalmology. He worked with one of the leading New York ophthalmologists Dr. Conrad Berens. This connection helped in planning my next year of postgraduate studies. Dr. Berens knew well Dr. Irving Wright who was an acknowledged expert in anticoagulant (blood thinning) drug studies and in peripheral vascular disease. Dr. Wright agreed that the following year I would do a year of graduate studies in his department at the New York Hospital-Cornell Medical Center. Close to the New York Hospital was the Sloan Kettering Center for patients with cancer. There Dr. John Maclean, who helped me in Winnipeg to recruit patients for my research with Dr. Doupe, was taking postgraduate training. He gladly met with me and gave me some helpful hints about life in New York.

I finished my work with Dr. Nickerson in 1956 and completed my thesis. As a result of my work I was awarded a Prowse silver medal and prize, named after an eye, ear, nose, and throat surgeon, who was the Dean of the Faculty from 1917 to 1931. When the academic year was over I set out for New York. I traveled with my classmate Gerry Winkler, who was our class' gold medalist. He had a Studebaker car and was heading to do postgraduate training in neurology in Boston. The trip was enjoyable. Before the last stage of the trip to Boston we spent a day or two at the Atlantic coast in Ogunquit, Maine and listened to the sound of the surf. The tourist season had not yet begun.

New York and Mayo Clinic 1956—1958

I found a room in the student residence associated with the New York Hospital and lived there through most of my year in New York. The atmosphere of New York was exciting with its crowds and bustle. For the first time since my happy days on the sandy beaches of the Baltic Sea in Poland I tasted the delicious Italian lemon ice sold in stores on First Avenue not far from where I lived. I often visited my aunt, uncle and cousin. I became reacquainted with Julliete, the daughter of my Winnipeg "family" and her husband and two children. I met other members of her extended family. Among them were a journalist Ethel and her brother Ben, an engineer. They were brilliant people with wide interests. They lived on the lower east side of Manhattan with their mother who was suffering from severe complications of diabetes and died during my year in New York. I visited them often. I went with Ethel to see the play *The Iceman Cometh* by Eugene O'Neill at a theatre in lower Manhattan and was tremendously impressed. Ben once took me to a baseball game at the Polo Grounds where the New York Giants played. I saw the great Willie Mays and Bobby Thompson, who hit "the homer that was heard around the world" to win the pennant in 1951. My visits with Ethel and Ben were always most enjoyable with stimulating discussions on a number of topics. I maintained contact with them over many years to come.

At the laboratory of Dr. Wright I met a Dr. Marc Verstraete from Belgium, who was finishing his fellowship with Dr. Wright. He had become a prominent medical scientist in diseases of the blood and of peripheral blood vessels in Liege in his native Belgium. I was to meet him a number of times at future international medical meetings. There were also two graduate fellows from Columbia; Enrique Urdanetta, a son of a former President of that South American country, and Jamie Borrero. We got along well together and Dr. Wright and his staff were pleased with our work. I spent considerable hours in the library studying and collecting information that I thought might be useful in conducting current and future research.

We saw patients with blood vessel diseases at the New York Hospital and regulated anticoagulant drug treatment of patients at the Bellevue Hospital, where the Cornell Medical Center had a division. I became quite attached to some of the patients that I followed. One was a quite elderly Italian gentleman with vascular disease and ulcers on his toes. I spent a fair amount of time with him and his family discussing various treatment options. I examined a man from the mountains of Colombia, who was thought to have been about a hundred and fifty-years-old. He was invited to the New York Cornell Hospital so that medical scientists could examine him. He was a lively short man, who liked to play his bongo drums. I checked his circulation and found that he had bounding pulses in his limbs indicating absence of any plugging of his arteries. I was moved when a patient at the Bellevue clinic gave me a present—a tie when I was finishing my duties there.

I was involved in the analysis of the results of anticoagulant treatment that resulted in a couple of publications in prestigious medical journals. I also started an experimental study of the effect of dietary fats on the clotting in the veins of dogs. I found the experience quite interesting though it did not lead to conclusive results. One day I went to visit Dr. Otto Loewi. Dr. Doupe, who must have known this Nobel Prize Laureate in medicine of 1936, who was originally from Germany, suggested the visit. By the time of my visit he was quite elderly and not well. He received me kindly. In the past he had to flee the Nazis before settling in the USA.

While in New York I decided to take advantage of its amazing choice of cultural events. I went to concerts and plays. I saw *Long Day's Journey into the Night* by Eugene O'Neill, the musical *Candide* with music by Leonard Bernstein, enjoyed open-air summer concerts at the Lewison Stadium. I even managed to see *My Fair Lady*, one of the most successful musicals on Broadway, it was still going strong in New York and it was very difficult to obtain tickets. With my colleague Jamie Borrero we went around 6 o'clock in the morning to line up for standing room only tickets that were being sold for the evening performance that night. I was enchanted by the show; Julie Andrews' understudy played her role that day. During that year the residents of the New York Hospital staged a performance of skits. One of them was a take-off on the song "The Rain in Spain" from *My Fair Lady*.

A Dr. H. G. Wolff was a renowned neurologist working at the New York Hospital. The students "transposed" the song to "The Pain is Felt Mainly in the Brain". I also wanted to see a ballet performance, something I never saw live before. Finally as the New York City Ballet's season was coming to a close I bought a ticket to a performance. I was so enchanted that I quickly bought a ticket to another one of the remaining shows. In the spring I spent a short vacation with my classmate Gerry Winkler, who was doing his graduate work in Boston. We went to Washington, D.C. and saw that wonderful city in bloom of the cherry trees. We visited several landmarks such as the Washington and Lincoln Memorials, the Smithsonian Institution, and the National Art Gallery.

During my year in New York I went on several dates. My dates were interesting but no close relationship developed. I felt somewhat awkward. Perhaps my teenage years lost during the war and the years spent in Winnipeg mostly studying, left me handicapped in dealing with relationships with the opposite sex. In February I went on a date arranged through my fascinating friend Ethel, who knew the family of my date. Her name was Emilee. I went to pick her up at an apartment in the Bronx where she lived with her parents. We had dinner at an English restaurant in Manhattan and went to see a musical *Li'l Abner* on Broadway. Afterwards we had a snack and a fascinating conversation. I learned that Emilee was teaching in a city high school and had wide interests, including Norse mythology that I knew nothing about.

I was impressed by Emilee and perhaps somewhat overwhelmed. While nothing between us developed at the time, more was to unfold in the future.

During my year in New York I tried to arrange for further studies. Eventually I wanted to return to Winnipeg and work there. I contacted Dr. Doupe, who suggested that I enjoy doing physiology and not worry about a future position, as there would always be a place for competent individuals. Eventually Dr. Doupe arranged for me to obtain a fellowship of the National Research Council of Canada to spend a year at the Mayo Clinic in the Laboratory of Dr. E. H. Wood to learn new techniques of heart catheterization useful in the diagnoses of various heart abnormalities. I eagerly took up the offer. It also happened to dovetail with a meeting I had with Dr. Beamish, the Winnipeg cardiologist with whom I worked previously, at a meeting of the American Heart Association that I attended during the year. He told me that there were plans to set up a foundation that would support research by young investigators in Manitoba.

* * * *

I arrived in Rochester, Minnesota where the Mayo Clinic was situated in late June 1957 in a second hand Chevrolet that I bought from a graduate student in New York. Dr. Earl Wood's laboratory was in the Medical Sciences Building, which contained a human centrifuge. In it Dr. Wood and his staff studied the effects of high gravitational forces to which pilots were subjected during the war. After the war the laboratory was active in pioneering various techniques to study the function of the heart and circulation in normal subjects and patients with heart disease. These were important in the procedures of heart catheterization carried out by Dr. Wood and his colleagues to help diagnose patients with heart problems and thus assist in arriving at optimal treatment for them.

Graduate students like myself participated in the diagnostic procedures and presented the results to a panel of distinguished specialists that included the cardiac surgeon John Kirklin, cardiologist Howard Burchell, pathologist Jesse Edwards and others. There were several graduate students in the laboratory including some from countries such as Austria, Ireland, and Yugoslavia. Among them was Irwin J.

Fox, who remained a graduate fellow in the laboratory for many years and became one of my companions. His work on an important dye used in the study of the heart function led to the dye being nicknamed "Fox green" in the laboratory. The green dye was newly discovered and improved the results of the studies of heart defects.

All students were involved in various research projects. Some of these entailed experiments on normal subjects, which led the students involved in the projects to "recruit" their fellow students for the experiments. Thus it came that I reluctantly agreed to be a subject for a project that involved several tubes or catheters placed in my arteries and heart. I was definitely apprehensive, but there were no ill effects. Being a subject for the experiment was a valuable experience because it made me realize how patients feel in similar situations and how a kind word or a question that acknowledges that one is there can make a big difference in how a patient feels. In retrospect it was also an example of the state of research on humans, healthy and ill, in which the subjects were induced to take part in experiments that had some, even if small, chances of untoward effects or danger. Such attitudes prevailed for decades after World War II despite the Nuremberg Code, which was formulated at the Nuremberg Doctors Trial in 1946. The western clinical researchers seemed to have assumed that the code was needed for the barbaric perpetrators of the atrocities of the German Reich, but not for the reasonable investigators under "normal" conditions. It was not until considerably later that thorough guidelines and ethics committees were put in place in the medical centres of most of the western countries to protect the subjects and patients and to insist on the subject's informed consent before proceeding with the research.

The work at the Mayo Clinic was very interesting and I met many bright physicians, students and staff members. I lived in a rented room close to the Medical Sciences Building, which was previously occupied by a Winnipegger, Dr. Glen Lillington. He graduated a few years before me with a gold medal. He specialized in the diseases of respiration and was to become an expert in the field. I chummed with Dr. I.J. Fox of the "Fox green" dye fame and Ken Hosie a British student. The three of us would go out for dinner almost every day to a local Chinese restaurant before returning to the laboratory for a few evening hours of further work or study. The projects that I was involved with led to some interesting findings that resulted in publications during the next couple of years.

There were some extracurricular activities. I went for drives in the country in my car and attended some artistic performances including one by the Ballet Russe de Monte Carlo. My classmate from Winnipeg, Sheldon Sheps and his wife were in Rochester, where Sheldon was a fellow in medicine. I visited them often. I met a very interesting couple Dr. Gerry Vogel, a fellow in psychiatry, and his wife Evelyn. Emilee, my date in New York, told me about them. They led a discussion group called Great Books, a programme conceived at the University of Chicago, from where the Vogels and Emilee graduated. University of Chicago was a very progressive institution led by its charismatic chancellor Robert Hutchins. The institution eliminated grades and course requirements, replacing these with broad-based general education classes and a series of comprehensive exams. Hutchins advocated the relocation of the BA degree to the sophomore year of college, focusing the bachelor's degree on general or liberal education, and leaving specialization for the master's programmes. Hutchins also became known for his emphasis on the "great books", through the evening courses he co-taught with Mortimer Adler, and his support of the adult groups, which mushroomed throughout the country in the 1940s. I found the book discussions in Rochester very stimulating and became acquainted with some classics of world literature.

In the fall the Vogels told me that Emilee was coming for the Thanksgiving weekend and invited me to dinner. There I saw Emilee again and we went out on a date. I was very impressed with her. She told me about a play *Six Characters in Search of an Author* by Luigi Pirandello. I read it and was fascinated. I started corresponding with Emilee regularly and soon realized that I wanted to marry her. I decided to go for a visit to New York in January. I asked her out and proposed. My proposal was a lengthy one as I felt that she ought to know about Winnipeg, its climate and other realities. She accepted and I decided I would first introduce her to my cousin George. While we were in his apartment I suddenly said, "By the way George, Emilee and I want to get married." Taken by surprise he said, "Do you have to?" I answered, "No. We just want to."

Emilee wanted me to know more about her roots and we drove north of the city to the area near Peekskill where she showed me an old farmhouse that belonged to her parents and where she spent her youth. They usually spent their summers there. A huge barn and smaller farm structures were converted into living quarters, which the family rented to New York City dwellers for vacations during hot summers. Emilee told me about her family and friends. Her mother was Jewish. She married a Protestant, who happened to have been born in Toronto. Emilee's maternal grandmother was a member of the International Garment Workers Union in New York. She died suddenly on the family farm in 1939. Emilee had an older sister married to a man who built paper mills in countries scattered across various parts of the globe.

Emilee was also an artist. She drew, painted, and sculpted. She spent time in the studio of the well-known sculptor Freeman Schoolcraft in Chicago and attended the Students' Arts League in New York. She took graduate courses in New York, worked at various jobs including as a commercial artist, and obtained her teaching certificate. When I told my aunt Pauline that I was going to marry Emilee, she refused to meet her because she was only half-Jewish! My aunt was dead set against mixed marriages and disapproved of the Gentile girlfriends that cousin George dated. My uncle met Emilee briefly when we stopped at his office. Then it was time for me to return to Rochester to complete my studies. Emilee's family, with her input, decided to give an engagement party for us in the spring. We were going to get married later in Rochester with a small ceremony and without any family members. Emilee felt that if my aunt would not attend then her family would not be present either.

* * * *

The informal engagement party took place on Easter Sunday April 6, 1957 at the Horn family farm on Croton Avenue off route 202 in the Peekskill area of the New York state, about forty-miles north of the Big Apple. It was raining cats and dogs and the lane from Croton Avenue to the farm, which was not paved, became a sea of mud. Dozens of people came from the city and the neighbouring areas trudging through the mud. Emilee's parents, however, with the help of family friends gave a lively party. Some people were partying in the main farmhouse, while others were having a good time in the huge barn. Celebrations went on well into the night. One of the revelers was found asleep the next morning in one of the rooms. One or two of my classmates who were in New York attended including Dr. Morris Loffman and his wife Sonia. Morris was to become a successful neurosurgeon in California. There were long distance congratulatory telephone calls from other classmates. I was not in the position to buy an engagement ring. Instead I bought for Emilee a long-playing record of Gregorian Chants that she liked. We received engagement gifts of long-playing records of Mozart's string quintets and one of his piano trios.

Many friends of the Horns came from the Colony, a remarkable community, just across the nearby route 202. The Mohegan Colony was established at the South end of the lake Mohegan in 1920s as a utopian attempt to provide an egalitarian way of living and raising one's family. It was an offshoot of the Stelton Colony established in New Jersey by the followers of the Ferrer School of thought. Its members were anarchists and libertarians of European origin.

The property for the Mohegan colony was acquired with help from the Baron de Hirsch Fund, which sponsored Jewish agricultural settlements in various parts of the world including Manitoba and Saskatchewan. Part of the modern school movement, Mohegan Colony was a hotbed of new thinking, established its own school, and had some three hundred families. There were many Jewish families, but quite a few people at the colony lived in interfaith and interracial marriages and others that did not believe in formal marriage. The colony contained a large variety of views on the political left from anarchists to socialists.

The nearby town of Peekskill had a population of about eighteen thousand. Though, with a relatively high percentage of WASP's, it was fundamentally a town of lower middle-class people who worked in the local shops and small industries. Its economy was stagnant apparently because its inhabitants rejected expansion of the industry to preserve the rural character of the area. That made the area attractive to the New York City dwellers that spent their summers in the Mohegan Colony and the surrounding district. During the summer the population of the areas around Peekskill swelled to some thirty thousand. Emilee attended the progressive school in the Colony and a high school in Peekskill, where she witnessed a performance by the original Von Trapp family singers, later made famous in the movie *The Sound of Music*. During summers a day camp was held at the Colony and Emilee served there as a counselor when she was a teenager.

In 1949 notorious events took place in the region. A concert headed by Paul Robeson was scheduled in late August. Robeson, a Negro singer and activist was a controversial figure who lauded the Soviet system after he traveled extensively in the Soviet Union and criticized the USA in the early years of the cold war. Preparations for the concert were disrupted by the rightist Peekskill elements that broke and burned chairs that were being set up forcing the cancellation of the concert.

At that time a Gentile girlfriend of Emilee's was coming home from work and came across the heavy traffic of cars belonging to the rightist veterans and their supporters, who had a variety of weapons such baseball bats. Emilee's friend looked somewhat Jewish and she was suddenly pushed into the road where the cars were moving with an epithet that covered all the bases: "God dam nigger loving, commie kike!" She avoided the cars but fell scraping her knees.

The concert was rescheduled for the following Sunday September 4, and large numbers of New Yorkers and people from surrounding communities came, including a "security" group that consisted of members of the unions to try and protect the performers and the audience. Outside a thousand veterans and their followers shouted insults and threw stones at cars and buses entering the concert grounds. The police, however, prevented them from entering the grounds. The concert proceeded without incident. There were other performers including Pete Seeger before Robeson sang Negro spirituals and "Ol' Man River". Then the sunny Sunday afternoon turned into a nightmare. Police routed the vehicles leaving the concert grounds through various connecting roads where protesters armed with piles of stones hurled them at the cars shattering windows and injuring many. A few cars were overturned. The violence spread to surrounding areas where large stones were dropped from highway overpasses leading to New York. Roger Williams wrote in the *American Heritage Magazine* in 1976 that the Peekskill riots were caused by anti-communist phobia combined with anti-Semitism and racial animosity, and that it foreshadowed the McCarthyism and its communist witch-hunt that dominated American public life in the early 1950s. As mentioned earlier it was owing to the McCarthyism that Winnipeg was rewarded in being able to recruit the well-known researcher Dr. Mark Nickerson to set up a strong Department of Pharmacology.

After the engagement party I returned to Rochester and Emilee continued her teaching. We were married on May 31, 1958 in Rochester by a justice of the peace. The witnesses were my classmate Sheldon Sheps and his wife Pearl, and Emilee's friends Gerry and Evelyn Vogel. We spent a brief honeymoon in a lake resort in the Brainerd region of Minnesota. Then it was once again back to finish our work in New York and Rochester respectively.

I corresponded with Dr. Doupe, who wanted me to return to Winnipeg to the Department of Physiology and set up new cardiovascular diagnostic facilities at St. Boniface Hospital where Dr. Morley Cohen was preparing to bring open-heart surgery to Winnipeg. I went to Winnipeg for a few days to check the equipment that was in use at the hospital and to decide what other equipment would need to be acquired. My second-hand Chevy's tires were getting worn out and I bought new ones. I kept busy completing my research projects at the Mayo Clinic and looked forward to Emilee coming to join me. She mentioned once that she liked cornflowers. I found a pot of blue cornflowers and brought it when I went to pick her up at the airport.

We lived for the remainder of the academic year in my single room apartment in Rochester. Emilee kept it neat and was helping me by typing the manuscripts of my research projects that were later published. Then, and gradually over the years, I found out more about Emilee's past. She was only five feet tall, but no slouch at sports. She was one of the best hitters on the boys' baseball team at Mohegan Colony. She played basketball at the University of Chicago. Once, a tall opponent pushed her hard and knocked her down during a game almost against a brick wall. The big girl paid for it by later receiving Emilee's sharp elbow in her chest.

Most impressive was Emilee's teaching experience in the "blackboard jungle" of New York. She taught in Long Island City High school in the New York borough of Queens. It was a large "600" school, which meant that there was police outside the school. Police were stationed inside the "700" schools. Emilee taught English to several classes in grades ten and eleven. Some were very unruly and difficult to control. Some girls were streetwalkers and once two burly policemen dragged a fighting and screaming girl into Emilee's class. Emilee persevered and achieved a lot. In October one of her supervisors commented that she carried the bulk of the English teaching "that would be a challenge to experienced old hands".

She was interested in her students and helped those that needed special help. Among her duties was taking turns to supervise the cafeteria. Once, Emilee noticed a big student going around the cafeteria and collecting something from the other students. She confronted him and thus broke up a protection racket. The towering student that she caught said, "I am going to get you Miss Horn." Her supervisor said, "Try to stay alive for the next two weeks!" as apparently the student was going to be transferred to another school. In the spring of 1958, a school's chairman sat in during one of her classes, which was a normal way of following teachers' progress. Emilee previously challenged the class to write short plays and then perform them. The chairman saw the class performance and discussion of the plays that Emilee conducted. He then asked her, "Where did the students get the scripts?" He was amazed when she told him that they wrote them themselves. In his report he congratulated her on a milestone in her development as a teacher and the courage to try something new. He wrote, "You came inexperienced… but you came through with flying colours. You became a confident, competent, successful teacher, loved by her students, appreciated by your supervisors, respected by your colleagues. My only regret is that some other school system—and some other nation—rather than ours, will be able to profit from your ultimate maturity as a teacher". One day near the end of the academic year, when Emilee was supervising in the cafeteria, there was a commotion or "rumble". Resolutely Emilee marched to investigate. As she approached the crowd of the students, they parted and she came to a table on which there was a celebratory cake for her!

When my year at the Mayo Clinic was over we set out in my car for Emilee's parents' farm in New York State. We stopped in Chicago where Emilee's friends from the time of her studies at the University of Chicago organized a party that gave me an opportunity to meet them. Emilee told me about a curious experience she had when she was a student in Chicago. One evening her date said to her, "Emilee, I like you but I cannot see you anymore because you are Jewish." The very next evening she was told by another date. "Emilee, I like you but I cannot see you anymore because you are not Jewish!" I do not know how children of mixed marriages are affected by such experiences, but they must have an effect.

A couple of days later we arrived in Peekskill and spent a couple of weeks on Emilee's parents' farm. I met a number of friends of the family, who were staying there and in the Colony and the surrounding area. In the evenings people who stayed on the farm would gather around an outdoor fire. There were hamburgers baked over the fire with fresh corn and delicious locally grown tomatoes. Then people talked about many subjects and at times sang. I was told that the legendary folksinger and political activist Josh White and young Eartha Kitt, who was to become a prominent singer and actress, once came to

Emilee's parents' farm and sang there after they had given a concert at a venue nearby.

We went to the beach in the Colony and swam in the Lake Mohegan. I also visited with my family in New York City and we saw Juliette, the daughter of the Kitzes family that sponsored me to Winnipeg in 1948, and their relatives who lived in the area.

Finally we set out on the long drive to Winnipeg where my job was soon to begin. Emilee's parents gave us various items, which filled the car. We drove and entered Canada at Fort Frances. I wanted Emilee to see Western Ontario with its forests and lakes before entering the flat prairie of Manitoba.

CHAPTER V
BACK IN WINNIPEG

We arrived in August and stayed for a few weeks with the Kitzes family on St. Matthews Avenue while we were looking for a place to live. We found an apartment on River Avenue near the Assiniboine River and a small park. It was located conveniently close to the St. Boniface Hospital where I was spending most of my working time. I was a member of the Clinical Investigation Unit that Dr. Doupe helped set up there. Dr. John Maclean, with whom I previously crossed paths and who became a wonderful colleague and friend, headed it. The unit also included Dr. Danny Snidal, who was starting a respiratory unit. I set out to put in place a laboratory to study patients with diseases of peripheral blood vessels and, importantly, techniques for the study of patients with heart disease that I learned at the Mayo Clinic.

I started doing heart catheterizations working with one of the cardiologists at the hospital and with the cardiac surgeon Dr. Morley Cohen. Doing heart catheterizations in those days was quite different from the procedures of today. I had to make a small incision over an arm vein, introduce a tube-catheter into it, and push it into the heart, while watching its progress on an X-ray screen. The X-ray machines at that time were emitting a fair amount of radiation so that I had only about ten minutes of the viewing time to pass the catheter into the chambers of the heart, and record pressures, and collect blood samples that were needed to make the diagnosis. At times it was difficult to get the catheter through the chambers of the heart into the main artery leading into the lungs, which was necessary to obtain meaningful data. One felt very badly if the attempt occasionally failed.

As new X-ray machines, which emitted less radiation, were developed through the years, the procedures became easier. Dr. Cohen did graduate work with Dr. Walter Lillehei in Minneapolis, where he participated in pioneering work on methods to develop open-heart surgery. He teamed up with Dr. Richard Burrell, Head of Surgery at St. Boniface Hospital, to set up an open-heart surgery team that would bring the benefits of this type of surgery to Manitobans. In 1959 Dr. Cohen performed the first open-heart surgery in the province at St. Boniface General Hospital. I was privileged to assist by monitoring the patient's intra-arterial blood pressure during the operation. Dr. Cohen was a highly skilled surgeon, principled teacher, problem solver, and community citizen who by example inspired others to better themselves and their communities.

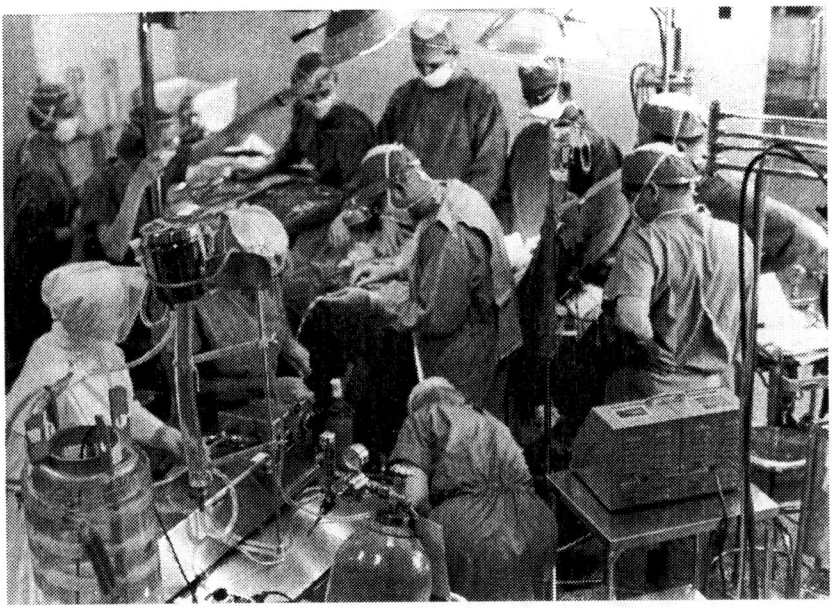

FIgure 16. First open-heart surgery in Manitoba. Dr. Cohen [center], sister Daigle in habit [left], S. Carter [right with back to camera], 1959. (Photo courtesy of St. Boniface Hospital Photo Archives.)

Emilee and I started enjoying various aspects of life; going for walks on both sides of the Assiniboine River, attending various art performances, and entertaining friends at our apartment. They included some of my classmates, colleagues and others, including John Hirsch whom I met during my early days in Winnipeg. Meanwhile Emilee started various activities. Through George Werier, who was an actor, she became involved with the recently formed Manitoba Theatre Centre. John Hirsch directed it. Emilee worked backstage with the props and wrote articles for the theatre newsletter. She recalled how once John was making numerous changes during a technical rehearsal at the old Dominion Theatre in 1959 that entailed the scenery, sound, cues, and props. He then asked if somebody had an aspirin and said that his hands were freezing and he was going to put on his gloves. His uncanny ability resulted in many memorable performances. The one that I was most taken with was *Of Mice and Men* with Gordon Pinsent. It created a moving experience that to me was not surpassed by many excellent productions that followed over the years. The company was the first Canadian regional theatre and, at the time of its founding, one of a handful of such theatres on the continent. It soon became professional and an ongoing part of the Manitoba arts scene. It was probably responsible in part for the explosion of regional modern professional theatre, which occurred in the late 1950s in North America.

At the same time Emilee enrolled at the University of Manitoba taking courses and working on a thesis on Sean O'Casey. She actually wrote a letter to the by then elderly author, which he did answer! The letter is stored in our safety box. Emilee also joined a group associated with the Winnipeg Art Gallery that was housed in the Winnipeg Auditorium, the same building in which the Winnipeg Symphony Orchestra performed. She took prints of paintings to a number of Winnipeg schools to expose the students to the beauty of visual arts and to give them ideas about how to appreciate them. In 1960 Emilee became pregnant and started hunting for a house. In the fall we moved to our new home on Elm Street in River Heights, a delightful neighbourhood with tall trees. Our son Joel was born in January 1961.

My work turned out to be very interesting and had different components. A doctor might be thought of as a professional who primarily takes care of patients. But since ancient times physicians engaged in studies or experiments to bring about new, hopefully better, ways of determining what a patient is suffering from and how to treat him; as well as teaching students who were to become doctors. Thus research and teaching were essential in addition to taking care of patients. Some doctors only took care of patients whereas others combined patient care with research or teaching or both. My work included all three of these activities, which I found stimulating and rewarding.

Working at the hospital with patients with various types of heart disease involved a close cooperation of a multidisciplinary team of surgeons, cardiologists, physiologists, radiologists, and anesthesiologists. The cases were discussed during conferences and the volume of cases grew rapidly. It became obvious that we needed a full-time cardiologist based at the hospital. We were able to recruit Dr. David Mymin, who joined us in 1961. Soon after he arrived, Dr. Doupe invited him, us and other guests to his cottage on an island on the Lake of the Woods in Western Ontario.

We became aware that it was a custom of many Winnipeggers to drive to "Zee Lake" for the weekend. "The Lake" was usually a cottage of varying sizes, often built by the owner on the shore of one of the thousand Manitoba lakes. Lake of the Woods was a good three hour drive east of Winnipeg. A black storm cloud followed us as we drove. Dr. Doupe waited for us at the pier and took us in a motorboat to the house on his island. It was a memorable weekend marked by a fierce storm. Dr. Hildes, who had a cottage on another island stopped for shelter. Then he, Dr Doupe and some other men set out to escort Dr. Hildes to his island while the storm raged. I stayed with women and children who included Joel our infant son. Joel decided to learn to climb out of his crib that weekend, and likely was only prevented from wandering alone in the middle of the storm and into the lake thanks to Emilee's alertness.

Professional Work

RESEARCH

After the arrival of Dr. Mymin the cardiac programme at St. Boniface Hospital progressed rapidly and other cardiologists were recruited to join it. This allowed me to concentrate on the investigation of peripheral vascular disease. I was interested in patients with arteriosclerosis or hardening of the arteries, a process that might lead to serious complications such as heart attacks and strokes. With the encouragement of Dr. Doupe I started studying changes in the stiffness of the leg arteries reasoning that arteriosclerosis would result in their greater stiffness. Dr. Doupe was extremely helpful in many ways. When I became frustrated with one of my technicians and said to him "I do not understand people," he responded, "You can never understand people, you can just learn to accept them."

My research was supported by a grant from the Manitoba Heart Foundation, which recently came into being in the province. I remained a recipient of its grants for the next three decades. The work was very interesting and involved consideration of the elasticity of the walls of the arteries and involved mathematical calculations. To improve my mathematical skills I joined with a group of my colleagues, which included my classmate Ted Cuddy, a cardiologist and Dr. Peter Gaskell, who was in charge of the vascular laboratory at the Winnipeg General Hospital. We hired Professor of Mathematics Bernard Noonan from the University of Manitoba who gave us a series of talks. I found the experience most interesting and recall getting quite excited about the properties of the exponential number e. I had to make calculations that involved some eighty equations in my research project. These were made using an electric calculating machine and were quite time consuming. We did not yet have computers. Eventually the work led to a publication, although it did not lead to a useful diagnostic test.

I then turned to studying patients with plugged arteries to the legs due to arteriosclerosis. I started by using recordings of skin temperature in the toes and fingers of patients to assess their circulation, a technique I used previously in my work as a student when I worked with Dr. Doupe. This technique did not turn out to be very useful in detecting plugging of the arteries, as many such patients had normal skin temperatures. Therefore, I turned to the measurements of blood pressure in the legs. These patients often experienced pain in their legs while walking that forced them to stop repeatedly for a brief period of time, every time they walked a short distance from about fifty meters to a few blocks, a symptom called intermittent claudication. A small proportion of patients could develop gangrene that might lead to amputation, especially among those that had diabetes. Earlier there was no definitive treatment except for an amputation, if necessary. By mid-twentieth century, however, new surgical techniques were being developed, which allowed for the removal of the obstructing arteriosclerotic plaques or a bypass of the obstruction using patients' own veins or tubes made from a synthetic material. This development made the assessment for the presence and severity of the obstruction in such patients practically important.

Measurements of blood pressure in the arm were a routine method in the physical examination of patients since the beginning of the century, but only isolated experimental studies of blood pressure in the legs were made prior to 1950. Then new studies began to be published. They were showing that, as would be expected, the pressure in the legs with narrowed or plugged arteries was lower compared to the arm pressure. Among others Dr. Peter Gaskell started doing such measurements at the Winnipeg General Hospital. In the usual measurement of pressure in the arm, the doctor determines the pressure by listening with a stethoscope for the appearance of sounds over the arm artery while slowly decreasing the pressure in the cuff wrapped around the arm, after first pumping the pressure in the cuff up to squeeze the arm artery shut. In legs with plugged arteries no sounds were audible. Early measurements including my own used other methods such as detecting an increase in the volume of the limb by a plethysmographic method. The pressure was read when the blood started flowing into the limb while the cuff was being deflated as shown by the increase in the volume of the leg, by detecting the appearance of oxygen in the skin below the cuff, or by use of sensitive gadgets that detected the appearance of a pulse. Some of these techniques were cumbersome. I decided to use an ultrasonic probe that easily detected the beginning of blood flow as the pressure in the cuff was gradually reduced. I carried out measurements on a large number of patients, who also had angiographic X-ray studies, which showed the presence and severity of the blockage of their arteries. This work showed that the measurements were reliable and led to them being accepted as a routine method for the diagnosis and assessment of the disease of the leg arteries.

The research took a considerable amount of time. It entailed writing repeated applications for grants that allowed the research to continue, and writing up the results for publication. Research results often provide answers, but also generate questions that might lead to further research. Thus, my study of blood pressure in patients' legs led to an unexpected finding; in two patients I found that the pressure in their legs could not be measured because, even when I pumped the cuff around their leg up to a very high pressure of 300 millimeters of mercury, their arteries were not compressed as shown by continued flow of blood into the leg detected by an ultrasonic probe. A plain X-ray of their legs suggested the explanation: the X-ray showed dense calcification of the wall of the arteries, which must have made them rigid like stem-pipes so they could not be compressed by the inflating the cuff. These patients had diabetes and patients with this disease often have calcified arteries. In these two patients I felt strong pulses in their feet showing that their arteries were not plugged up. Situation became more complex, however, when I subsequently encountered a patient who had no palpable pulse in his leg indicating the presence of plugged arteries, yet, his blood pressure was measured as normal. The X-ray showed that the walls of his arteries were calcified; yet, they were not completely incompressible allowing eventual compression by the cuff. This "partial incompressibility" resulted in a falsely high pressure value. Thus, I realized that in some patients the leg pressure measurement could be wrong and therefore misleading.

To try and obviate this problem, I turned to measurements of pressure in the toes. This could be accomplished by applying small cuffs, which I made from thin rubber tubing, and pumping pressure into them to compress the arteries entering the toe. I then determined the pressure in the toe arteries by noting when blood started to flow into the toe beyond the cuff. Measurements of pressure in the fingers were carried out previously in various experimental studies and I was aware of them particularly because my colleague, Dr. Peter Gaskell, was studying them in patients with high blood pressure. I detected the beginning of flow by noting the appearance of oxygen in the skin, as did Dr. Gaskell in his studies, but then found that it was less cumbersome and faster to use a plethysmographic strain gauge or a photocell that detect an increase in volume in the end part of toe beyond the cuff. Before I could apply the method to patients with plugged arteries, I had to determine the value of toe pressures in normal subjects. I then documented that toe pressures are a reliable method to demonstrate the presence of plugged arteries to the legs in patients, by relating the measurements to the findings of plugging of the vessels in angiograms showing the plugged vessels in a series of patients. My results were carried out with the assistance of nurses and technologists, who worked with me in the Vascular Laboratory at St. Boniface Hospital, and were published in reputable medical journals. I presented my findings at scientific medical meetings among doctors and researchers who had the opportunity to become acquainted with the work of others and to exchange ideas with colleagues from many medical centres. I attended meetings at the military station in Suffield, Alberta where experiments were conducted during World War II as well as in Banff and other Canadian and US cities.

My work attracted some attention. After I presented my findings at an international meeting in Liège, Belgium, I was invited to a meeting in Copenhagen. There, leading researchers in the diseases of the peripheral blood vessels from various European and North American centres gathered. My exposure in Liège and Copenhagen led to an invitation, by research surgeons from the west coast of the USA, Drs. Eugene Strandness and Eugene Bernstein, to another international meeting in San Diego in 1977. Other participants and I were each asked to write a chapter on the subject of our expertise; in my case the measurements of pressures in the legs with arterial disease. These chapters were to be handed in on arrival at the meeting otherwise one's expenses were not paid. The chapters were then published in a book. Working on my chapter was a major undertaking, as I wanted it to be a thorough review of the subject. It led to my working numerous extra hours that usually included both Saturdays and Sundays. Thus, over a number of months that it took me to complete the manuscript, my wife and family saw little of me.

Over the following years I participated in further meetings in San Diego and in a number of other international meetings in the USA, Scandinavia, Toulouse, London, Athens, and Basel. I was asked to contribute chapters and reviews to a number of publications. I visited laboratories of several colleagues in the USA, London, Scandinavia, Switzerland, and Israel. In 1982 I received a letter from a Polish vascular surgeon, Dr. Arkadiusz Jawień, who was interested in my work. I corresponded with him and then met him in Poland in 1988. While in Poland I visited various sites and medical centres and I became friendly with Dr. Jawień. I invited him to Winnipeg for a visit while he was spending a year in Dr. Strandness' laboratory in Seattle.

My studies continued by investigating the ability of the measurements of pressures, and of other parameters of circulation, to predict the prognosis to the leg, such as estimating the chances of amputation. I found such estimation useful in the management of patients and determining whether or not surgery was necessary. Interestingly, I also found that such measurements had a prognostic value in estimating patients' mortality. The reason for it turned out to be the fact that the presence of atherosclerosis in leg arteries had a strong association with the presence of the same condition in the arteries supplying the heart and brain, which in turn might lead to a fatal heart attack or stroke.

Patients who had obstruction of the arteries to their legs usually could walk only a short distance before experiencing the pain that forced them to stop for a minute or so, which quickly led to the pain subsiding. This condition, known as intermittent claudication, could be treated by surgery. Surgery had limitations, however, and entailed some risk. The limitations were that plugging up of the artery or of the bypass did reoccur in a significant proportion of patients. I became interested in reports that supervised walking improved the walking ability of individuals with plugged arteries. I studied a group of such patients; had them walk at a certain pace under supervision and encouraged them to do some walking on their own. I was gratified to find that their walking ability improved amazingly, as the majority after a period of three to six months of such training could walk a mile or more without stopping and with little or no pain, as long as they did not walk very fast. Such walking ability was quite adequate for many patients and obviated the need for surgery.

I also became interested in Raynaud's phenomenon, a condition in which fingers and sometimes toes become "dead" white when cold, a fairly common condition in our Canadian climate. It is also fairly common as a complication of the use of vibrating tools such as pneumatic hammers. These were used extensively in Manitoba by the miners in Thomson and Flin-Flon, and by lumberjacks. I studied a large number of such cases for the Worker's Compensation Board of Manitoba, who found my measurements of the sensitivity to cold in the circulation of the fingers useful. I published my findings and then my research output slowed down as the end of the millennium was approaching, and I started winding down my professional activities. Because of a quirk of fate my last article in a peer-reviewed scientific journal did not appear until 2006, fifty years after my first publication.

Teaching

As soon as I began working in Winnipeg in 1958, Dr. Doupe assigned a couple of my colleagues and me to teach physiology to the dental students. I was asked to teach the function of the heart and circulation, in which I was well versed, but also of the kidneys and the respiration.

Teaching required considerable preparation to acquaint myself well with these areas of medicine. After I came home from work and had dinner, I spent most of the evenings studying and preparing for my lectures. Such time commitments, that were to continue through most of my professional career, must have made life difficult on my family and I have been grateful for their support.

My early teaching was a learning process. I think that at first I was imparting to the students a large amount of information at a pace that they must have found difficult to follow and absorb. I was also asked to teach medical students. Dr. Doupe instituted teaching of normal and abnormal physiology of various organs to second year students. Other faculty members, who taught circulation included Dr. Peter Gaskell, and cardiologists including Dr. Robert Beamish and my classmate Dr. Ted Cuddy. In addition, we were asked to provide some research experience to medical students during their physiology course by having them work in the laboratory or participate in a research project during a period of some weeks for a few mornings a week.

Sadly Dr. Doupe died of complications of diabetes in 1966. These complications included blindness that he suffered from for a period of time. I was shocked and saddened when I realized his condition during one our meetings. I was showing him some graphs of my data and he looked at them and said, "It is no use." I recovered from my shock quickly and said, "OK, I shall describe them," and proceeded to do it. At Dr. Doupe's funeral I served as one of the pallbearers.

Dr. Arnold Naimark became the Head of the Department of Physiology. He decided to institute innovations in teaching, to recruit new members to the department to teach, and do research and thus to build an even stronger department. The staff including myself was teaching physiology also to first year medical students. We lectured and participated in small group tutorials during which students were discussing various aspects of the subject guided by the instructor. As I lectured I realized that the sheer amount of the expanding knowledge was difficult for students to absorb. They had to listen and take notes for future review. To help, I decided to give students printed notes that outlined the subject covered and indicated what they needed to know. Other colleagues also were giving notes to students. Dr. Naimark challenged us to consider creating demonstrations instead of just doing didactic lecturing. I thought that hemodynamics or factors that govern the flow of blood in the circulation, which I was teaching, might lend itself to a demonstration that would stimulate students and improve their understanding. I devised a model of the human circulation made of tubes of various dimensions and properties that imitated those of blood vessels. We used a cylinder of compressed air over a fluid reservoir to cause fluid to flow in the model. There was a choice of various tubes through which the flow, that we measured, took place. I measured about a dozen of these flows during the session. Before each flow I asked the class to predict how large each flow was going to be using their knowledge of the subject that they were asked to study beforehand. I wrote on the blackboard the numbers that various students suggested, as if they were bids on a horse race, and the closest "bid" to what the flow turned out to be was the winner. My class on this subject turned out to be very popular. One of the students said, "It is like magic". The positive student-feedback was deeply satisfying. The model was constructed with the help of Eugene Hamel, my chief technologist in the vascular laboratory at St. Boniface, who worked with me effectively and faithfully for more than three decades. I dubbed the model "Princess" or "Prince" on alternate years, because the fluid that we used was stained blue with ink, so that the "princess" or "prince" had blue blood in their veins.

The whole system was stored at St. Boniface and we lugged it each year, for at least twenty years, to the Medical School for the demonstration. Amazingly it never broke down or gave us any serious trouble. I finally decided that we should create an instructional video equivalent. The audiovisual department of the University of Manitoba carried out the task in an excellent way. I greatly enjoyed the creative process that included an actor hired to speak the lines I wrote, because my diction left a lot to be desired.

One of the colleagues that Dr. Naimark recruited to the Department of Physiology was a muscle physiologist, Dr. Norman Clinch, originally from Great Britain. I found that Dr. Clinch was a very bright and interesting person with whom I became very friendly. During the 1960s the university decided to overhaul the medical curriculum and to improve the quality of teaching. Physicians, who were not necessarily good teachers, although they were experts in their chosen specialty, taught the medical students. At the time, two professors from the Faculty of Education, Clifford Wood and Robert Hedley, offered a trial course to a group of eight teachers from various faculties to improve their teaching skills. Wood and Hedley previously used the method in their work with teachers in the public school system. The course took place during consecutive mornings over two weeks on the Fort Garry campus of the university. Dr. Naimark suggested that Norman Clinch and I participate. We did and found the experience extremely worthwhile and gratifying. We all made five-minute presentations on various topics. The presentations were videotaped and then during the replay the group made suggestions, comments, and criticisms in a supportive manner. We also were exposed to exercises in learning through discussion, with analysis of various role-playing in a small group setting, and to interview techniques. Each morning we all went to the university cafeteria for a mid-morning break, which helped forge a strong collegial bond within our group, including our counselors Cliff and Robert. The training was so successful that it led to a continued programme of such courses. The members of my original group were asked to lead other groups of university teachers, which I did a few times. The programme became a regular feature and continued to run for a long time, including a satellite programme that took place at the medical school.

The overhauling of the medical curriculum began with reports made by a committee constituted for that purpose and chaired by Dr. Lionel Israel. The committee suggested widespread changes, including a recommendation to teach normal and abnormal structure and function of the body's organ systems early in the curriculum using specific body system committees, such as cardiovascular and respiratory instead of traditional courses in anatomy or physiology. The recommendations were accepted and, under Dr. Naimark's directions, subcommittees for each system were constituted to come up with proposals for the content of the courses. I became the chairman of the cardiovascular subject committee. To come up with a detailed proposal three colleagues and I checked into a motel for a long weekend and worked intensively to reach our goal. The new curriculum came into effect around 1970. The faculty curriculum committee, dubbed "curriknics" by Dr. Naimark, appointed co-coordinators to come up with a detailed schedule of teaching and to oversee the running of the courses. Norman Clinch became the coordinator for the first year and I was asked to coordinate the second and the didactic part of third year. I think that Dr. Naimark thought that I would do a good job because of my tendency to pay meticulous attention to details. The work entailed designing annually a detailed schedule of the teaching sessions in proper sequence, which took long hours to prepare. Some years later computers facilitated this onerous task.

One of the problems that I encountered in scheduling the courses, soon after the new curriculum was instituted, was the fact that early in January an important national medical meeting took place that was attended by a large number of the faculty members who were needed to teach at the time. Thus, I did not have enough teachers available to fill that week's teaching schedule. I came up with a solution, probably because of my previous experience in the course with Professors Wood and Hedley. I decided to organize a Curriculum Evaluation Seminar (CES) to obtain student feedback for the teaching faculty. Students were divided into groups and each group discussed their opinions of the teaching of one of the subjects, initially among themselves. Then they presented their findings to two members of the faculty who taught that subject. The sessions were followed by a general informal session of all participating students and staff members over refreshments. The students were also asked to prepare a final written report based on their deliberations, which was then available to each teaching subject committee and the coordinators and the curriculum committee. The CES proved to be quite successful and continued over the years. Dr. Naimark dubbed them my "student love-in". The feedback that they provided was found to be as good, or better, than the results from questionnaires that students were given to fill out, and helped bring about improvements to the curriculum. Manitoba students who attended a national student meeting felt that the University of Manitoba had a superior curriculum feedback system. Dr. Naimark encouraged me to write up the experience with CES. As a result my report was published in the *Journal of Medical Education*.

Apart from my administrative academic work as the chairman of the cardiovascular committee and as curriculum coordinator, I continued to teach cardiovascular function to first year medical students and peripheral vascular disease to second year students. I did the latter with my classmate and friend Dr. Allan Downs. Allan became a vascular surgeon and later the Head of the Department of Surgery in the faculty. We taught peripheral vascular disease together for many years in the form of lectures and small group tutorials. The group tutorials became a routine format that was included in the teaching of most subjects. I also taught physical examination of patients for peripheral vascular disease. This took place at St. Boniface Hospital. I asked some of the patients that I saw at the hospital if they would be willing to be examined by the students and most of the time they agreed. Teaching of peripheral vascular disease to students, interns, and resident doctors also took place in connection with my clinical work at the hospital.

Another form of teaching I became involved in was to supervise medical students who were doing research over two summers in the B. Sc. (Med) programme. If they wrote up their work in the form of a thesis and presented their findings to plenary sessions of students and faculty members, they would obtain the additional degree of upon graduation from Medicine. This was what I did as a student with Dr. Doupe. Now I was guiding students in such endeavours. Over the years I had several students who successfully completed their projects with me. Working with these bright young people was very satisfying, even though we spent at times very long nights putting finishing touches on their thesis and presentations before the deadline. One of my B.Sc. student projects came about in a curious way.

My colleague Norman Clinch was interested in biofeedback, a phenomenon that showed that humans seem to be able to change "involuntary" functions of the body, for example blood pressure. At that time, the high school of one of my sons had a programme called School Without the Walls in which individual students or small groups engaged in a field experience with students' parents, who would volunteer to guide them. I brought my son and a friend of his to the vascular laboratory at St. Boniface Hospital and decided to see if they might be able to modify their skin temperature by biofeedback. I put them in a very cold room, which would produce in them a large and quick drop in skin temperature, as part of the body temperature maintaining mechanism. I attached sensitive skin temperature indicators to their finger tips that gave them the feedback of their skin temperature, and asked them by "thinking of warm situations" to try and prevent the temperature drop they were seeing. Their temperatures dropped rapidly, but each time they thought warm thoughts, the decrease slowed down markedly. This led me to conduct a proper study of this phenomenon, first in a group of normal subjects and then in patients with Raynaud's phenomenon. The results were positive. Both normal subjects and patients were able to modify their skin temperatures, and the patients that practiced the biofeedback reported fewer episodes of cold-white fingers. Apart from the B. Sc. (Med.) students, I also had a few students from the Department of Physiology, who were not medical students, but did research projects in my laboratory that led to a degree of Master of Science or a Ph.D. The work of a number of my students led to publications, and one student was invited to an international meeting.

Reporting the results of my research in published articles and at national and international meetings, and writing book chapters and reviews is also a teaching function, as it contributes to the spread of new knowledge, and provides opportunities to subject one's findings to the assessment and criticism of others. In addition, faculty members are asked to give presentations at rounds, which are conferences held at teaching hospitals or at the medical school. I did my share by presenting a number of my findings at such rounds or seminars on subjects related to my line of work. Faculty members also participate and organize national or international meetings, which take place in the city. I remember well a meeting of the Canadian Society of Vascular Technologists, which we organized in Winnipeg in 1991. With my chief technologist Eugene Hamel and other members of our laboratory we organized an excellent meeting. We invited guest faculty from among local specialists and Dr. Eugene Strandness from Seattle, one of the world's leading investigative vascular surgeons. The most memorable meeting that I was a part of was the International Multidisciplinary Vascular Disease Symposium held in Winnipeg in 1996. The principal organizer was my colleague, classmate, and friend Dr. Allan Downs, an excellent vascular surgeon and the Head of the Department of Surgery. He succeeded in obtaining the support for bringing about this huge three-day meeting. I was helping him to invite vascular physicians that I knew and in planning the programme. We were able to put together a forum of over 140 speakers. They included leading world experts: five from Europe and Australia, twenty-seven from the USA, thirty-six from Canada outside Manitoba, and fifty-three from Winnipeg. Among them were Dr. Marc Verstraete from Belgium, whom I first met in 1956 while I was doing my postgraduate studies in New York, Dr. Strandness, and vascular physicians and surgeons from leading medical centres such as the Mayo Clinic. The symposium covered the full range of topics on vascular disease. It included sessions for physicians as well as for vascular technologists and nurses. There were attendees from Canada and the USA, who were specialists or family practitioners.

CLINICAL WORK

As soon as I arrived to work at St. Boniface Hospital in 1958 Dr. John Maclean, who was my direct superior, arranged the space for my office and laboratory on 3C, an area that was previously a patient ward. He also arranged that I see patients in the outpatient department. There I had a clinic in which I was regulating the dose of blood thinning (anticoagulant) medications in patients who were taking such drugs on a long-term basis. I acquired training in this field while doing my postgraduate work in New York. Patients had a blood test (prothrombin time) every one to three weeks, which tested their anticoagulation level. I would adjust the dose of drugs that they needed on the basis of their test results. The indications for long-term anticoagulant treatment have evolved as new knowledge has become available. At first patients who had heart attacks were among those treated. In later years they included those that had artificial heart valves implanted. A complication of the anticoagulant treatment is bleeding that may occur in an occasional patient. During one of my first clinics I saw a man on an anticoagulant drug, who told me that he had some rectal bleeding. Although such bleeding can occur in people who do not take anticoagulants I felt that an examination required. On rectal examination of the patient I felt a tip of a mass that was a rectal tumor and I referred him for treatment. Some other drugs that patients might be prescribed can alter the effect of anticoagulant drugs. I found that a couple of drugs increased the anticoagulant effect, which was not known previously. The increased effect potentially could cause bleeding. As a result of my findings, one of the drugs was taken off the market. I supervised the anticoagulant therapy for numerous patients in the clinic at St. Boniface Hospital for more than thirty years.

We tested large numbers of patients with diseases of their blood vessels in the Vascular Laboratory that I set up on 3C at St. Boniface Hospital. The most frequent tests consisted of measurement of blood pressure by noninvasive techniques. Other tests included measurements of skin temperatures, estimation of other parameters of blood flow to patients' limbs, estimation of sensitivity of blood vessels to cold, and of blood pressure to the penis in cases of male impotence. These various tests were useful in helping to determine the diagnosis and to estimate the degree of severity of the disease. This knowledge was useful to the patients' physicians as it helped them reach decisions on how to best manage the patients' condition. The tests were also used to evaluate the results of surgery and of other treatments, by comparing the results before and after therapy. After their surgery, patients were often followed-up by measuring their blood pressure at regular intervals such as six months or a year to check on their condition. Thus, the laboratory was busy with more than a thousand of these tests performed every year.

I was asked to see an occasional patient, who was in the hospital, in consultation for peripheral vascular disease. At times this entailed taking charge of their treatment. It was in an outpatient clinic, however, where I saw patients with peripheral vascular disease in consultation on a regular basis. I held the clinic once or twice a week. The patients were referred for my evaluation by colleagues, who were internists, surgeons, other specialists, and by those who were in family practice. I was in a good situation in that I was able to arrange my schedule so that I could spend up to an hour to take the history from a patient and to examine him or her. I also took time to make sure that patients understood my opinion about their condition at the time, what tests I would like to arrange and why, what was the significance and prognosis of their condition, and what options were available for the treatment of their condition. I felt that spending time talking with the patients was important in order that they know as much as possible about their situation. Some naturally were apprehensive, and some scared because they might have been told, for example, that they will need an amputation if they do not stop smoking. I always encouraged smokers to seriously consider stopping and explained that smokers had a higher chance of increasing severity of the disease and of the possibility of developing other complications of their arteriosclerotic condition such as a heart attack. I suggested various ways that they could follow to achieve cessation of smoking. I thought, however, that it was not right to tell them that they will lose their limb if they continue to smoke. Well-documented studies showed that the chance of requiring an amputation were quite low in non-diabetic patients with plugged leg arteries. Although patients with diabetes formed a large proportion of those that needed amputation, yet even among those that had diabetes amputation was relatively uncommon although more frequent than among those without diabetes. I told patients that I would send a copy of my final detailed report to their own doctor. In most cases I arranged for the patient to be tested in the Vascular Laboratory to confirm the presence of plugging and assess the severity of their disease. I dictated letters to the patients' physicians after seeing results of their test with my diagnosis and recommendations. Frequently clinical clerks, who were third or fourth year medical students or residents who were doing their graduate work, participated in my clinic. I would assign to them a patient to assess and then review, and as needed checked their findings. Frequently I found that patients appreciated the time I took to examine them and talk with them. I thought that this might have been due in part because they often first saw my colleagues, who did not have as much time to spend with them, as a result of a tremendous workload and pressure of full waiting rooms of patients waiting to see them in their offices.

Throughout my long career at St. Boniface Hospital I found the people there to be helpful, caring, and effective co-workers. Among them Dr John MacLean, to whom I was responsible over a number of years after I started working at the hospital, was the most important for me and he always remained a true and wise colleague. I think that he was one of the most underestimated members of the staff. He was a good teacher, a compassionate physician caring deeply for his patients, and an expert in endocrinology. He also established the Department of Nuclear Medicine. Foremost, however, to all that he worked with and very much to me, he was a trusted friend to whom I turned many times for advice and help when I encountered problems of various nature; both related to work and personal. It was very sad when he died suddenly in 1991 on the verge of retirement. Many of us felt his loss profoundly.

As years went by and I was nearing the age when many retire, I gradually started to decrease my professional commitments and began working part-time. I did less teaching and research, but continued to oversee the vascular laboratory. A year into the new millennium, I gave up running the laboratory and retired completely a couple of years later. I was associated with the University of Manitoba for a long time—eight years as a student and forty-five as a faculty staff member. It was a most rewarding experience. I met and cooperated with numerous colleagues at the faculty of medicine, at St. Boniface Hospital, and at the Fort Garry campus. Even after retiring I had audited courses at the university and availed myself of its facilities for physical activities. The year when I retired I was pleased and surprised to be honoured with a Heart Care Award by the St. Boniface Institute of Cardiovascular

Sciences and Research Foundation. The gala award dinner was a wonderful evening. I was accompanied by my two sons and introduced by William Norrie, the former Mayor of Winnipeg and Chancellor of the University of Manitoba. He used to live in our neighbourhood and our sons were friends of his boys. I felt humbled, particularly since Dr. Morley Cohen, the great heart surgeon who introduced open-heart surgery to Winnipeg, was given the same award at the dinner.

Chapter VI
Changing Medical Landscape

Health care and medicine have evolved tremendously since my early years in Poland. The first drugs effective for bacterial infection, the sulfonamide drugs, appeared just a few years before World War II and were followed by the discovery of penicillin. Since then other antibiotic drugs were developed that were effective against a variety of bacterial agents. More recently antiviral drugs became available to combat viral infections. Indeed the medical landscape has continued to evolve rapidly since the time when my classmates and I were young physicians half a century ago. During that time joint replacements became a reality for sufferers with arthritis, one of the most effective and successful therapeutic advances that eliminated pain and improved the quality of life in many patients. Bypass surgery and other less invasive procedures to deal with obstruction in the arteries supplying the heart, the brain, and the lower extremities became generally available. Organ transplantation to replace diseased kidneys, hearts, and other organs, and bone marrow transplantation to treat certain forms of malignant leukemia are also routinely available. Surgical procedures became more effective for certain forms of cancer and other conditions. Developments of more effective diagnostic tests such as ultrasound, cat-scans, and magnetic resonance imaging (MRI) have played an essential role in these advances. New drugs were developed to combat a variety of diseases including high blood pressure and diabetes.

When my classmates and I graduated in 1954, we believed that ongoing research would bring about solutions and eradicate diseases over time, and that proved to be the case to a considerable extent. We were also generally devoted to medicine, intended to make it a primary purpose of our lives, and gave relatively little thought to our earnings, though we assumed that we would make a reasonable living. The advances in health care took place in large part along with extensive research of the basic structure and function of the cells and body organs, of the abnormal function in the disease states, and of potential effectiveness of various new forms of treatment. The developments resulted in great improvements in the health of the population and have been accompanied by a generally increased longevity. At the same time these developments led to new challenges and changes in the administration of health care delivery. When we were doing our graduate studies in the 1950s there were hospital wards filled with "public" patients that we took care of under the supervision of the staff physicians, and "private" patients who had health insurance. The staff physicians with our participation cared for the latter. The quality of care was probably quite similar in both types of patients. In 1969, more than a decade after we graduated, universal health care, Medicare, became a reality throughout Canada and all patients were cared for similarly. The emergence of Medicare occurred during a period of economic expansion and was accompanied by an increased support for research and development of a variety of new diagnostic and therapeutic methods.

There were other changes in the health care system including at St. Boniface Hospital, where I spent the largest proportion of my working hours. The Grey Nuns, who built and owned the hospital, wore their unique and striking habits and performed a number of important clinical and administrative functions when we were students and during the early years of my work on the staff of the hospital. As medical care became more sophisticated, complex and expensive, the hospital was taken over by the provincial health authorities, the habit of the nuns changed to a more "civilian" form, and fewer nuns were participating in the expanding workings of the institution. When I first started working in 1958, there were only three geographically full-time physicians at the hospital. The majority of the medical staff were doctors who cared for the hospital patients, but had private offices elsewhere. Gradually more and more full-time doctors were recruited to work at the hospital as medical care became more and more complex.

Medical research is supported by the federal and provincial agencies such as the Medical Research Council, the Manitoba Heart Foundation (later Heart and Stroke Foundation of Manitoba), the Kidney Foundation, and others. It was also felt that more support for health research was needed and that it would be advantageous if it were to take place in close association with and proximity to the hospitals. To accomplish that goal, foundations were formed by several city hospitals in order to raise funds for the bricks and mortar to house more researchers and to support them. Among these the St. Boniface General Hospital Research Foundation started its activities in 1971 and was very successful. Established to fund a new building, devoted to housing a variety of health related research and to recruit basic and clinical researchers, the research foundation began by holding international fund raising dinners. At each dinner a prominent researcher or a person who made important contributions to human welfare was awarded a St. Boniface Hospital Research Foundation prize with a substantial monetary component, and gave an address to the audience. Among the recipients were Dr. Jonas Salk, the inventor of a polio vaccine, Dr. Christian Barnard, the pioneer of heart transplantation, the first lady Rosalind Carter, Prince Philip, Anwar Sadat, Dr. Andrei Sakharov, a Nobel Prize Laureate, scientist and peace activist, and several other prominent people and researchers including the best in Manitoba. The hospital award was also given to Mother Theresa and Pope John Paul II, though they did not attend a dinner. As a result of these efforts a research building arose on the hospital grounds and was soon populated by a growing number of researchers. Those who have been conducting their research there included members of the cardiovascular section of my Department of Physiology headed by Dr. Naranjan Dhalla. He became a world famous researcher, and his Institute of Cardiovascular Sciences at St. Boniface organized huge world meetings for heart researchers.

As time went on, it became apparent that what we did not appreciate as young physicians were the unforeseen and unintended consequences that often follow new developments. For example, the development of antibiotics led to the emergence of new antibiotic resistant strains of bacteria. This in turn led to the development of new generations of antibiotics. They were effective, but then bacteria would again become resistant. Thus, the battle against infectious agents has to continue. New drugs were effective against a large variety of ailments, but in some cases they had to be recalled because they led to untoward side effects that impaired patients' health or could even be fatal. The effectiveness of improved diagnostic and treatment methods led to longer life span, but the aging population is more susceptible to various degenerative ailments: the ravages of arthritis, heart attacks, strokes, and dementias including the Alzheimer's disease. This in turn leads to ever increasing needs for health care resources that are not unlimited. Thus, society and governments are put into a position of having to make difficult choices. One of my prominent colleagues used to say that we teach students about what we know, but not about what we do not know, which is much greater. Indeed despite the tremendous progress in technology, biology, and medicine, what we do not comprehend continues to seem unlimited. As we make progress new challenges arise. Seemingly a case of "receding goalposts," it might be based in the reality that every change we make results in another change or consequence that must be faced and dealt with. The life and the universe continue to unfold.

Although tremendous progress has been achieved, health care is ever faced with new and difficult challenges. We are said to be in the age of so-called "evidence based" medicine, which is meant to signify that it is practiced on the basis of studies that document the value of drugs and other treatments. Some of the evidence, however, does not stand the test of time, as newer studies at times show negative side effects of treatments, or new better treatments emerge. Therefore, as has been the case previously, we practice on the basis of the best available evidence. It is very costly and time consuming to prove effectiveness of new treatments or that one is better than another. The evidence of large studies that involve at times thousands of patients may show that, for example, twenty-five percent fewer patients develop heart attacks with drug A compared to drug B. Statistical methods may indicate that the probability that that difference occurred by chance are small, less than one in twenty, or one in a hundred. This however, does not mean that drug A will be better than drug B in every patient or in any given patient. Advances in genetics suggest that it might be possible at some future time to predict individual responses to treatments. We do not know how long that might take to achieve and how costly it might be.

The increased complexity and plethora of medical technology and therapeutics led to more and more specialization. The specialists, often based at the main teaching hospitals, play an ever-increasing role in patient care. The role of the family practitioners, who are patient's primary physicians, tends to diminish. When I was seeing patients in the vascular clinic who were often referred to me by specialists, I always inquired who was the patient's family physician and indicated that I would send to him or her a copy of my report. Although today's family physicians and specialists tend to be as well intentioned and compassionate towards their patients as we were, the pressures of limited time available to physicians and the fragmentation of patients' care may lead to unfortunate outcomes as at times some patients fall "between cracks". I will mention two examples. An elderly patient developed severe pain in the left side of his lower back below the waist. A thorough examination was done in a hospital emergency department, which among others showed a normal hip X-ray. The pain continued and was associated with a considerable limp. The patient saw a prominent neurosurgeon that did an MRI and a couple of nerve injections that brought no relief. A considerable time later the patient saw a well-known orthopedic surgeon who at once diagnosed a hip-joint degeneration of an especially severe variety, and said that he would send a referral to a colleague who specialized in hip surgery. When the family enquired several months later, the referral was never sent. The hip surgeon would not take the delay in referral into account. When he finally saw the patient several months later, he planned the surgery for a year or more hence. Because the pain was of practically unbearable severity, the patient's family made inquiries and another orthopedic surgeon arranged and carried out successful surgery in about four months. Apparently, at the time, there was no effective system to coordinate hip surgery. The other example is that of a forty-two-year-old man who developed carcinoma of the tongue. He was given localized radiation treatment on three occasions in a hospital in the US. Apparently the treatment is very complex and incorporates extensive computer technology. It turned out that the patient was given ten times more radiation than intended on all three occasions, perhaps because of a computer malfunction. This tremendous dose led to the destruction of patient's various nerves and tissues, which in turn resulted in the deterioration of his vital functions. The man died after suffering tremendously for about two years. These examples illustrate some of the problems associated with medicine. Since doctors and machines are both imperfect unintended effects will happen, and had taken place throughout the history of medicine. Unfortunately some of them might be preventable.

The difficulties facing health care include the delivery of treatment and prevention of disease to the largest proportion of the population.

The governments and health care professionals continue to wrestle with these problems. Since I graduated, the areas that have been addressed in Manitoba and in Canada overall include the provision of better institutional care for patients with chronic conditions, and in personal care homes; the institution of home care and of palliative care; and the progress made in better coordination of the resources by regional health care authorities. Various models of healthcare, like universal Medicare in Canada, primarily private health insurance in the USA, and various mixed European systems, have their own advantages and disadvantages. The cost and administration for profit-health care organizations and affordability are all inherent in these processes. The physicians generally make a very good living and a number of specialties have proven to be quite lucrative. At times, however, costly litigations against physicians and health care professionals, lead to exorbitant costs of professional insurance that might result in doctors being unable to practice, particularly in the USA.

With the explosion of information technology in recent years, patients are becoming more sophisticated. This tends to enable them to participate in taking care of their health, to utilize their health care resources better, and to make more rational decisions regarding their health care and life style. Considerable effort has been made by physicians and health care authorities in trying to promote healthy life styles. In Manitoba and the rest of Canada prohibition of smoking in public areas that was followed thoroughly in an uncompromising manner contributed to a considerable lowering of the proportion of the population that smokes compared to many other countries. The efforts to promote healthier eating habits and encouragement to exercise and to be active mentally and physically are also being made, but have not been pursued nearly as effectively as the prohibition of smoking. Attainment of these goals is likely to result in a healthier population that would require less of the health care resources to the benefit of the whole society.

Our society will have to decide how the resources at its disposal should be utilized. For example, should all persons of certain ages, even if they feel quite well, have regular health checkups and tests of various types? Many quite elderly people relate that they have not been to a doctor for most of their long lives. If all elderly people and other selected groups were to be checked and tested regularly, the physicians might not have sufficient time to attend to the sick.

As stated above, the progress in technology and specialization led to the diminished role of the family doctor, who used to be of primary importance in dealing with patients' problems. The family practitioners used to make frequent house calls. Nowadays this is rare and patients more often use walk-in clinics and access health centres in the community. Early in the twentieth-century the family doctor had a high standing and the respect of patients, and his presence and confident manner imparted optimism to the patient that likely had a salutary effect by mobilizing the body's own defense systems that might have been otherwise impaired by greater stress and anxiety. The great Canadian physician William Osler recognized this change in the doctor- patient relationship and penned an article entitled "The Faith that Heals". Dr. Hans Selye, who showed that negative emotions could have detrimental effects, championed this concept. The well-known book *Anatomy of an Illness* by Norman Cousins recognized and popularized the concept of the body's natural defenses and factors that might affect them.[1] There is an ongoing interest in the body-mind connection and evidence that stress reduction by various forms of relaxation, yoga, biofeedback and others, might have beneficial effects on health. Further work supported the notion of the interactions between emotions and health. For example Dr. Jon Kabat-Zinn, Professor of Medicine at the University of Massachusetts Medical School, has directed a stress reduction clinic for patients with chronic pain, cancer and other diseases, as well as for professionals including physicians, and other groups in society. He described the experience in the clinic in the book *Full Catastrophe Living: Using the Wisdom of Your Body and Mind to Face Stress, Pain and Illness.*[2] The research in which Dr. Kabat-Zinn participated showed that stress reduction has a salutary effect on the treatment of psoriasis, a skin condition, and was helpful in cognitive psychotherapy. The methods used in the stress reduction clinic are available in some hospitals in the USA and in Canada. The Ontario Health Insurance Plan decided to fund mindfulness-based stress reduction from the public purse. Recently a programme was started at St. Michaels Hospital in Toronto called Mindfulness Based Chronic Pain Management. Video conferencing programmes are offered from Sunnybrook Health Centre to various remote locations in Ontario. Stress reduction courses are offered in many locations in Toronto by medical doctors, psychiatrists, psychologists, and nurses. Some courses are also available in other provinces in Canada.

The effects of various forms of stress reduction are not easy to demonstrate objectively and there tends to be a resistance to their acceptance by mainstream medicine. Also, the availability of funds for research has become more limited since the decades that followed my graduation and led to the universities increasingly resorting to the "partnership" with the industry. This in turn tends to result in more financial support for the research of treatments such as drugs that have a potential to benefit the pharmaceutical industry and probably less for other projects that might elucidate ways to mobilize the body's natural defenses by various methods. The increasing popularity of yoga and of various forms of meditation might be driven in part by the fragmentation of patient care that followed the explosion of medical technology, associated erosion of positive aspects of patient-doctor relation, and reduction of the role of the family physicians, and of the time that doctors have available to spend with their patients. It might be a sign of the population trying to take a more active role in maintaining their health. In his book published in 1979 Norman Cousins wrote: "True, not everything is known about the placebo. But enough is known to put its continued study on the medical and human agenda." Yet twenty-five years later in 2005, after great strides in medical science, Professor of Medicine at the University of Ottawa, Dr. W. Grant Thompson in his book *The Placebo Effect and Health: Combining Science and Compassionate Care,*[3] again calls for more research into the beneficial effects of placebo, and for efforts to increase the time that physicians spend with their patients. Hopefully society will continue to build on the progress attained during the past century by continuing research to discover new and better ways of maintaining good health, treating illness, and delivering the benefits of new discoveries to the whole of society.

CHAPTER VII
SOCIAL AND FAMILY LIFE

In 1960 we settled into our life in the two-story house on Elm Street. Emilee designed and arranged for a number of changes to the building that made it more functional and practical for our lifestyle. Three years after we moved into our home our second son Andrew was born. Emilee was busy taking care of the family and I carried on with my work and did some chores at home. We enjoyed gardening and went for walks around our neighbourhood. We attended social evenings hosted by my colleagues and gave a few parties at home. We took our boys to the beautiful Assiniboine Park and its zoo.

Over the years we took advantage of the many cultural events that Winnipeg offered, the number and scope of which grew as time went on. We were able to go out in the evenings leaving our boys with babysitters. At times we seemed to be too busy going out three or four times a week. We subscribed to the Manitoba Theatre Centre, The Royal Winnipeg Ballet, The Contemporary Dancers, The Winnipeg Symphony Orchestra, The Manitoba Chamber Orchestra, and The Warehouse Theatre and attended other performances. We enjoyed many memorable evenings. One was a part of the CBC Music Festival during which Beethoven's *Archduke Trio* was performed with Gary Stucka playing cello, Irmgard Baerg on piano and Charles Dobias on the violin. We were ardent fans of the Royal Winnipeg Ballet and witnessed its almost meteoric rise to great prominence guided by the Winnipeg's own Arnold Spohr. They performed many relatively short and most entertaining ballets before going on to perform full-length works such as *The Swan Lake*. To me, Christine Henessy was the greatest ballerina of the cast before the rise to fame of Evelyn Hart. With time Manitoba Theatre Workshop became active.

Our younger son, who was artistically inclined, attended classes there. He was in the pilot performance of the TV programme *Let Us Go*, which went on to air over a considerable period of time. Later he performed at the Manitoba Theatre Centre and on Rainbow Stage, a delightful summer theatre in Kildonan Park, where we enjoyed many splendid musical theatre shows. The Manitoba Theatre Workshop eventually moved from their original venue near the City Hall to Portage Avenue and became the Prairie Theatre Exchange, but not before mounting some great performances at the original venue. More recently, and among others, The Jewish Theatre was started with Beverly Aronovitch as artistic director and became an important part of the local theatre scene. The Virtuosi Music series began presenting concerts at the Eckhardt-Gramatté Hall of the University of Winnipeg. Among other cultural events the Agassiz Music Festival, the Winnipeg Chamber Music Players, and the Musical Offering series came into being.

We were very happy with the quality and variety of cultural opportunities and events available in the city. We enrolled our sons in a private French immersion course in St. Boniface. We enjoyed our interest in arts; Emilee's more in visual arts and mine in music. We attended the Winnipeg Art Gallery, where over the years Emilee took classes in painting and stone sculpture. She also availed herself of classes in ceramics and yoga at the River Heights Community Centre near where we live.

My interest in music was relatively dormant during my undergraduate and postgraduate studies and was then revived when my colleague Dr. Marcel Blanchaer, who later became head of the Department of Biochemistry in the faculty of medicine, introduced me to the recorder, the *flauto dolce* or "sweet pipe." It is an instrument very easy to start playing and enjoying, but difficult to master. Yet we were able to get together and form a group or consort that through the years varied in number from three to five players. We usually met weekly to play together as our abilities allowed.

On a few occasions we played at special events, for example at the Winnipeg Art Gallery and at the Assiniboine Park and we participated in the Winnipeg Music Festival, an annual event in which many school children, and young and older performers show their musical prowess. The festival was founded in Winnipeg in 1918 by the Men's Musical Club and grew from 274 entries in the first competition to over 3000 thousands participants. A number of young participants in the festival went on to prominent professional musical careers including the pianist Emmanuel Ax, singer Tracy Dahl, and singer and harpist Loreena McKennit.

We introduced our sons to music; the older took up the recorder, switched to the clarinet, and tried his hand on the saxophone and guitar, while the younger played viola in addition to singing and acting. I had the satisfaction to play with my sons for pleasure and in the festival. Our younger son played with the Manitoba Youth Orchestra and both took part in the performances of musicals put on by their high schools, River Heights Junior High and Kelvin High School. Playing the recorder became popular and was introduced into the school curricula by the teacher Muriel Milgrom who also played an important role in the recorder movement for adults in the province. A chapter of the American Recorder Society was formed in Winnipeg and was active for many years, before giving way to the Early Music Society. I was a representative of the chapter. This worked well for me personally when I attended medical meetings in the USA. I would contact local members of the Recorder Society and they would invite me to play with a group for a delightful evening of music making. That was the case when I attended a meeting in Washington, D.C. in 1968. It took place during the turbulent Democratic Party convention. I watched some of the proceedings of the convention with "Lute" and Pierre, relatives of the Kitzes family from Spain, who were in Washington. Pierre was a prominent journalist interested in th public affairs.

A number of years later in Winnipeg I bought and started learning how to play a *tenor viola de gamba*, an instrument of an old string family that was in common use before the violin family took over. Although my proficiency on the *gamba* was never as good as on the recorder, I was able to play with colleagues in a quartet or a trio of viols and found it rewarding. Our family interest was not limited to classic music. I was always fond of the Viennese waltzes and operettas. We all were fans of the folk singers, especially Pete Seeger and The Weavers. We heard them in concerts in Winnipeg, during vacations in the New York State, and on television and the radio, and acquired their recordings that we still listen to now and then.

My interest in sports was rather dormant at first, though I followed the exploits of the Winnipeg Blue Bombers and attended some games with Ben Kitzes. We were in contact with the Kitzes family and visited them regularly. They sold the store on St. Mathew's Avenue and moved to a house in southern River Heights. My interest in sports began to increase when our older son started to participate in various sports. I enrolled him in a baseball team and to my great surprise was told that I was the coach! I had never played baseball in my life. I did my best, however, and got help from an assistant coach, a father of one of the boys on the team, and very valuable help from Ben who knew the game well and helped a lot with practices. Surprisingly we won the local club championship in the last inning of the last game, which made everybody happy. Perhaps I might have been "the most happy fellow." I know that I lived through my son, compensating for what I missed as a youth because of the war. I also know very well that it made things difficult for him. My wife and both sons did not have it easy living with me and my inexperience in many aspects of life, which to some extent, must have been affected by my experiences during World War II. Despite some ups and downs we managed and have grown as individuals and as a family. I learned a lot from my wife, who knew much better than I did how to handle various situations. She was able to express her emotions spontaneously and sincerely as situations demanded. On the other hand, my emotions were held deeply in check, perhaps since the trying times in Europe when I was a teenager. I also learned a lot from both our sons as they kept growing in age and as people.

My older son has been a good athlete. He won trophies and a championship as a speed skater, played hockey on a select Winnipeg team that went east to a tournament, in which a ten-year-old Wayne Gretzky was turning heads, was a good runner and participated in other sports. At one point he bought me a pair of running shoes and said "Dad, here is a pair of running shoes for you. Have some fun and leave my running alone!" It was a good advice. It started my jogging career, which is still continuing though less and less. Although I never regularly ran very long distances, I did run about three times a week relatively slowly and accumulated a total of a few hundred miles per year in my hey days. Running probably contributed to my well-being and relatively good health in addition to providing many positive experiences. I took my running shoes with me on my travels to medical meetings and on vacations and they served me well over roads and pavements in many cities in North America and in places such as The Hyde Park in London, in Hawaii, Greece, France, and other countries.

In Winnipeg I did participate in many road races and ran two half-marathons. I thought at first that a full marathon was too strenuous an effort, as many runners find out. After I ran my second half-marathon at the age of sixty-one, in less than two hours and felt well, I thought that perhaps I could do one full marathon. I remember well the legend of the Greek runner that ran from the village of Marathon to Athens to let the Greeks know of their army's victory over the Persians and died after delivering the news. In 1990 I trained more over the winter and spring leading to the annual Manitoba Marathon, an important community event that raises funds for people with intellectual disabilities. It proved to be an exhilarating experience. As I jogged along Lyndale Drive I heard a voice on a portable radio "an elderly male, number three hundred and seven." "That's me!" I thought. The hot sun shone down as the volunteer support crews kept track of runners they thought might get into trouble.

My experience began some three hours earlier at the University of Manitoba. I parked in a lot near the University of Manitoba Stadium, where the run starts and finishes, shortly after six in the morning and where many people already arrived. The crowd swelled with thousands wearing colourful running outfits ranging from small fry to elderly women and men of various sizes and shapes. The scene was uplifting; people are talking, stretching, and taking the last drink of water. Greetings were exchanged and I caught a glimpse of the favoured runner from the USA, Dennis Rinde. Along the route through the city there are aid stations manned by numerous volunteers, who try to keep the runners cool with sponges and cool drinks, and groups of onlookers that cheer them on. Soon after leaving the start line at the stadium we ran by a series of humorous signs: "It is all downhill from here," "Steroids for sale" and others. At the eight-mile aid station at Harrow Street and Wellington Crescent I saw Emilee with our dog. They came out despite the early hour. I hugged my wife and pet the dog before resuming my trot and heard a man calling, "There is a winner!" I come across a few bands that played to cheer us on. My son appears on the bicycle around mile sixteen, keeping an eye on me, encouraging me, but keeps telling me to walk through the aid stations and take in plenty of water. I finished slowly and deliberately. It felt good to enter the stadium and the sore legs and bruises under my toenails were a small price to pay.

I was a hockey fan and followed the teams on which my son played and the Canadian National Team that was based in Winnipeg for a time under the direction of Father Bauer. In those days Canada was not allowed to use professional players and was at a disadvantage because some countries, especially the Soviet Union, had "amateurs" who trained all year round. A world championship was to be held in Winnipeg in 1970 and I was looking forward to it. Poland was to participate and I recalled that my cousin George was the captain of his high school hockey team in Kraków before World War II. Canada was, for the first time, allowed to use nine professionals from the ranks of the National Hockey League When the International Ice Hockey Federation reversed that decision, however, Canada withdrew and boycotted the championships until 1976 when professional players were finally allowed to take part. Regretfully there was no championship in Winnipeg.

We followed the Winnipeg Jets in the World Hockey Association and were thrilled with their winning the Avco Cup. Finally they were reluctantly allowed to join the National Hockey League, a decision influenced by the western Canadians' boycott of the Montreal beer. We followed the 1972 Summit Series of Canada's professionals against the Soviet team and attended the game in Winnipeg. The whole family was involved in attending and participating, in various ways, in sporting and cultural events. Emilee and I did a lot of car pool driving for the boys to and from sport, theatre, and musical events and practices.

I also sampled the game of curling, a popular Canadian winter sport. I participated in a doctor's league, which curled once a week at the Granite Club downtown near Assiniboine River. I once participated in a weekend bonspiel with several games that left me tired and with sore muscles. However, I found the experience enjoyable. During one of the meetings of the Canadian Physiological Society in Quebec there was a friendly competition between teams from various provinces. Our team, which included my colleague Dr. Clinch—a complete novice, myself, and Jack Jezack, who was my student and a fairly good curler, did well and won the competition.

I did some cross country skiing too. At first I took a few lessons with my younger son. That was followed by more ambitious ventures that included skiing in provincial parks like Sandilands and the fable-like wonderland of the Spruce Woods Park. I also enjoyed skiing near and around the city at La Barriere Park, on the grounds of golf courses, and in the Assiniboine Park not far from where we live. When visiting our older son when he lived later in Duluth, Minnesota, I went skiing in beautiful neighbouring parks.

We always looked forward to vacations, but also took advantage of several beaches or resorts that were within a short drive of an hour or less from Winnipeg. When the boys were young we would drive to one of these nearby beaches after I got home from work for a dip in cool water and some fun. We drove to the beautiful Grand Beach on Lake Winnipeg and to Falcon Lake on weekends, and spent several brief stays at the Hecla Island Resort.

In the early years in Winnipeg we drove for our summer vacations to Emilee's parents' farm near the Mohegan Colony in the state of New York. This allowed us to see our families in the New York area; we visited with Emilee's friends from her youth, and spent pleasant hours at the Colony beach on Lake Mohegan. The drive to New York State with the children was arduous and took three to four days. I did most of the driving, which I enjoyed, though it was tiring. There were no interstate highways then and the going was rather slow. Once I drove for twenty-eight hours from Rochester, Minnesota to New York in one stretch. As the boys grew older we explored western Canada and visited beautiful foothills and mountains in Alberta including Banff and Jasper Park. We would stop at scenic areas for a picnic lunch. It provided a happy and relaxing time. We took pictures and I have one of me at such a stop sitting on a tree stump and posing very happily. On the way to New York State we often drove through Michigan, which provided welcome stops at lakes along the way and allowed for a quick dip to break up the monotony of long drives.

We also traveled through the eastern provinces and visited Toronto, Ottawa, Montreal, and Nova Scotia and neighbouring provinces. We attended Expo '67 and have a photo of our boys with a Mountie in Ottawa. It was in front of the Parliament Building that we saw a brief announcement on a bulletin board that read: "Visit of head of state cancelled." It was after the notorious "Vive la Quebec libre!" speech by General de Gaulle. We had a chance to sail on Long Island Sound near New York City in a boat of one of Emilee's relatives and spent time at the beach house of my cousin George and his family on Long Island looking out over the Atlantic.

In 1982 we decided to take a winter vacation. Emilee and I spent about two weeks in Hawaii where I jogged and star gazed. For a few years previously we joined the Winnipeg Chapter of the Royal

Astronomical Society. I spent some hours in the middle of the night in Hawaii watching the stars seen only in the southern zones such as the Canopus, the second largest star seen from earth, the Alpha Centauri, and the Southern Cross. During one of our sightseeing trips I was shown how to snorkel and got hooked on watching the plethora of colourful fish. I snorkeled at several wonderful snorkeling destinations on the beautiful island of Maui.

The following winter we returned to Hawaii with our sons and went there a few more times over the next fifteen years. In 1986, we went to the top of the extinct volcano Haleakala on Maui and I saw Halley's comet that looked about a quarter of the size of the moon. The next year Emilee and I went to the British Virgin Islands, where we took a trip on a yacht and I hiked, jogged, and snorkeled. While snorkeling on one occasion I encountered a barracuda. We looked at each other, I with some apprehension, and then swam our separate ways. Emilee and I admired spectacular sunsets and enjoyed gourmet dinners served at our resort. During that vacation we took the opportunity to visit Sandra, the daughter of Emilee's sister Thelma, who was living in Puerto Rico with her family. We visited Thelma in the past, during a trip to Guatemala when our first son was an infant, and met her and her family during our vacations at my in-laws' farm in New York State.

We spent vacations together with our sons when they were young. Later, often just Emilee and I went together. I attended the medical meetings most of the time on my own, although Emilee accompanied me occasionally. She came with me to a meeting in San Francisco. We took the opportunity to visit Los Angeles and other sites in California and met some of Emilee's friends who lived in the area. In Los Angeles we visited Stefan Halpern and his wife. He was my classmate in the secret school in the Warsaw Ghetto and had become a psychologist. Another time, we explored western Canada and the USA. We enjoyed the remarkable Waterton Lakes area in Alberta, where mountains with glacial lakes seem to arise in the midst of the flat prairie. We then took the famous Logan Pass into the States, and visited Seattle, where a friend of Emilee's from her student days in Chicago lived, before going on to Vancouver, Victoria Island, and Powell River where we visited my classmate Cam Hobson and his wife Marie. They took us in their boat for a dinner while sailing the Pacific. On Vancouver Island we happened to meet another of my classmates Howie MacDiarmid near the town of Tofino. Howie became a Member of Legislative Assembly (MLA) from the district in the provincial parliament and built a beautiful beach house on the shore looking out on the Pacific. He invited us for a great salmon dinner.

Among many trips to meetings that I attended, a few were especially memorable for me. In 1970 I traveled to Europe for the first time since I left it for Canada in 1948. Our flight arrived in London where I was reunited with my cousin Ryś for the first time. I met his wife Doris and daughter Sandra. It was great to see them. They met me at the extremely busy and crowded Heathrow Airport, took me to their home, and were most hospitable. This was also the case whenever I visited London over the subsequent decades. Ryś, who was eight years my senior, seemed always to consider me his little cousin, as was the case before the war.

In 1970, I set out from London for the continent and after crossing the English Channel proceeded to Italy by train. For part of the trip I was in a compartment with a few young men whose language I could not understand; they might have been Welsh. I stopped for a few hours in Pisa and went up to the top of the famous leaning tower before going on to Siena, where I participated in a recorder seminar run by an American recorder player. Siena is a beautiful medieval city with a rich history and architecture. The evening I arrived a special event was taking place. It is called *Palio*. It is a bareback horse race of three laps on an earthen track around a huge city square. The race is run twice a year in celebration of the Virgin Mary. A painting of her is paraded into the square in a carriage drawn by oxen. I made my way among crowds into the square. It was filled with close to 100,000 standing spectators. It was a warm evening and now and then medics carried out a spectator who fainted to administer medical help. From time to time different sections of the crowd waved colourful kerchiefs that conveyed an effect of a flock of birds. The colours represented the city districts or *contradas* that fiercely competed in the race. There were pre-race ceremonies with trumpets blaring and skilful flag throwers hurling the flags of their *contradas* high into the air. They would then float down gracefully somewhat like colourful parachutes. The race is run wildly. Several riders and horses went down.

After it was all over I walked among streaming crowds from the square through one of many side streets. The carriage with the painting of the Virgin Mary happened to pass by. Suddenly the oxen bolted and as I tried to get out of the way in the narrow street I got kicked on the leg by one of the animals. The bruise remained for a few weeks as a painful reminder.

After the seminar in Siena was over I spent a couple of days in Florence and took in many of its famous sites. I found that most impressive were the sculptures of Michelangelo; the famous *David* and four unfinished works—blocks of marble from which powerful human figures seemed to be struggling to come out. I then spent half a day in Venice and from there took a train to Paris. I explored many of the famous sites and met with my cousin George from New York who happened to be there. We spent a pleasant hour in an outdoor café on Champs Élysées. It so happened that while I was in Paris, I saw the movie *M*A*S*H* for the first time.

A very meaningful experience for me occured when I came across a building where my favourite Polish poet Adam Mickiewicz lived. A plaque marked it. I walked up the stairs, which he might have walked to his apartment, with awe. I then participated in an international meeting on vascular disease in Liège, Belgium. I renewed my acquaintance with Dr. Marc Verstraete whom I met first at the New York Hospital in 1957. My contact with colleagues there led to my being invited to Copenhagen a couple of years later. Then it was off to London for a World Congress of Cardiology.

During my trip I became aware that Mrs. Zofia Rechthand, a friend of my family from before the war and in the Warsaw Ghetto, was coming to visit her friends in Paris from Poland, but did not arrive there until I already left for London. This lady was the only surviving member of the family that immensely helped my family and me in the Warsaw Ghetto. As related earlier, her husband, one of the richest Jews in Warsaw, and his two wonderful daughters were betrayed and murdered by the Nazis while hiding in Warsaw. Without their help I would not have survived. I felt that I must see her. I took a one-day return flight from London to Paris after she arrived there. I went to where she was staying with her friends. We met for the first time since those terrifying days in September 1942. We were glad to see each other and reminisced. She lived out the rest of her life, mourning her husband and daughters whom she lost in the Holocaust, in a home for the aged in Warsaw. My aunt Pauline contacted her from New York and visited her in Warsaw in the 1960s.

In 1985 I was invited to an international vascular meeting in Athens to give a talk. I enjoyed the experience and found it very interesting to meet there colleagues from many countries. I visited the Acropolis and other ancient landmarks. I took a cruise to the remarkable island of Rhodos from where we could see the shores of Turkey. We saw the buildings of the Order of the Knights of St. John who participated in the Crusades. The view from the peak of the local Acropolis, where there were ruins of a temple to Athena, was breathtaking. I had a feeling as if I were on top of the world. Far down below were old ruins and a bay where St. Paul was said to have landed. We went on to Crete where we visited the remarkable excavations of an early civilization, and stopped at the unique island of Santorini. After the cruise I went on a bus tour led by a very knowledgeable guide. We visited Epidauros and its huge amphitheatre built into the side of a large hill. The acoustics were such that we could hear the pin that our guide dropped on the stage a long distance below while we sat far away high in the top row. Apparently the amphitheatre was built around 330 B.C. and it has 14, 000 seats. Nearby is the area of the shrines of Asklepios, the Greek god of medicine and healing. We continued on to the site of the ancient Olympia with the ruins of its many institutions. I was moved as I jogged around the excavated stadium where the ancient Olympic games were held, and found the site where the heart of Baron de Coubertin, the originator of the modern Olympic games, was buried nearby. We went on to Delphi, the site of a famous oracle, and there saw a very impressive and well preserved stadium and a hillside full of statues, apparently erected by Greeks to obtain their gods' blessings for an Olympic victory. Our tour then turned north where we saw cliffside monasteries on huge rock mountains in Meteora that arise abruptly from a plain terrain. The main access to the monasteries used to be by means of a net that was hitched over a hook and hoisted up by rope and a hand-cranked windlass to winch towers overhanging the chasm. Monks and supplies reached these places by means of nets or at times using retractable wooden ladders up to forty meters long. On the way back to Athens we stopped at the site marking the Battle of Thermopylae.

I flew on to Geneva, rented a car and explored the picturesque Swiss countryside looking very much like the scenes in the film *The Sound of Music*. I visited a colleague in the historic city of Berne. My host showed me the ancient city sites. I was surprised to note that he would turn the car motor off for brief periods of time at every red light apparently to reduce the pollution. I spent a magical day at the alpine resort of Spietz and rowed briefly on its lake before driving through mountain ranges to Zurich. I visited the laboratory of my vascular specialist colleague there, explored the city and its lake, attended a couple of concerts, and bought a good quality soprano recorder. Then I was off to London for a visit with vascular experts in that city, for sightseeing, and a special time with my cousin Ryś and his family.

From London I flew to Israel to see the Maccabiah Games in which my son participated running in the 800 and 1500 meter races. It was a very meaningful time. I visited Tel Aviv, explored Jerusalem and its many famous sites including the sacred sites of the three great religions. A colleague took me on a tour of the ramparts of the Old City and I saw excavations of an ancient Roman street. I visited Yad Vashem, the site that commemorates the Holocaust. It was a very moving experience. An eternal flame was burning in the area commemorating the victims and concentration camps. I walked along the avenue of the Righteous Among the Nations where trees with plaques commemorate the Gentile rescuers of the Jews, saw a small boat that symbolizes the rescue of the Danish Jews, and a monument to Janusz Korczak, who perished in Treblinka with the children of his orphanage from the Warsaw Ghetto. I went to the archives where one of the staff helped me find a document pertaining to my friend Staś with whom I played in the early months of the German occupation in Warsaw in 1939. I toured Masada and floated in the Dead Sea. I drove in a rented car north to see the Sea of Galilee. Nearby I visited a kibbutz near the border with Jordan, to which my aunt Pola made a donation for an orphanage in memory of my cousin Tadzik and uncle Edmund. I then followed a road through the mountains to the coast and north to the kibbutz of the survivors of the Warsaw Ghetto that initially included some of those that fought in the Ghetto Uprising. It contains Ghetto Fighters' House Museum. I met there a lady that knew one of my teachers in the *Spójnia* School in Warsaw before the war and found it very meaningful to talk about the times from my early years in Poland.

* * * *

As was mentioned above, we have kept in contact and visited friends, classmates, and family through the years. In 1980 while in New York, I saw Hanna Herfurt, the Righteous Gentile lady who played an essential role in the survival of my family and me, for the first time since early after the war in Kraków. She had finished medicine and specialized in hematology having taken postgraduate training in Boston. She married a hematologist Dr. Gerwel and lived in the city of Poznań, where she was in charge of transfusion services. That time in New York I recall us three; my cousin George, Hanka, and I walking down a broad avenue hand in hand.

We held our medical class reunions in Winnipeg five, ten, twenty-five, forty, fifty and fifty-five years after graduation, and some other reunions elsewhere. After graduation our class scattered throughout North America. It was always good to get together with classmates and their spouses. In 1979, twenty-five years after graduation, we had an ambitious reunion in Winnipeg that included a day of talks given by the class members on a variety of medical and other topics. It proved to be a great success. Shortly before our reunion, the Manitoba Medical College Foundation was formed, initially to commemorate the 100th anniversary of the founding of the Manitoba Medical College. The anniversary was to take place in 1983. Subsequently and to this day, the Foundation helps to organize class reunions in a manner similar to that of our reunion of 1979, and it also helps to raise funds to help support scholarship at the faculty of medicine. Perhaps our reunion in 1979 contributed in a measure to the growth of the foundation in that manner. We generally followed the format of our 25th reunion in the later ones. We had good turnouts, though our ranks dwindled as we lost some classmates as time marched on. At our 50th reunion there were thirty-two of the fifty-nine of our class members and ten others did not attend for various reasons. My classmate Dr. Allan Downs provided us with a detailed analysis of what our class did and where they settled to work.[1] Only about a quarter of the class ended up working in Manitoba. Some settled in Western Canada, most in British Columbia, and others worked in the USA, most commonly in California and on the East Coast. He indicated that the pattern that our class followed tended to continue, which has implications for the medical manpower in the province.

Volodia and later Mary Kitzes succumbed to heart disease in their late years, but enjoyed life for a number of years after they sold their general store and retired to a home in southern River Heights. One day in the 1970s, their son Ben developed some discomfort in his chest while bowling and did not feel well. His cousin Etta (who helped by getting Volodia and Mary to sponsor me to come to Winnipeg in

1948) phoned us about Ben's problem. I was at first unsure what to do, in part because experience suggests that it might not be good for a physician to be involved with the care of their own family and friends, however, Emilee suggested that I go to see Ben and I did. He went to bed soon after coming home—an unusual behaviour for him. Although his complaints were not typical of the common forms of heart disease, I phoned my classmate Ted Cuddy, an excellent cardiologist who told me to bring Ben to the Health Sciences Centre Emergency department, where he would later meet us. Ben was examined and Ted was looking at his X-rays late in the evening and wondered out loud concerning a potential diagnosis, using me as a sounding board. He arranged for an emergency angiocardiogram test, because he suspected a dissecting aneurysm of the aorta, the main artery through which blood flows from the heart to the body, a very serious condition. The test confirmed Ted's suspicion. He phoned Dr. Morley Cohen who scheduled Ben for an emergency open-heart surgery at St. Boniface Hospital next morning. The operation saved Ben's life and he enjoyed many years traveling, golfing, and attending football games of the Winnipeg Blue Bombers. Val Werier related this incident in an article that he entitled "A life for old kindnesses" in the July 11, 1977 issue of the *Winnipeg Tribune*. Val reported how Volodia and Mary Kitzes brought their niece Etta from Warsaw before World War II; that Etta worked as a nurse with the UNRRA (United Nations Relief and Rehabilitation Administration) in the Displaced People Camps in Europe, and how she asked her uncle and aunt to sponsor a young orphaned boy from Poland to Winnipeg. Then that boy, who was I, became a doctor and helped save Ben, although in reality my role was very minor. There was another, in a sense a reverse aspect of this story that followed a few years later. Ben had elevated blood pressure that was monitored by measurements at home. One day when I visited, I was asked to take Ben's blood pressure. Before doing it I wanted to check the equipment by taking my own blood pressure. To my surprise I obtained a very high reading on myself. I arranged to see a colleague who confirmed that I had high blood pressure, which has been treated ever since. Had that incident not taken place, it could well be that with untreated hypertension, I might not be alive today. Doctors often are not good patients themselves and might neglect their own health. Also, at times a high degree of stress caused by their work exacts a price by impairing their health and putting strains on their family life.

Chapter VIII
Lessons of the Holocaust

Remembrance

During the years that followed the end of the war my memories of its horrors abated or perhaps were suppressed. New life unfolded promptly in Poland, Germany, and finally in Canada and I seemed to immerse myself in it fully. I was in contact with the offices of the Winnipeg Jewish Community Centre around 1960 in connection with some proceedings related to reparations for the survivors of the Holocaust from Germany, but that contact was limited. I think that I was probably reluctant to deal with the memories. I believe that somebody from Europe connected with the events of the Holocaust visited Winnipeg soon after I returned from my graduate studies in the United States in 1958, but I was not interested in making contact. People that I came in contact with in Canada did not question me much about that part of my life. Many years later in my extensive reading about the Holocaust and its survivors, I found that mine was not an uncommon experience, although some survivors kept reliving the horrors and suffered nightmares all along. I believe that the Canadian Jewish Community spent their efforts in bringing survivors of the Holocaust to Canada and in helping them start their new lives, but were not fully aware or interested in learning about our experiences in Europe. As time marched on the attitudes of survivors changed.

My attitude underwent a change around 1980. It seemed to start with a novel that a colleague recommended to me. It was *Miła 18* by Leon Uris about the Warsaw Ghetto and the uprising there in 1943. I read it with interest. At about the same time I became aware of a symposium on the Holocaust held at the Jewish campus on Hargrave Street and I decided to attend. Further contacts followed. I became a member of the Holocaust Awareness Committee (HAC). Its mandate was to

145

promote the memory and history of the events of that unprecedented genocide that doubtless represents the utmost of men's inhumanity to men. I embraced that mission and continued as a committee member for many years. In similarity to many survivors I now felt that our story must be told and retold. The committee had been active for a number of years before I joined. It sponsored annual events associated with the anniversaries of the Kristallnacht and the Yom Ha Shoah commemorating the Holocaust in April and coinciding with the beginning of the Warsaw Ghetto Uprising. The committee was supported by the Jewish Winnipeg Community and met at its premises on Hargrave Street, but chairpersons and most of its members were at that time Holocaust survivors.

When I joined the chairman was Philip Weiss. I met his wife Gertrude, a kind and charming lady, in Munich at the Jewish Students' Union a year or two after the war. Philip was a survivor of twelve camps and passionately devoted to perpetuating the memory of the events of the Holocaust. One of the achievements in which he played a vital role was the erection of the Memorial Monument to the victims of the Holocaust, whose family members settled in Manitoba, on the grounds of the Provincial Legislature in 1990. It was the first such monument on public grounds in Canada. On its walls are engraved the names of about 4000 victims including the members of my family. A solemn ceremony is held annually at the monument on Yom Ha Shoah, in which government officials, and leaders and members of the Jewish community, and Jewish and non-Jewish school students participate. After Philip Weiss resigned from the committee in 1993, he relentlessly continued his mission by talking about his experiences and about the Holocaust to high school students and at universities. He also sponsored, at his own expense, performances of the film *Schindler's List* for a number of Winnipeg high schools classes. In 1988 the Second Generation Group of Winnipeg that consisted of children of the Holocaust survivors approached me. They were doing a project filming interviews with survivors documenting their experiences six years before Steven Spielberg's Foundation started a large-scale project for the same purpose. It was a long interview, recorded at the Channel Twelve-television studios. The tapes of the interviews of the Second Generation Group of Winnipeg form a valuable resource, which was made available to the US Holocaust Museum in Washington, D.C, in addition to being housed at the Jewish Heritage Centre in Winnipeg.

Also in 1988 the first March of the Living took place from Auschwitz to Birkenau. This programme is supported by the government of Israel and worldwide Jewish organizations and takes place annually in April for two weeks. Its purpose is to teach students of different religious and ethnic backgrounds about the dangers of intolerance through the study of the Holocaust, and to promote better relations among people of diverse cultures. The climax of the programme is the march, which is designed to contrast with the death marches, which occurred towards the end of the war when Germans forced Jewish inmates of the camps, already starving and stricken by oppressive work, to march huge distances in the sleet and snow, while those who lagged behind or fell were shot. The living that walk a path of a death march serve to illustrate the continued existence of world Jewry despite Nazi attempts at their obliteration. March of the Living programmes often conclude with travel to Israel to celebrate its independence day further underlining the contrast of Jewish life and death. Groups of Jewish students come for the march from all over the world and non-Jewish groups also participate. A Winnipeg "Second Generation" group, with Morris Henoch and others, has taken part regularly. In April 1993 there was the 50th anniversary of the uprising in the Warsaw Ghetto, which was commemorated in ceremonies around the world including Warsaw. I was briefly interviewed by the CBC, which ran the segment on their local news following the national news with Peter Mansbridge. Also in 1993, I participated for the first time in a presentation on the Holocaust and related matters at the Oak Park High School. Philip Weiss gave an impressive talk about his horrific experiences during the war, I talked about mine, and a recent refugee from the Balkan War talked about his experience. We received a positive response.

Barbara Goszer became the next chairperson of the HAC and steered it successfully. In 1995 the HAC began to print a biannual newsletter *The Holocaust Remembered*, which contained editorials, news of the related events, and features dealing with educational materials. Some Gentiles became members of the committee. For a period of time I became an acting editor and was responsible for the editorials. They dealt with the importance of preserving the memory of the martyrs and documenting them by submitting special forms to the Hall of Names at Yad Vashem in Jerusalem, the Jewish and Gentile heroism during Holocaust and other topics. I submitted the forms for my family members to Yad Vashem and asked others to do the same. In 1998 the Jewish campus moved from Hargrave Street to a new expansive site in the area of Tuxedo. Through the tireless work of Barbara Goszer and her colleagues a Holocaust Heritage Centre with a small museum, archives and offices was established at the new campus. There is a memorial wall with plaques that commemorate victims of the Holocaust, acknowledge contributions made by individuals and families, and pay tribute to the Righteous Gentiles. I sponsored a plaque that acknowledges Dr. Hanna Herfurt-Gerwel, Zofia Różycka, and Danuta Krzeszewska, the three Righteous Polish ladies without whose help and courage my family members and I would not have survived the war. Several other projects began to operate at the Holocaust Heritage Centre.

Perhaps the most important initiative has been exposing classes of high school students throughout the province to presentations on the Holocaust and its significance. A retired Winnipeg teacher, Hersch Zentner, a Canadian who did not experience the Holocaust himself, developed and ran that programme for many years with extreme devotion and hard work. For example, in 1995 he did twenty-eight presentations to 3000 students. Hersch was born in Winnipeg in 1937 and taught high school. In 1988 he went on a trip with B'nai B'rith that gave him an in-depth look at the concentration camps in Germany and Nazi death camps in Poland. The trip led to his interest in the Holocaust. He became passionate and devoted himself to presentations and discussions of the Holocaust to large numbers of schools in Manitoba over some twenty years, during which he spoke to thousands of students. Thus the Outreach Programme of the Holocaust Education Centre came into being. Hersch invited a survivor to tell his story as an important part of each presentation and I had the opportunity to do so. His passing in 2002 was a great loss. In a tribute to Hersch, Barbara Goszer said in part, "Hersch had strong convictions, great passion and determination. Hersch wanted to teach Holocaust to the non-Jewish world and thus became the architect of our Holocaust Outreach Programme. He taught justice by presenting truth and strove to bring peace and love to all humankind."[1]

More recently, presentations to classes of high school students continue to take place but now at the Asper Jewish Community Campus in the Holocaust Heritage Centre. In 1993 B'nai B'rith began a programme Unto Every Person There is a Name in Canada. The names of the victims of the Holocaust are read at a ceremony during proceedings on Yom Hashoah. In Winnipeg the names and places where the victims perished are read out loud at a ceremony in the Provincial Parliament Building. This personalizes to some extent the anonymous millions of the martyrs of the Holocaust. Members of the Jewish community and non-Jews including public and government figures read the names. I read in 2002. When I and other survivors read the names of the members of their own families they would personalize it further by saying, for example, "My mother ..." The monument at the Parliament Building, with the nearly 4000 names and the name reading ceremony, made me think that it might be very worthwhile to try to "bring back to life" to a greater degree the people, their lives, and culture that were lost during World War II. In 1997 I proposed to the HAC a Manitoba Holocaust Heritage Project to document the pre-war life in Europe of the murdered Jewish individuals whose names appear on the monument. The project was approved; questionnaires filled out by the survivors or their children were produced. Survivors or their descendents were asked to fill them out and also to provide stories about the pre-war life. A project co-coordinator was hired, an appeal to survivors was made, and responses were obtained. Despite the hard, unselfish work of a number of devoted volunteers, however, the project continued to linger until recently. A couple of years ago Belle Millo, who is currently the Chairperson of the Holocaust Education Centre, took it upon herself to put together the information and stories of over 50 survivor families. She spent countless hours typing and tirelessly working to obtain support for a book "Voices of the Winnipeg Holocaust Survivors", which was published in 2010.Over the past fourteen years I also participated in symposia and made presentations to classes of high school and university students. My presentation to the European Study Group at the University of Winnipeg was videotaped and its copies sent to the Winnipeg Holocaust Heritage Centre and to the US Holocaust Museum in Washington.

In 1995 two significant events took place that were related to the sentiment felt and repeatedly expressed by many Holocaust survivors: that teaching students and other groups about what transpired during the war should lead to overall tolerance and respect of other individuals and their views. In June The Manitoba Human Rights Commission hosted a conference Encouraging Tolerance in Canada, in which members of the commission, lawyers, human rights activists, and members of Civil Liberties Association took part. In August a Jewish-Mennonite-Ukrainian Conference took place at the St. Paul's College of the University of Manitoba called Building Bridges. The Jewish Historical Society, Manitoba Mennonite Historical Society, and Manitoba East European Society organized it and their members gave presentations. The theme of the conference dealt with the concerns and interactions of the three communities with a view toward the future and its proceedings were published.[2]

The Asper Foundation Human Rights and Holocaust Studies Programme began in 1999. It creates awareness of the Holocaust in grade nine students by education sessions at the Holocaust Education Centre and culminates in a trip to the Holocaust Memorial Museum in Washington, D.C. Both Jewish and non-Jewish students participate. The Freeman Family Holocaust Education Centre at the Jewish Asper campus also sponsors the Mina Rosner Human Rights Essay Contest that each year awards a price for the best essay on the Holocaust and the importance of championing human rights. Mina Rosner, whom we knew well, was a Winnipeg mother, grandmother, businesswoman, author, educator, and a Holocaust survivor. She grew up in the Ukraine and saw her friends, family, and community exterminated by the Nazis. She wrote a book about these experiences entitled *I am a Witness* and CBC produced a documentary of her revisiting the people and places where she lived before the war and where she experienced the atrocities of the Holocaust.

In 2002, members of the Holocaust Heritage Centre organized a huge Holocaust symposium for high school students. Their teachers, who were earlier provided with educational materials, prepared their classes for the symposium. The symposium was held in the Duckworth Centre at the University of Winnipeg. A thousand students with their teachers filled the huge auditorium and listened to a keynote presentation. After a lunch break they moved to classrooms at the university for break-out sessions where each group listened to a talk of a survivor of the Holocaust, who related to them hers or his story. The symposium was so successful that it had continued since on an annual basis. Its topics over the years were "The Camps," "The Righteous Among the Nations," "The Lessons Learned" and others. Also in 2002, a special celebration took place at the Jewish Asper campus. A Dutch Winnipeg resident Katy Simpson was honoured for risking her life to save Jews in the Netherlands during the war, and she received the Righteous Among The Nations Award. Emilee and I knew Katy as a very pleasant and courageous lady through contacts at cultural events. A year later I attended a meeting in Washington, D.C. at which the Holocaust survivors gathered and were honoured at various events including a ceremony at the US Memorial Holocaust Museum in which the colours of various US Army units that liberated camps in Germany were paraded, and dignitaries such as the Noble Laureate Elie Wiesel, and other prominent Holocaust survivors took part.

How could it have happened?

Over the years, when I participated in the activities related to the preservation of the memories and events of the Holocaust, I read extensively and thought about what transpired during those terrible times. How could the German state carry out a systematic killing of six million Jews, in addition to that of gypsies, homosexuals, political dissidents, and members of other occupied nations, and how could the rest of the world allow it to happen? This question has generated a huge literature and scholarly discourse. Despite the outpouring of scholarly writings for more than fifty years, there seems to be no simple answer to the question of how the enormous evil of the Holocaust could have taken place perpetrated by a highly cultural European nation. The events defy comprehension. Yet one must attempt to consider and try to understand it as thoroughly as possible. Even an incomplete understanding provides knowledge of the complexity of the events; it is relevant to other genocides, and provides some insights into human nature. Since the dispersal of the Jewish people in the Diaspora, their majority tended to live following their own religious and cultural customs wherever they settled rather than assimilate. Although some became very successful in various endeavours, and contributed to the economic and cultural lives of their adopted countries, they would repeatedly serve as scapegoats whenever things did not go well, were subject to persecutions because they were different and because of the anti-Semitic attitudes of the Catholic church, which most Protestant churches inherited without change. The persecutions included even the small numbers of Jews that assimilated. As alluded to earlier, repeated large-scale annihilations of the Jews took place in the forms of slaughters of thousands upon thousands by the crusaders on their way to Palestine; by Swedes, Poles, and Cossacks in the seventeenth-century Poland, in pogroms in the imperial Russia and so forth. These horrific events seemed almost "logically" to set stage for some form of Holocaust affecting the Jews. The world, however, did not imagine that it would be perpetrated by the highly cultured German state that followed its maniacal Fuehrer. Certain political and economic circumstances and a "scientific" discipline contributed to its occurrence. The worldwide anti-Semitic attitudes among individuals and government leaders and the unprecedented, and thus hard to believe nature of the highly organized, mass annihilation contributed to the world's indifference towards the Holocaust as it was occurring. These factors were combined with difficulties in the logistics of trying to bring about effective interventions that might have resulted in saving Jews under the Nazi yoke.

The ascent of Hitler to power is said to have taken place at least in part because of the economic depression, and the resentment of the Germans resulting from their loss of World War I and the conditions imposed on them after that war. It appears, however, that seeds that might have aided in the formulation of the thoughts that eventually led to the systematic murder of Jews and others appeared considerably earlier and were related to the developments in biosciences and medicine. Darwin's theory of evolution led to the development of eugenics aimed at improvement of the human race by intervention to prevent the reproduction of humans judged to be "defective" and thus detrimental to the human species, if allowed to reproduce. These considerations, briefly summarized below, were presented at a conference and published in 1996.[3] An International Society for Racial Hygiene was formed in 1907 and led to further developments after the First World War with close relationships between the United States and many European countries including Great Britain, France, and Germany among others. Utilitarian views were adopted, which held that it would be acceptable to prevent reproduction and even exterminate the physically or socially unfit. Sterilization of thirty-eight thousand mostly mentally disabled people took place in the United States between 1908 and 1941 and was deemed constitutional by the Supreme Court. Today, compulsory sterilization programmes are usually seen as overly coercive and blunt attempts at genetic engineering, which focus on poor and disenfranchised groups. The best-known compulsory sterilization programmes were those of Nazi Germany, which sterilized over four hundred thousand individuals in the 1930s and

1940s, the United States, which sterilized over sixty-four thousand individuals from 1900s through the 1970s, and many Scandinavian countries. Among the latter, Sweden sterilized the highest proportion of its own citizens; from the 1930s mostly through 1950s and to some extent until the programme was formally abolished in 1976. In Canada close to three thousand women were sterilized mainly in Alberta, where Sexual Sterilization Act first passed in 1928 and was not abolished until 1972.

In addition, as previously indicated, the US Congress passed an Immigration Restriction Act in 1924 that barred immigrants from Asia and Eastern Europe largely for racial reasons. These various developments were followed by the Nazis, who used them as models to protect their "superior" Nordic race and led to the atrocities, which they carried out. In carrying out the large-scale annihilation of the Jews and others (mentally ill, physically deformed, Romas, and some Slavs) the German medical profession took on an essential role. Its members planned and supervised the exterminations and took opportunities to carry out inhumane research experiments, of which Joseph Mengele's "work" is the notorious example. The dangers of scientifically "improving" the human species have recently raised concerns that ethical considerations must be included in various projects. The Human Genome Project holds a promise of salutary results that have potential to bring about improvements to human health care, however, it also contains potential for engineering characteristics of human beings that raise questions that could affect the basic nature of the human species.[4]

The actual degree of the annihilation of the Jewish population in various parts of the Nazi dominated Europe varied from country to country. By far the largest estimated number of victims was about three million Polish Jews followed by a million in the Soviet Union. In other countries the numbers varied. There were between two hundred- and three hundred thousand victims in Romania, Czechoslovakia, and Hungary. Jews fared better in France, Italy, and Bulgaria, which though allied with Germany, remained independent. The Bulgarian authorities took a courageous stand and circumstances resulted in the large majority of Bulgarian Jews being saved. In Denmark a remarkable secret evacuation of most of the Jewish population to Sweden took place by the effort of the Righteous Danes just before Nazis were to send the Jews to concentration or death camps.

These figures need to be considered in relation to the numbers of the Jewish population that lived before the war. Out of the fifteen to seventeen million Jews alive in the world in 1939, six million or about forty percent were annihilated. Counting only the Jews of Europe, the percentage is about sixty-five percent. In Poland, Austria, Germany, and the Baltic countries around ninety percent were murdered. The percentages were between fifty and ninety in a number of the other countries that fell under German occupation or were Germany's allies. However, less than thirty percent of Jews from France, Luxembourg, Italy, and Bulgaria perished and hardly any from Denmark.

There were some Righteous Gentiles in every country including Germany who helped Jews. In Poland, where I was, the anti-Semitic attitude of some groupings within the Polish underground, of some members of the Polish Government in exile in London, and of a large proportion of the population of the country undoubtedly were detrimental. Polish hooligans attacked Jews early during the occupation in large pogroms incited by the German occupiers. Later after the Ghettos were liquidated many underground Polish detachments, especially those of the National Armed Forces, a separate entity from AK i.e. Home Army associated with the Polish Government in exile, attacked and killed Jewish partisans in the forests. Some country peasant groups participated in German raids on Jews hiding in the forests and some did it on their own accord. Germans rewarded anybody who delivered hiding Jews to them. Jews who were hiding in the Aryan part of Warsaw and in other cities were in constant danger of being blackmailed by the anti-Semites and criminals, rendered penniless, or denounced to the German authorities. The chances of survival were enhanced by the perfect command of the Polish language, financial means, "good looks" and confident deportment, which many hunted Jews lacked.

An example of somebody with a good chance was my peer Wanda Rechthand, a well-educated, intelligent, resolute, and cheerful girl. I remember that she made light of an encounter with a German guard, when we were still in the Ghetto. She had "good looks", and worked as an Aryan after leaving the Ghetto. Another Jewish fugitive, who met her on the Aryan side, described her high spirits.[5] At the same time, it is important to emphasize that some Polish parties and many individuals were not only sympathetic to the plight of the Jews, but actively helped the victims, risking and in a number of cases losing their lives in the process.[6,7,8] An organization for the purpose of helping the

Jews—Żegota was formed. It included Righteous Poles who worked with members of Jewish organizations. It helped many Jews in hiding. Heroic Righteous Gentiles were responsible for the survival of many Jewish people including members of my family and myself. Paulsson estimated in an extensive well-researched study that about eleven thousand and five hundred or forty percent of the Jews who hid in the Aryan part of Warsaw survived the war,[9] which is comparable, for example, to the survival rate of Jews in Westerns European countries such as the Netherlands.

A Jewish member of the Polish Government in London, Isaac Schwarzbart, was having a hard time representing Jewish interests to the Allies. Despite the position of the Polish Government in London, a large proportion of Polish officials in the underground were opposed to the equal rights for the Jews in Poland, remarkably even after Germans killed the majority of the Jews in the Polish territories.[10] The inconceivable nature and the unprecedented inhumanity and extent of the Holocaust made it difficult to believe that it could be true, and contributed to the resistance to accept that it was really occurring. That was the case with the Allied authorities in the west as well as a number of Jewish leaders in England, USA, and Palestine. Apparently some Jews even believed that it was safer to be in the territories under Germans—a highly cultural people, than under Russians, who used to engage in pogroms over the years in the past.[11]

Yet reports of the annihilation of the Jews that was taking place near the eastern front and in Poland were transmitted early to the West. First there were reports of the mass killings by the German *Einsatzgruppen* in the occupied Soviet territories in 1941. Then a German industrialist Eduard Schulte informed western representatives in Switzerland in 1942 about the imminent threat of Hitler's "Final Solution"[12] and couriers from Poland reported to the Polish Government in exile in London and to British and American authorities. Jan Karski was the first of the Polish couriers. He went into the Warsaw Ghetto in August 1942 when a large proportion of the Ghetto population was being taken to Treblinka and then he was smuggled into a transit camp near the death camp of Bełżec. There he witnessed masses of Jews being robbed, treated inhumanely, and sealed in rail boxcars lined with lime to die.[13] His and his followers' reports, however, tended to be met either with disbelief or indifference, including some Jews in the west who were unable to believe the grim reality. A second Polish courier Jan Nowak reported that Schwarzbart begged him to minimize the numbers of deaths in talking to the British, because they would not believe them, even though Schwarzbart himself must have been aware of what was going on, as for example, there were accounts in the Polish press in Winnipeg in 1943 and a booklet about the Warsaw Ghetto Uprising was published in the West in 1944.[14] Similarly, Nowak reports that the cousin of my mother, Adam Pragier, a member of the Polish government in England, told a fellow Jew, Szmul Zygielbojm, to decrease the number of reported Jewish deaths by dropping a zero from a report of seven hundred thousand deaths, as he, Adam, and others thought that it had to be propaganda.[15] Zygielbojm later committed suicide in protest over the indifference of the Western Allies towards the fate of his fellow Jews.

Together with the difficulty to believe, the indifference to the fate of the Jews pervading the western countries must have played an important part. Jan Karski transmitted the pleas of the Jews of Warsaw for the Allies to take a number of concrete measures that might have resulted in saving significant numbers of Jewish people at least in some territories.[13] The pleas and the information about the atrocities did not bring about any practically meaningful actions, and the reports were actually suppressed. The following quote from Nowak's book about his meetings with western officials in England illustrates it.

In all the meetings I myself introduced the subject of the extermination of the Polish Jews and the destruction of the Warsaw Ghetto. The crime of genocide, the slaughter of hundreds of thousands of people, the scale and methods used, unprecedented in history, seemed matters of the highest importance. Everybody had listened with interest mixed with disbelief. Thirty-odd years later, looking through the notes and reports of those interlocutors, I found all the references to the Jews omitted. Jan Karski, my predecessor, arrived in London from Poland in 1942 with extensive first-hand eyewitness information about the fate of the Jews. Before he left Poland Karski, posing as an Estonian policeman, risked his life by getting into the concentration camp at Majdanek (*actually a transit camp near Bełżec—S.C.*) to see with his own eyes what was happening to the Jews sent there. Karski met with Anthony Eden on his return to London and told me that at his audience he described at length the systematic and progressive extermination of the Jewish population. The undersecretary of state considered the conversation so important that a report on it circulated to all members of the war cabinet. I looked this up at the Polish Records Office and was astonished to find everything Karski had said about the extermination of the Jews omitted from the document. Why?[16]

The indifference of the Western Allies towards the plight of the Jews seems to be borne out, for example, by the refusal of the Allied Armed Forces to bomb the railway lines leading to Auschwitz and the camp itself. That would have made it difficult for the Nazis to transport Jews to their deaths. Yet, Allied Air Force planes bombed a German industrial complex close to Auschwitz in 1944 and some bombs fell accidentally on the camp! Apparently the refusal to bomb was based on the pretext that bombing the railway lines to the camp "was not a military objective", that the air force could not bomb with accuracy or could not afford the planes or risk the lives of the airmen. Yet, they flew further over or very close to Auschwitz to drop supplies to the fighters of the Polish Warsaw Uprising in 1944, who were holding only parts of the city. The dropped cargo often fell into German hands. If the Allied Air Force did bomb Auschwitz or the rails leading to it, which they certainly could have done, more than a hundred thousand Jewish lives might have been saved. As it was, the Germans continued to gas Jewish victims in Auschwitz until almost the end of 1944 and large numbers died and were shot there until the Soviet Army reached Auschwitz on January 27, 1945.

Martin Gilbert extensively documented the relationship of the Western Allies to the Auschwitz-Birkenau deaths camps in his book *Auschwitz and the Allies.*[17] He concluded that the Allies failed in responding because of lack of imagination, initiative, intelligence, and coordination and that the long lasting German deception concealed the killings in the camp also contributed the Allies' failing.[18] The latter assertion is debatable. He adds that there was at times failure of sympathy. It is also clear, however, that British indifference was related to their concern about increased Jewish immigration to Palestine, if large numbers of Jewish refugees from German occupied Europe were to be admitted. The essence of the matter may be gleamed from the following passage: "From a map in Churchill's papers, the flight paths to Warsaw can be seen passing just to the west of Kraków, virtually over Auschwitz itself. But it was the agony of Warsaw [referring to the Polish Uprising of 1944], not the agony of the Jews, that had come to dominate the telegraphic exchanges of the Allied leaders"[19] and resulted in the British sending some planes to Warsaw to supply the embattled 1944 insurgents—despite the Soviets refusal to allow them to land for refueling on the nearby territories that they controlled.

Dealing with the legacy of the Holocaust

Individuals that lived during the Holocaust appear to fall into three categories: the criminal perpetrators that ordered and carried out the murders, the "silent" majority that followed the perpetrator's orders or stood by and remained indifferent to what was happening, and the Righteous that at great danger to themselves actively resisted the crime and acted to try and save the victims. Those three groups were represented in all countries including Germany, and to an extent among the Jews. There were some Jewish criminals who exploited their fellow Jews. The notorious "thirteen", who ran a luxurious club in the Warsaw Ghetto, are an example. There were Jewish informants, who betrayed other Jews to the authorities. My cousin George had an experience in Warsaw with one such informant. Shortly after meeting a Jewish acquaintance on the Aryan side, he was questioned by the police but managed to talk his way out of trouble.

Throughout most of the civilized world criminal anti-Semitic elements have been a constant for close to two millennia, and unfortunately seem to continue their activities undeterred by the occurrence of the Holocaust. The survivors of the Holocaust and their descendents have talked and written about their experiences to memorialize their murdered brethren and to bring about greater tolerance, and thus a better world. They are achieving the first objective, but unfortunately the second remains elusive as anti-Semitism continues unabated and other genocides are taking place. Teaching people about the Holocaust in schools and in the media, in Winnipeg and throughout many countries of the world, generally evokes expected and appropriate reactions from audiences. Personally, I received heartfelt letters from students of the schools where I made presentations and was thanked by many individual students and teachers after I told them about my experiences. Many felt moved and one would hope that at least some would adopt more positive attitudes towards students of other backgrounds, than those they held previously.

However, teaching people about the Holocaust does not seem to have resulted in an overall change in anti-Semitic attitudes. Otherwise enlightened people at times seem to imply that it is all right to hold anti-Semitic views, when that is the "norm" of the time. "Never again" emblazoned on memorial stones at the site of Nazi's death camps in several languages rings hollow. Indeed Peter Novick wrote that "never again" only means "never again would Germans kill Jews in Europe in 1940s"[20]. The populations of various countries hold different views on the Holocaust and racism. Each country has struggled with the fallout of the Holocaust. Germany has faced it, probably first and with a lot of soul searching. It has made attempts to come to terms with it by paying compensation to its victims, organizing get togethers with the survivors and building memorials or museums to commemorate the events. Austrians, many of whom were eager and cruel perpetrators of the atrocities, tried to paint themselves as the "first victims" of Hitler, and have had great difficulties in coming to terms with what actually transpired, i.e. that overall they were no better, if not worse, than the Germans. The Dutch have had difficulties coping with the reality that the majority of the country was eager to cooperate with the Nazis, though there was active resistance by the Righteous individuals. France struggled with the divide between members of its resistance and collaborators of the Vichy Regimen. Indeed there were segments of the population of every country in the German occupied Europe that collaborated with the Nazis. The de-nazification process in Germany, Austria, the Netherlands, and other countries failed to a considerable degree, and some members of the Nazi party or its collaborators have risen to high posts and many have lived in peace and freedom. At the same time there is resentment among segments of the population, including those that were born after the war that they need to deal with that part of history. There are also frequent attempts at revising history and "Holocaust denial". Others including some Jews and Holocaust survivors feel that enough is enough.

In the Soviet Union, Jewish annihilation during World War II had been officially ignored, as the government considered Jewish victims together with the deaths of millions of all their citizens during the war against Nazism. Poland seemed to have had as much or more difficulties in acknowledging what transpired there during the war and afterwards than other countries. Yet, since the 1970s positive steps are being taken. For example, in 2001 Polish bishops apologized for Polish Catholics' crimes of murder against the Jews. Among several institutions, the Polish Center for Holocaust Research at the Polish Academy of Science in Warsaw appears to have chosen another helpful pathway. Its aim is to continue to conduct Holocaust-related research. Their website states that Holocaust happened on Polish soil, in full view of the Polish society and that Holocaust is an integral part—whether one wants to believe it or not—of Polish history.

For Poles, the experience of the Holocaust remains a unique event and carries with it extraordinary responsibilities. Nevertheless, in terms of social awareness, Shoah seems to belong to Jewish rather than to Polish history. Even today many Poles feel ill at ease, threatened or outright disappointed by the Jewish perceptions of the Holocaust and often times the Jews are seen as rivals in the martyrology competition. Despite the recent historical research and public debates, culminating with the discussion around the crime in the village of Jedwabne, Polish society largely ignores the issues related to the Holocaust. Still too many myths and lies are finding their way to the public sphere and enter public circulation. The Polish researchers believe that this should change. Among their activities the group produced the excellent book "The Warsaw Ghetto: A Guide to the Perished City", which details the life and events in the Warsaw Ghetto.[21] They collaborate with researchers in various countries and with Jewish scholars in Poland and elsewhere. Also, a Museum of Polish Jewry dealing with the thousand years of its history is about to be built in Warsaw. There is interest in Poland in Jewish culture. Various events are presented in annual festivals enacted by Poles and Jews. A small Jewish community is now active in Poland. Recently Jewish survivors in Warsaw honoured Polish Holocaust rescuers of the Jews. Some of the rescuers receive financial assistance from Jewish organizations. It was a Polish Righteous Gentile, the wartime courier Jan Karski, who stated in his 1981 address at the Conference of International Liberators in Washington that:[22]

> The Lord assigned me a role to speak and write during the war when—as it seemed to me—it might help. It did not.

Furthermore, when the war came to an end, I learned that the governments, the leaders, the scholars, the writers did not know what had been happening to the Jews. They were taken by surprise. The murder of six million innocents was a secret …

Then I became a Jew. Like the family of my wife—all of them perished in the Ghettos, in concentration camps, in the gas chambers—so all murdered Jews became my family.

But I am a Christian Jew. I am a practicing Catholic. Although I am not a heretic, still my faith tells me the second original sin has been committed by humanity: Through commission or omission, or self-imposed ignorance, or insensitivity, or self-interest, or hypocrisy, or heartless rationalization.

This sin will haunt humanity to the end of time. It does haunt me. And I want it to be so.

Karski's statement reflects the unique place of the Holocaust in history and the inaction of the world that silently stood by. His saying, that the world was taken by surprise, however, is only partly true.

The western countries Britain, then USA, and Canada overall remained aloof towards the plight of the Jews since Hitler came to power and during the war. That was related to their primary attention to the war effort and because of anti-Semitic views of the officials that were in positions that would have allowed them to assist and save Jews. They interned Jews from Germany in the prisoner of war camps, just as they did with German nationals and those of Japanese origin. The news of the Nazi atrocities was suppressed in the US State Department. Ruth Gruber confirmed this in her book *Haven*, a story of the rescue of about a thousand Jewish refugees from Italy in 1944.[23] These people were almost deported back to Europe, but in the eleventh hour President Roosevelt intervened and allow them to stay in the United States and apply for immigration from within the country. The plight of the Jewish inmates of the concentration camps liberated by the US Army near the end of the war generally continued to be dismal for several months after liberation. The US Army was ill prepared for the task and did a grossly inadequate job with respect to Jews, who were the most physically and psychologically depleted of all the displaced persons. They received the poorest treatment, in part because of widespread anti-Semitism in the US Army. General George S. Patton was among the least sympathetic and considered Jewish displaced persons "lower than animals."

My cousin George was liberated by the Americans and worked with a US Air Force unit as an interpreter. Two Jewish GIs came one day to talk to him. They were concerned about Jews in the nearby camps of Dachau and Buchenwald continuing to die at a high rate because of the lack of adequate food supplies and medical care, while American officers were taking their time organizing their agendas with the help of the readily available and willing assistance of the German fräuleins. The enterprising and determined efforts of the two American soldiers, despite insurmountable odds against them, eventually led to a presidential commission by Earl G. Harrison in the summer of 1945. It reported that conditions in the camps were terrible and this led in turn to the intervention by President Truman. Robert Hilliard, one of the two American soldiers who talked to my cousin, discusses this story in the book *Surviving the Americans: The Continued Struggle of the Jews After Liberation*.[24] These events are also commemorated in a documentary film.

Canada today is a country that became to a high degree a multi-ethnic mosaic and a sanctuary for the oppressed from various parts of the globe. Winnipeg near the geographic centre of the country exemplifies particularly well the change that transpired in the country. Its population contains people from most countries of the planet. Multicultural events such as the Folklorama and others emphasize the cultural diversity. The Arthur V. Mauro Centre at St. Paul's College at the University of Manitoba is dedicated to research, education, and outreach to foster global peace and justice. It explores diverse dimensions of social life at the local, national, and international levels, including conflict resolution. I attended a meeting there in recent years, which included a presentation about the Polish organization Żegota, which saved many Jews hiding from the Nazis in the Aryan area of Warsaw during the German occupation.

Canada's previous record on immigration and human rights, however, was very different than it is today. A CBC television programme of October 6, 1982[25] revealed that during World War II the Canadian government did everything in its power to bar the door to European Jews trying to flee Nazi persecution. Irving Abella, co-author of the book *None Is Too Many*,[26] demonstrated using archival research that Canada did less than other Western countries to help the Jews despite mounting reports of Hitler's genocide, which were known to the Western officials by 1942. Small countries managed to rescue fifteen to twenty thousand Jews, compared to the four to five thousand Canada rescued. At the heart of the closed-door policy was Frederick Charles Blair, a civil servant, who as the head of immigration in the Mackenzie King administration was in charge of upholding immigration restrictions. His correspondence in federal archives is rife with anti-Semitic remarks. In one letter, Blair compared Jews clamoring to get into the country to "hogs at feeding time." Saul Sigler, a Toronto businessman, told the CBC that he tried in vain to get his brother and sister into Canada. Blair's response, according to Sigler was: "Why don't you people learn to live with your neighbours wherever you are? Why are you hated?" But Blair did not act in isolation.

Mackenzie King, the wartime prime minister, and Vincent Massey, Canada's high commissioner to Britain, supported a tight cap on the number of Jewish immigrants. Blair was responsible to Thomas Alexander Crerar, a Western Canadian politician who was born in Ontario, but moved to Manitoba at a young age. He represented the northern Manitoba riding of Churchill and was appointed to King's cabinet, serving as minister of immigration and colonization and in other positions. When on occasion the prime minister or Crerar were moved to try new initiatives to save the lives of the Jewish victims of Nazi persecutions, Blair usually succeeded in persuading them to desist. Furthermore, he or other civil servants were able to thwart admission of a significant number of Jews to Canada by strictly applying the existing stringent criteria for eligibility or by interpreting them in such a way as to make it impossible that more than a pittance of the threatened people could be saved. For the meritorious service Crerar was appointed to the Canadian Senate in 1945 and in 1973 was made a companion of the Order of Canada. Similarly, upon his retirement in 1943, Blair was given a prestigious award for meritorious public service.

Canada's immigration policy did not change appreciably even after the war ended, for at least two years. The entrenched anti-Semitic attitudes of the civil servants, politicians, and of the large proportions of the public continued to resist admission of Jewish people. This approach changed by 1948 as businessmen pushed for large immigration to assure adequate supply of labourers and consumers for the expected economic boom. Thus, Canada came to start admitting refugees and displaced people from several countries, including some Jews because of the national economic self-interest. At first close, members of the immediate family were allowed to join their kin. Then labourers needed in various industries were recruited from among the displaced persons. In these groups a strong, though unspoken, anti-Jewish bias severely limited the numbers of Jews. The Canadian officials felt that Jews did not assimilate well and tended not to remain in various labour camps in Canada but soon would leave for the cities. The Jewish groups in Canada continued to be frustrated in their efforts to bring some of the remnants of the European Jewish people from the refugee camps. They finally received an agreement from the government for immigration of tailors and other needle-workers, in which Jewish people dominated. Even in this case, however, when Canadian officials realized that a large group of primarily Jewish workers would be arriving, they instituted a ruling that no ethnic group could form more than fifty percent of the workers. It was not until the 1950s that Canada allowed Jews again in large numbers, as had been the case in the 1880s and before the First World War. Restrictions on Asian immigrants outlived the limits on Jewish newcomers lasting until the 1960s.

In a 1995 speech to Holocaust survivors in Toronto, Prime Minister Jean Chrétien said: "We turned our backs on Jewish refugees from Europe when we could have saved lives, when we should have saved lives. Instead, we washed our hands of the matter."

The attitude of the Canadian government largely reflected Canadian public sentiment towards the Jews at the time. Anti-Semitism was rife throughout Canada and there were concerns that Jewish and other refugees would compete for jobs and not fit into the community. Thus, it would be politically disadvantageous for the politicians to allow Jewish immigration. In some places Jews were not permitted to hold particular jobs, own property or stay in certain hotels, a situation eerily reminiscent of the conditions existing in the pre-World War II Poland. Anti-Semitism was most strident in Quebec, however, where right wing, nationalist French-language newspapers castigated Jews.

Canada has also been criticized for ignoring the plight of more than nine hundred European Jews aboard the ship *SS St. Louis* in 1939. The refugees' plea for safe haven was refused by Canada, Cuba, and other western hemisphere nations. The ship was forced to return to Europe where almost half the Jews later died in camps or from other war-related causes. In Ottawa in 2000, several Canadian Christian leaders apologized to twenty-five of the *SS St. Louis* survivors. One of the clergymen who apologized to the survivors of the *SS St. Louis* was Doug Blair, a Baptist minister and the great-nephew of Frederick Blair, the bureaucrat who orchestrated Canada's limit on Jewish immigration and who personally advised the government to ignore the pleas of the Jews aboard the *St. Louis*. "I'm sorry. Will you forgive me?" Doug Blair asked the gathered survivors, the CBC reported. In January 2011, a monument called the *Wheel of Conscience* was unveiled in Halifax at pier 21 to commemorate Canada's fateful decision not to let the passengers of *St. Louis* to disembark in 1939.

The Canadian Jewish Community was unsuccessful in its efforts to save Jews from the Holocaust by bringing them to Canada before and during World War II. Similarly for a couple of years after the war it was unable to bring refugees. They had no political weight. As stated by the authors of *None is Too Many*: "Canadian Jewry sought to tap into the wellspring of human kindness, only to find it dry. The Western world, including Canada, was prepared to eulogize the Jews; it was not prepared to offer them a home".[27]

Thus, people and countries that were involved in the Holocaust directly in continental Europe and the Western Allies Britain, Canada, and the USA continue to find it difficult to confront the incomprehensible horrors of the Holocaust and how they acted during it. To avoid the discomfort of facing it, they often tend to diminish it, deny its uniqueness, and some people crudely deny that it happened. Anti-Semitic attitudes then come to the fore. Anti-Semitism is entrenched too firmly over most parts of the world and in the Christian traditions to dissipate; it is likely that it will always remain. In Poland where there is only a minimal Jewish presence, anti-Semitism continues "without the Jews".

The creation of the state of Israel, which came about probably in large part because of the Holocaust, became an additional factor in feeding anti-Semitism, as the Jewish state is forced to take strong measures to defend itself from the neighbouring countries that want to destroy it. In Canada, anti-Semitic incidents as compiled by B'nai B'rith have increased from the annual rate of seventy-seven in the early 1980s to 258 in the 1990s and to 658 in the new millennium. In Manitoba there were fewer than ten incidents annually from 1996 to 2001, and more than twenty annually since. While writing these memoirs, I came across an article in the March 16, 2007 issue of the *Winnipeg Free Press* (p. B1) about a vicious hate letter sent to a Winnipeg teacher, who worked with students on an anti-racism unity group and who was recognized by an award from the Manitoba Human Rights Commission. Along with anti-Semitism, racism, and genocides in the Balkans, Rwanda, and Darfur continue to occur while the world remains largely indifferent and impotent, despite the efforts of many enlightened individual and groups in various countries and communities.

The Righteous Among Nations, who were the shining light during the darkness of the Holocaust and other atrocities, need to be considered, as possibly holding clues that might be helpful in the humankind's efforts to improve the society of nations. The stories of their valour are inspiring. While large numbers of their heroic deeds will never be known, the more we know about them the more we are likely to appreciate them and benefit from them. A new book about a remarkable rescue of German Jews appeared recently, *The Greatest Invention of the Leitz Family: The Leica Freedom Train*, by Frank Dabba Smith, a California-born rabbi currently living in England.[28] The Leitz family who manufactured the Leica cameras before World War II rescued huge numbers of Jews by smuggling them out of Germany as their "employees" to be stationed abroad. Some members of the Leitz family were imprisoned. Until the death of the last member of the family their wishes did not allow the publication.

The following considerations about the Righteous are largely based on the article written by Professor Daniel Stone in Winnipeg.[29] While Hitler's Nazis and their collaborators murdered six million Jewish people, the majority of the more than 300 million in Germany and Nazi occupied Europe stood passively by. There were heroic Gentiles, however, who by their actions were instrumental in saving thousands of Jews.

The ten thousand Gentiles recognized by Yad Vashem in Jerusalem, as "Righteous among the Nations" for saving Jews from the Holocaust are only the tip of the iceberg of Gentiles who helped Jews. Many heroic Gentiles eluded recognition because the Jews they protected died without giving testimony, because some of the Gentiles preferred anonymity, and because Yad Vashem's definition is restrictive. Additional thousands or even much larger numbers performed small acts of heroism and simple decency that helped Jews survive.

Some important saviours were not officially recognized because their diplomatic status shielded them from arrest. Sempro Sugihara, a Japanese consul, distributed two thousand to three thousand transit visas to Lithuanian Jews against his government's instructions, allowing them to escape to the Soviet Union and beyond. His Portuguese counterpart, Aristide de Sousa Mendes, violated his government's instructions by granting ten thousand transit visas to Jews fleeing France. Francis Foley, a British agent now recognized by Yad Vashem, issued thousand of visas to Jews in Berlin. Yad Vashem probably violated its own guidelines by recognizing Raoul Wallenberg, whose diplomatic immunity shielded him from Nazi arrest. Many deserving Gentiles risked death at Nazi hands but missed official recognition because they took money from Jews to feed them and to bribe suspicious guards.

Henryk Grynberg, now a Jewish-Polish writer, described the less definitive and quite typical heroism of twenty or thirty peasants in three Polish villages who took turns feeding his family for more than a year while they hid in the woods. Dozens of other villagers knew what their neighbours were doing and chose not to turn the Jews in, or their Christian protectors. Similarly Susan Thumin Silk recalls that poor Polish peasants shared their own limited food with her and her father while they were hiding in the forest from the Germans.[30] There must have been thousands of similar situations. A large proportion of the Holocaust survivors owe their lives to the assistance of heroic Gentiles and to numerous Gentiles, who chose not to act villainously despite rewards that the Nazis offered.

The extraordinary heroism of those recognized by Yad Vashem deserves special recognition, of course. Anne Frank and her family were hidden by Mies Giep and several other Dutch citizens who fed them in their hiding place at great risk to themselves. Indeed, the police arrested two Gentiles along with the Franks and put them in camps—luckily, they survived. Two villages earned collective recognition: Chambon-Sur-Lignon in France and Nieulande in Holland. The Council to Help the Jews, Żegota mentioned earlier, organized by Catholic activists in Poland hid eight thousand Jews in Warsaw and other large cities, supplying false papers, feeding them, and finding trustworthy doctors for them when they were sick. Among individuals that were part of Żegota was Irena Sendler, a health worker and remarkable woman. She saved twenty-five hundred Jewish children by smuggling them out of the Warsaw Ghetto between 1942 and 1943 to safe hiding places and found non-Jewish families to give them shelter. Although she was caught and tortured, she would not divulge any information.

There were many reasons for such heroism. Some Gentiles saved friends and neighbours. Some saved strangers because they hated injustice. Some saved Jews to resist Nazis. Some responded when a Jew came to ask for help. Some responded to an approach by a Gentile friend to share the burden of saving a Jew. Some devout Christians saved Jews in accordance with Christian dogma to love their neighbours, including priests who supplied baptismal certificates. Some atheists saved Jews out of socialist idealism. Some belonged to resistance organizations.

It would be wonderful if we could distill the essence of Gentile Heroism and inject it into the world's population to protect all peoples from racism. One way is to promote socially conscious activities of all kinds. One major predictor of Gentile heroism was membership in a socially active group: religious, political or even recreational. Group membership promoted social solidarity and broke down the isolation that kept individuals from resisting Nazis. Luckily, Winnipeg's character as a multicultural city of volunteers tends to protect it against racist behaviour, although dangers continue to exist.

Another way of applying the lessons of the Holocaust is promoting education about it and about racism and its consequences—activities, which are taking place in Winnipeg and in countless centres elsewhere. Other strategies that have been identified as important in promoting understanding and respect for people who are different from oneself include: understanding of one's own emotions, the ability to think critically, and opportunities to meet with members of other communities. There is a need for more interaction among various ethnic groups. Personally, I would welcome a meeting of Polish and Jewish groups in Canada. I feel an affinity with and appreciate the cultural contributions of both these nationalities.

The Holocaust stirred the conscience of the people of the world by the stark demonstration of men's ability to inflict evil on their fellow beings and probably plays an important part in bettering harmony among humans. Thus, Winnipeg and Canada are now in the forefront of the promotion of the human rights, a tremendous progress compared to sixty years ago. It will always be necessary, however, to fight prejudice and to try preventing genocides and human rights abuses. We must continue our efforts and take measures in these endeavours. Among them we must always keep remembering the Holocaust, because it is our "solemn" trust to commemorate its victims, and because the Holocaust provides a focal point that lends itself well as the trigger to counteracting hate and racism. To forget it would foster indifference, which was an important factor in its perpetration. At the same time it is essential to include together with the Holocaust many other catastrophes, genocides, and large-scale injustices. Even though the Holocaust was unique in the extent and "scientific" methods that the highly cultured Nazis used, the deaths and suffering of many millions of the victims of other genocides, catastrophes, and injustices is an equally essential ingredient of our collective human remembrance and important in the common fight for freedom from discrimination and injustice.

Extreme human suffering must be acknowledged and there is no need for competition for martyrdom. Thus, the killing of the millions of the Polish, Soviet, and other nationals during World War II, the starvations of the Armenians and Ukrainians before the war, the more recent tragedies in the Balkans and Africa, the suffering of the victims of the atomic bombs in Japan, of the aboriginal peoples of the Americas and Australia, and even of the German civilians in the fire storms of the bombed cities during last World War and other persecutions, must be included in the lessons that need to be heeded, and hopefully in the Museum of Human Rights to be built in Winnipeg.

Chapter IX
Visits to Poland
and Retracing the Past

In 1988 after taping the interview of my experiences during the war in Winnipeg, I was invited to an international medical meeting in Toulouse, France to give talks related to my research interests. The meeting was stimulating as I met many colleagues including one from the Soviet Union, and we had an opportunity to sightsee in this mediaeval French city. What was more important, however, was that I decided to go on to visit Poland. I felt that if I were ever to return to the country where I was born and grew up, now was my opportunity. I took it and flew to Warsaw. My younger son Andrew wanted to come with me and he flew to Warsaw from New York, where he was studying. He arrived the day after me.

In my hotel during my first evening after arriving I was looking through the telephone book. The book was old, worn out and a few years old. At the time Poland was still ruled by a communist government and infrastructure, services, and amenities were not easy to obtain. Round table discussions were taking place, which lead eventually to a change in the country's political regime. Leafing through the telephone book I found a listing for my teacher of Polish literature from the Warsaw Ghetto, who I knew survived the war. I phoned him and he remembered me well. We decided that I would contact him later during the visit and hopefully we would get together.

Next day I met my son at the airport and was glad to have him with me. We had a connecting flight booked from Warsaw to Kraków within an hour or so after he arrived, but found that it was leaving from another airport. We dashed there and just made the connection. We were in a small plane. A striking sight was a guard with a rifle in his hands stationed at the back of the compartment. We landed at a small airport outside Kraków and boarded an old bus for the city. It made frequent stops and was full of Polish country farmers. Arriving in the city centre, we went to a tourist office and with the directions we obtained finally chose to stay at a recently built hotel on the outskirts of the city.

During the forty years that I spent mostly in Winnipeg I spoke Polish rarely, only when I visited my family in New York and to a few older patients of Polish or Ukrainian origin in Winnipeg, who did not speak English. Within a couple of days of my arrival my ability to speak Polish seemed to have come back and I spoke it fluently. Many people found it surprising, including my son, and at times forgetting myself, I would start to speak Polish to him. With my son I revisited the famous sites including the city square with the Church of St. Mary, where the trumpeter played *hejnał* from the church tower and the remarkable wooden carvings of the altar sculpted during the fifteenth- century by the famous artist Wit Stwosz. We toured Wawel the grand and remark- able castle of the kings of Poland with its many beautiful structures and many historic sites including the graves of the Polish kings and of its other famous citizens such as the poet Mickiewicz and Marshal Piłsudski. It felt good to see these sites again after fifty years, which I witnessed previously as a youngster during my happy childhood before the war. At the same time it felt somewhat bittersweet, when I thought about seeing them again soon after the war in 1945 when I found my aunt Pola and uncle Edmund and first learned about the death of my dear cousin Tadzik.

Prior to my trip to Europe I contacted a few Polish medical scien- tists. That led to my giving a talk about my work in the department of medicine in Kraków. A very meaningful event was finding and visiting with Mr. Józef, my uncle's family's faithful driver and Mr. Józef's wife. The elderly couple was very glad to see us and most hospitable. It was an emotional experience for my son and me, and most likely for our hosts. Mr. Józef was so helpful to my family from Kraków before, dur- ing, and after the war. We took the opportunity to see an opera *Halka* by the Polish composer Moniuszko. My son, a trained dancer, had a chance to witness a dance rehearsal led by a gracious Russian teacher from the old school in Moscow.

I contacted the local Jewish community and one of its members took us to the Jewish cemetery, where we went to the grave of my cous- in Tadzik, after whom my son Andrew was given his middle name.

Standing there again, decades after his burial, I deeply felt a sense of great loss and sadness. We managed to locate the building that was the villa in which my Kraków family lived before the war.

Figure 17. With Mr. Jósef and wife, Kraków, 1988.

We then set out in a rented car with a driver-guide for Auschwitz and Birkenau and toured these infamous sites of the camps of death. The government built a good highway from Kraków to Auschwitz. The campsite contains well-organized exhibits. There are local guides that take groups of tourists through the camp. We were naturally deeply affected by the sight of the crematoria and other structures and exhibits that bear witness to untold atrocities that took place there during several years of the war. On the wall in a building in Auschwitz we saw the quotation "The one who does not remember history is bound to live through it again" by Santayana.

We then went on to the resort of Rabka and saw the building that before the war housed a sanatorium, which was co-owned by my uncle and where I spent some winter vacations as a young boy. Memories of these happy times poured back into my mind. We continued to Zakopane in the Tatra Mountains. I saw the familiar peak of the Giewont Mountain with its large cross, visible from the town below, which I saw previously in 1939 a few weeks before the outbreak of the war. The village seemed different than how I recalled it. It now reminded me of the crowded streets of Banff. There was a local *góral* (mountaineer) with a sheep dog for rent to take photos with. We did take a photograph and I wondered if the dog might have been a descendant of the one in the picture of my family that I had taken in Zakopane shortly before the outbreak of World War II in August 1939.

The next day the driver took us on a rather long drive to Treblinka. The Nazis destroyed that death camp northeast of Warsaw, where my parents likely perished. Now there are at its site symbolic structures and a field of a huge number of large stones, which represent countries and villages from where the victims that were murdered in the camp's gas chambers came from. One of the rocks is in memory of the educator Janusz Korczak. We left flowers and lit memorial candles that the driver helped us obtain on the way to the camp. I felt overwhelmed by a flood of emotions thinking of my parents and thousands of other compatriots who died here a horrible death. I thought that my son was probably overcome by the emotions at least as much as I was.

The driver then took us to Warsaw where we met a man who worked at the Jewish Historical Institute. The man, Mr. Jan Rochwerger, arranged an apartment for us in the suburbs where we stayed during the rest of our visit and was very hospitable and helpful to us in many ways. I showed my son numerous sites that I knew from before the war. Since most of the city was destroyed during the war, the actual buildings were mostly erected after the war. I found the place where the building Leszno no. 22 stood opposite Orla Street, where I spent my early years. There was there now a small building, which I found out a few years later, is the home of the Warsaw Chamber Opera. We walked through the *Saski* (Saxon) Gardens, where I often played before the war. Close by was the site of the Tomb of the Unknown Soldier with the honour guard and a remnant of the original building that stood there.

We went to the Elektoralna Street where my grandparents lived before the war and where we, as well as the Rechthand family, stayed in the Ghetto. I found the site where my *Spójnia* School was. The place looked similar to how I recalled it. I found the Smolna Street near the large and wide thoroughfare of Nowy Świat (New World) and the building at no. 36, where we lived for a couple of years before the war. Only the upper stories of the building had been destroyed. Again memories of these far away times flashed before my eyes. We went to the beautiful *Łazienki* (Baths) park where I played before the war with chestnuts and where my father took me in a boat on the artificial lake around a summer palace of Poland's last king Stanisław August Poniatowski. Near it was a stage of a summer theatre. My son struck a ballet pose for a photo. We attended a performance at the Warsaw Opera House.

We went to the old city square, where old colourful buildings that I remembered from before the war were well restored. I remembered that my father, when I was about seven- years-old, once took me to the famous winery of *U Fukiera* and let me taste some old Polish mead, the famous drink of Polish nobility over centuries of history. I found a place nearby where we drank a glass of hot mead. We saw the castle of the Polish kings and the residence of its presidents before World War II. The Germans destroyed it during the uprising in 1944. It was beautifully restored after the war and contains many splendid objects of art.

We went to the Jewish Historical Institute named after Emmanuel Ringelblum, the visionary historian who led the collecting of historical materials in the Warsaw Ghetto some of which were found after the war in the ruins of the Ghetto. The institute possessed three paintings by my aunt Stanisława Centnerszwer, which she painted in Białystok where she went with her family after the outbreak of the war and where she and her family later perished when the Białystok Ghetto was liquidated in 1943. A Dr. B. Czajkowska donated the paintings after the war. Who she was I was unable to find out. Unfortunately we could not see the paintings, because they were being exhibited in another city at the time.

I went with my son to the area where my mother and I were attached to a German factory in August and September 1942 and followed our way to the *Umschlagplatz* where I saw my mother for the last time. I felt a feeling of sadness and a sense of awe. My son was affected very much. There was no field there now, but a symbolic marble gate with a rectangular enclosure has been built as a memorial. On the inner walls were etched first names from A to Z of the hundreds of thousands of people who went through that site that led them to their deaths in the gas chambers of Treblinka. Not far from there we found Miła (Pleasant) Street, where there was the bunker of the command of the staff of the Jewish Military Organization in the Ghetto, headed by Mordechai Anielewicz, where he and many fighters perished after fighting Germans for more than two weeks in May 1943. Nearby were two significant structures: a hill with a memorial stone marking the command post and a large monument to the Warsaw Ghetto Fighters in the middle of a large field.

We then visited my professor from the Warsaw Ghetto and his wife; it was a bitter sweet reunion as we talked about the times forty-five years earlier, and about many colleagues and what happened to them. I found out that my bright friend Stefan Kraushar, who wrote a letter to the president of Poland before the war, was now living in Urbana, Illinois, in the USA where he was on the staff of the university. My son, who had no knowledge of Polish, managed to speak French with my Professor's wife, who was very charming. I spent several hours with Dr. Arkadiusz Jawień, who contacted me previously in Canada about my work He came by train from the city of Bydgoszcz, to see and speak with me about our mutual interests and work in the field of vascular disease.

Another moving experience was meeting a lady, who was the widow of a member of the Polish Underground Army during the German occupation. Her husband participated in an abortive attempt to help the Jewish fighters in their uprising of April and May in 1943 to break out of the Ghetto. She lent me a book that dealt with these and related events that I read with interest. We then returned to North America with many memories and photographs.

Later in 1988, I attended a medical meeting in Chicago. Prior to going I was able to contact my friend Stefan Kraushar in Urbana, and Emilee and I drove to visit with him and his family. His wife was a Polish Gentile. They both were social scientists and Stefan, often accompanied by his wife, made many trips to Europe and Poland. He gave lectures in Poland. I was surprised that his mother was still alive and lived with them. It was memorable that I was able to see and speak with this frail ninety-one-year-old lady, who knew my mother and went to the same school with her in Poland. She remembered me as the little "Stefanek", a boy from the pre-war years and referred to me in that way.

Twelve years elapsed before my second visit to Poland. At the time my older son Joel, who was working as an emergency room physician in Duluth, Minnesota, became very interested in seeing the places where his father came from. We met at the airport in Minneapolis and flew to Warsaw in 2000. On the plane we struck up a conversation in English with a Polish man. He was very kind and helpful, almost beyond the call of duty. After we landed he helped us with money exchange. Since he had time, because his train to Poznań was to leave some hours later, he went with us to the train station from where we took a train to Kraków.

Going by train enabled us to see the Polish countryside. Soon after we left Warsaw the train went through a small station of Pruszków. I pointed it out to my son and told him about the events in 1944, when among thousands of Warsaw inhabitants; I went through a makeshift camp in that town set up by the Germans as they were winning the battle for Warsaw from the Polish Underground Army insurgents.

In Kraków, we walked around the inner city ribbon of parkland of Planty and explored the numerous historic sites of that medieval city, which by now was getting blackened by the fallout from the industrial complex of the town Nowa Huta, built nearby after the war. We visited the cemetery where my cousin was buried, and located the building where I lived with my uncle and aunt shortly after the war. I again relived the moments of those far away times and shared them with my son.

The restaurants provided good and interesting fare. We had dinner one evening at a restaurant where a young singer and two accompanying musicians provided entertainment. I asked the singer if she knew my favourite song from before the war "Oh bloom my rosemary". She did and sang it beautifully. The song was appreciated by the dining patrons, but especially by me, as I recalled my childhood when I sang it decades earlier; and by an elderly man, who made a gesture of appreciation towards me.

Various services in Poland were now much more modernized than during my previous visit in 1988 with many easily accessible ATM's and Internet cafes. We visited the Auschwitz-Birkenau complex and my son and I set out on foot for our own "March of the Living", which we completed after initially getting lost. In Birkenau I closed my eyes on the platform where the Nazi's selections for the gas chambers were made. I seemed to be in a daze of light. My son thought that it might have been related to the "selection" at *Umschlagplatz* in Warsaw, where I was separated from my mother in 1942. My son was particularly affected as the atrocities committed on the Jewish people by the Nazis were driven home.

Our driver then took us to the site of the unique and famous salt mines in the town of Wieliczka near Kraków, which I never saw before. We walked hundreds of steps down deep into the mine and saw amazing sites including elaborate sculptures made from salt rock. We then took the train to Warsaw and settled in a hotel. We made a trip by car to Treblinka where I spent moving moments with my older son.

Figure 18. In Treblinka, 2000.

In Warsaw our hotel was in the northern part of the city, not far from the site of the Ghetto and the *Umschlagplatz*. We visited these sites and went to the Jewish Historical Institute. A lady there, with whom I was in communication before coming, had the three paintings of my aunt waiting for us to see. One of them was a portrait of her daughter and my cousin Elżbieta. I was also given a folder full of listings of numerous other paintings of my aunt with Xeroxed copies, presumably from catalogues. I showed my son the sites from the time

Figure 19. With son Joel in Treblinka, 2000.

when I was a youngster in Warsaw. They included the Łazienki (Baths) Park, where my son struck a pose for the photo that resembled the one that my younger son assumed there during the visit in 1988.

Somehow I found out that the Righteous lady, Hanka Herfurt-Gerwel, who lived in western Poland happened to be Warsaw. After speaking with her on the telephone we took a cab to where she was staying with friends. It was an emotional reunion. Besides Hanka, whom I knew well, I met two women about whom I heard a lot from my cousin George after the war but never met them previously. My son was very interested in meeting all three ladies, all of whom knew my cousins and had been their good and helpful friends during the war. Hanka knew exactly the place where my cousin Tadzik was killed in 1944. We went there later and saw a plaque on a building that commemorated the site of the deaths of my cousin and his friends together with many members of the Polish fighting company, which was stationed at the same site as the hospital, in which my cousin worked with distinction during the armed uprising. We stood for a long time in silence near where my cousin was tragically killed in 1944. I remained in contact by mail and telephone with Hanka, who lived in the city of Poznań, over a number of years until she passed away in 2007.

Figure 20. Cousin Elżbieta's portrait by aunt Stasia.

Since my return I have tried to find out more about my relatives and people I knew before the war. I obtained some of the information through contacts with the US Holocaust Museum in Washington and through Professor Daniel Stone of the University of Winnipeg. I came across a book *Revisiting the Shadows* by Irene Shapiro[1], a lady who was one of few survivors of the Białystok Ghetto. I contacted her. She was living in the New York state and so happened that at one time she worked at the Mohegan Colony summer camp, where my wife Emilee worked a number of years earlier. Irene did not know my aunt Stanisława Centnerszwer or her husband, however, she put me in touch with a few people from that city, some residing in Israel, and

Figure 21. With three Righteous Gentiles, Hanna (center) and two friends, Warsaw, 2000.

a Professor in Poland, who specialized in the study of the liquidation of the Jews of Białystok. These contacts and my attempts to find out who was Dr. Czajkowska, the woman who donated my aunt's paintings soon after the war, did not at first succeed.

Apparently the current generation living in that city has no connection to the time some sixty years ago. I found some information about the work of my uncle before the war and about my aunt setting up an exhibit of various items produced by the workers of the Białystok Ghetto to demonstrate to the German authorities the usefulness of the Ghetto's inhabitants. Also, one source reported that my cousin Elizabeth married a Gentile, but remained with her parents and perished with them, rather than trying to save herself by staying with her husband. I do not know who her husband was. I wondered whether Dr. Czajkowska might have known.

Through Yad Vashem I found out about a man who made a deposition about my aunt. He lives in France. I was able to speak with him on the telephone. He knew my aunt but not well. He narrowed down the date of her demise to the second action of the liquidation of the Ghetto in August 1943. I continue trying to see if I might be able to find other paintings of my aunt or a score of my uncle's musical compositions. It is a difficult task. I was able to find out a considerable amount of information about some of my family members and that has made me understand and appreciate them even more. Not surprisingly, the process has been a long one and at times frustrating, because of the long time of a generation or two that elapsed. Yet, it has been most worthwhile and on a couple of occasions I received new information when it seemed that it would not be likely to happen. Only last year I found out that Dr. Czajkowska who donated my aunt's paintings was actually Dr. Berta Szaykowska, a known pediatrician in Białystok during the war, and that a landscape painting of my aunt that was exhibited in Warsaw in 1919 was saved and is in Warsaw. Thus, I intend to persist and continue trying to learn more

The book *Winter in the Morning: A Young Girl's Life in the Warsaw Ghetto and Beyond 1930-1945* by Janina Bauman[2] attracted my attention. She described several of my peers from the Warsaw Ghetto. I contacted her in Britain; we talked about common friends and might well have known each other. She gave me the telephone number of one my peers in Poland and so it came that after sixty-four years I spoke again with Hanka Kon in whose mother's apartment we briefly stayed in 1940 when the Ghetto in Warsaw was first created. A Polish-Jewish Foundation published her memoirs in Canada in Polish. She sent me a copy of her book. We then spoke again a few times and exchanged emails. I was unable to contact Alinka who emigrated to Israel or Ela who went to Australia. I made contact with the group of scholars in Warsaw, who study the Holocaust, and sent to them information on the members of my family. That information is now included in their database of Jews of Warsaw on their website, which contains a lot of valuable data. I also made contact and exchanged information including scans of photographs and documents with the Museum of the 1944 Warsaw Uprising and with the Polish Jewish Museum that collects artifacts to display them when the museum is built in the next two or three years. These contacts made me think again about Yad Vashem and its Hall of Names. Years ago I submitted the names of the members of my family who perished in the Holocaust. There are about three million names in it. I realized, however, that there are some people that I knew who perished but who are not in it. Therefore, I submitted the names of three members of the Rechthand family and of my friend

Staś Koppel. It seems likely that there are others who might know of people who perished in the Holocaust, but who did not think about submitting them; hopefully as many as possible will.

It might be recalled that I was friendly with a fellow survivor; the student Adam Rosenblum in Munich in 1947 and that I lost contact with him after he left Montreal, where he stayed just for a year or so around 1951. After I retired I found the copy of his musical composition, "Symphony", which he gave me when I was leaving for Canada, and thought that I should try to do something about it. I contacted composer Sid Robinovitch, who looked at the score and thought that it was worth pursuing. I arranged for the hand written manuscript to be transferred by a professional copyist into a more manageable form and gave it to Sid to see what he might be able to do with it. He converted it into a piano version. A concert took place at the Berney Theatre at the Asper Jewish Campus on February 17, 2005 as part of the series *Music 'N Mavens* under the title "Recovering Our Musical Heritage". The programme included remarks by Sid Robinovitch and some music by him and by Ernest Bloch. I spoke about Adam Rosenblum, the person I knew long ago. The main highlight of the event, however, was the spirited rendition of Adam's work by the pianist Cheryl Pauls, which was encored at the end of the concert. Bringing Adam's work to life seemed a worthwhile endeavour and a part of the overall effort of many survivors to "bring back to life" the rich heritage of the Jewish people of the continental Europe, and in my case of Poland, where so many Jews resided through most of the thousand years of the Polish history.

CHAPTER X
NEW ENDEVOURS - EPILOGUE

In 1990 we were in New York visiting our families. Emilee wanted to buy a gift for her sister's children and we went into a large bookstore. While Emilee was looking for a proper gift I browsed. I noticed a fairly thick book with a dark blue jacket entitled *The Mozart Compendium*. I bought and read it slowly and thoroughly. It is a detailed guide to Mozart, his life, his times, his personality, and his music, edited by the musicologist H.C. Robbins Landon. The compendium was put together because 1991 was the 200th anniversary of Mozart's death. It occasioned writings, performances, and a great number of celebrations of that musical genius. As I read and reread the book, I listened to very thorough and enjoyable broadcasts by the CBC that dealt with Mozart's life and covered all genres of his music. It stimulated my interest in Mozart, the man and his wonderful music, and over the following decade I read a number of new biographies and listened to and collected recordings of Mozart's music. That experience led to my decision to audit a course in the history of music of the eighteenth-century at the University of Manitoba in 2001, when I was close to a complete retirement and shed most of my professional responsibilities.

The professor, Dr. Kurt Markstrom, was excellent and auditing the course was an exhilarating experience. It was good to attend classes with a group of eager young students. I chose to participate fully, including taking tests and examinations. I encountered some hurdles. I expected the course to deal with the history of the musicians of the time, including Mozart, however, it was clear from the beginning that the course entailed an analysis of musical compositions and required some knowledge of music theory that I did not have. Therefore, I enrolled in additional preparatory studies, one-on-one, with a teacher to quickly pick up some rudiments of the music theory that would allow me to follow the course requirements, which included an assignment of a detailed analysis of a musical work.

The work I chose was Mozart's "Clarinet Trio", because I heard and liked it, but also because our older son played the clarinet and the younger the viola, an unusual pairing of instruments that Mozart composed this work for with a piano. It is a unique and wonderful composition. I threw myself passionately into analyzing it, for which I needed the essential help of my theory teacher, which she willingly provided. I did rather well in that assignment and in the course in general and found the whole experience most gratifying. I also hoped that learning about the musical structure of compositions would allow me to understand and appreciate listening to music even more. To some extent it did in that it provided, as our Professor put it, "a road map" which allowed me to follow compositions and understand what was happening as the music flowed on.

It has been said that music is "a spice of life." It brings joy and pleasure. Yet, men had also used it for other purposes. Music encouraged soldiers to rush into battles through the ages and the Nazis even used it in the death camps, such as Auschwitz to put the arriving victims "at ease" and thus make the work of sending them to their deaths more orderly. In Treblinka, where both my parents likely perished, concerts of classical music were staged, selected by the Nazi henchmen, and performed by the Jewish inmates.

My parents were musicians and I kept returning to music throughout my life. I turned to it again as my professional activities decreased. Personal preferences determine one's favourite compositions. Although I had enjoyed various types of music and compositions by many classic composers, I found now that Mozart's music moved me deeply and as a rule more than that of other composers. It had been said that a large number of words had been written for each note that Mozart composed, but words and music are in different domains, as music is essentially emotional, rather than intellectual. When the course that I audited finished, I felt that I somehow wanted and needed to continue. Mozart as a person, apart from his music, fascinated me. What was that man like, who gave us these invaluable gifts of his genius? As the American biographer Marcia Davenport wrote "Mozart gives ever more impressive proof that there really is immortality; first in his music; then in the fascination that he holds for people of all persuasions and ages." At the same time I found differing opinions about him in various biographies. I decided, therefore, to continue my own study of Mozart and his music. I delved into Mozart family's correspondence and other sources and started writing a Mozart biography for myself.

I also found that there was a close association between music and medicine. In antiquity, music was used to treat disturbed patients; students training to become physicians were required to study music until the seventeenth-century; the healing power of music has been explored more recently to a considerable degree; and a deep interest in music had been held by many physicians. Clyde Gilmour, the late CBC broadcaster, wrote to me, "I don't know how physicians can do it. Our obstetrician had to rush off to the rehearsal of his string quartet, after he delivered our baby." A number of famous doctors whose names we learned, when I was a medical student, I realized much later were also musicians, and physicians have engaged in writing about the health and demise of the famous, including musicians. I myself became interested in Mozart's health and his and his father's deaths.

Mozart was a very human person and struggled with vicissitudes of daily life including family relationships, economic, and other hardships. He tended to be an honest and socially conscious person. He was friendly with a number of Jewish people, and was not concerned that the empress in Vienna, where he lived and worked, was strongly anti-Semitic. His music seems to speak to the soul. His works encompass the whole range of emotions: pure and simple beauty of early divertimentos and the violin concertos, exuberant joy, romance and tenderness in the *sinfonia concertante* for violin and viola and a number of the piano concertos, foreboding and dark moods in the first movements of the piano concertos K. 466 and K. 491 in minor keys, and inner emotional struggles reflected in several string quartets and quintets. Probably foremost, is the feeling of longing felt in the slow movements of several piano concertos. It seems to be the longing for happiness, beauty, and bliss which humans can experience but fleetingly. Mozart's music has a universal appeal. Schubert, quoted by the biographer Solomon, wrote in his diary on June 13, 1816:

> As from afar the magic notes of Mozart's music still gently haunt me....They show us in the darkness of this life a bright, clear, lovely distance, for which we hope with confidence.

O Mozart, immortal Mozart, oh how endlessly many such comforting perceptions of a brighter and better life hast thou brought to our souls!

Allan McPhee, a broadcaster of the Canadian Broadcasting Corporation put it simply: "A day without Mozart is like a day without sunshine."

As I made my way through studies and writings related to Mozart, a few years went by and in 2005 I realized that 2006 was going to mark his 250th birthday. It occurred to me that perhaps there might be some interest in what I wrote. I made enquiries and lo and behold a local publishing company, Heartland Associates, was interested. The process of working with the editors and rewriting and improving my manuscript was a new and interesting experience.

The year from the launch of the book in November 2005 through 2006 was memorable. I attended concerts, signed my book, and gave several talks and presentations about Mozart and his music. Talking about Mozart was for me delightful. To paraphrase what I heard Menahem Pressler of the Beaux Arts Trio say: "I would pay to talk about Mozart." Among others I enjoyed very much being master of ceremony at a special concert of Mozart's music at the St. Bartholomew's Anglican Church in Winnipeg in October 2006.

* * * *

My uncle Edmund, the ophthalmologist and aunt Pauline from Poland lived for a long time in New York. My uncle was busy with his ophthalmology practice. My aunt in her late years visited Poland, where she saw Mrs. Krzeszewska, mother of Danuta, who was killed together with my cousin Tadzik, Pan (Mister) Józef, the family's faithful driver from before the war, and Mrs. Zofia Rechthand, a distant relative, whose family helped us in the Warsaw Ghetto. My uncle and aunt died; he in 1959 and she in 1967. I flew to New York to be with their son, my cousin George (Zdzich) and his family on those sad occasions. George practiced ophthalmology for a very long time. Among his patients were a number of famous people. When he retired several patients wrote to him and expressed their deep appreciation. He is well, travels, and enjoys life in New York City.

As will be recalled my uncle and aunt lost their younger son, my cousin Tadeusz (Tadzik) in the 1944 Warsaw Uprising. He was a wonderful young person. They grieved him when I joined them soon after the war and they continued to feel his loss through the years. This was more evident to me when I was with my aunt. She was the more reserved and withdrawing person of the two. Her feelings are evident in the letter of January 12, 1962, which she wrote to us when our first son was a year old:

> My dear ones,
> For the birthday of the sweet child I send you my heartfelt wishes.
>
> That he be healthy, that he grows to give joy to the family, benefit to people, and distinction among his co-devotees.
>
> It is a pity that I cannot be with you that day. I think about the child very often and miss him. I see in him Tadzik and ask The Highest that he possesses his strength, honest character, noble, sensitive heart, sincerity, courage, intelligence, deep faith, honourable personality and that exceptional charm that gives him the love of those who know him.
>
> I let my thoughts flow, but I do not have people to talk to about him. You know and love him and I know that it is not a product of sick motherly imagination, but sincere truth and that you yourself want to see in him Tadzik's qualities.
>
> Hearty kisses,
> Pola [Grandmother Janka's sister]

My uncle was a rather outgoing and cheerful person, who appeared to adjust fairly well to the new conditions and his life in New York. It was therefore a surprise when many years after his death his son, my cousin George, showed me paper clippings of articles and beautiful poems in rhymed verse that my uncle contributed under a pen name to *Nowy Świat* (New World), a popular Polish newspaper in New York. The poems and articles dealt with his unabated grief concerning the death of his son, Tadzik. They revealed a part of my uncle's nature that was not evident to us from his generally cheerful demeanor in his daily life. An example translated by the author follows.

LETTERS THAT YOU WILL NEVER RECEIVE
IN MEMORY OF A SON

I

I write these words because I miss You
And won't believe that you're gone forever.
My hair grows gray from the sad thoughts
And a hot tear flows from my eye.

It seems to me, that you're among us
That any moment you'll open Your mouth.
Devout dream deceives my senses
Surrounded by silence, sad, dead and empty.

I see Your face, cheerful and radiant
And hear Your voice, humming merry tune.
But in my brain pulses but one thought
That you left and never ... will return.

I cannot forget Your flaxen hair
And I won't believe that You're so far
Graveyard thoughts race through my head
And a hot tear flows from my eye.

II

I wish that You knew that here on earth
I live and always think of you.
My feelings for You will never change
Till my remains rest in a cold grave.

I wish that You knew that I'm always with You
With my being and heart and soul
And I swear on all that is sacred
That I will never, never forget You.

I wish that You knew: love shall prevail
Until the blood drains from my veins.
Ah, when You left me in this world
Happiness for me had ended.

III

And yet I live, though can't understand
How one can live, with my heart
Ripped from my body; a precious life.
But without my soul that flew with You.

You were for me, like fertile depths,
Without which there can be no life here on earth.
No wonder that emptiness permeates all without you
That despair blasphemes at times in prayer.

At times Your soul deceives me in dreams.
I beg: that miracle might occur,
That you'll come to me alive, laughing,
That we'll embrace in a moment of life returned.

When my soul flew away with You,
I lost my heart, worthier than dear life.
How can the body live without one's heart?!
And yet I live, though can't understand.

IV

And when time comes for my life to end
I wish, that I dream of Your face
Easier will be to leave in my son's eyes
And lighter will be the grave above.

I wish to see you, as during uprising.
When you promised gravely in Warsaw:
"Father! In three days Poland will be free."
You imagined, dreamt, of true happiness.

I remember, how you stood tall
When full of hope and songs of victory.
Naive father's heart did not think
That You shall not return.

Let sadness ebb away, dress the body,
When time comes for my life to end.
Dress in the best what remains.
I wish to sparkle when meeting my son.

V

I dreamt again that I was with You.
You were delightful and so gay.
My heart beat happily with new vigor.
As if angels came with You.

I again dreamt that I was with You
And we talked as we did long ago.
We knew not, how time was passing,
You my happiness, my winged bird!

When You flew away from me in this world,
Consciousness left my body.
I was unaware of my dreadful loss
And nothing was left of my happiness.

There came grave doctors,
They began to examine my body,
I made a better diagnosis:
My heart loved too much and broke.

* * * *

Our older son Joel obtained his bachelor of physical degree in Calgary, and then worked in the cardiovascular section at the Children's Hospital in Winnipeg, took some additional courses and enrolled in medicine. He graduated in 1991 and was class valedictorian. He then worked for a number of years as an emergency room physician before taking a fellowship in palliative care. He now works in that field in Minneapolis.

In addition to his professional work he has engaged in creative writing, published a number of articles and a couple of books, and is interested in story telling as a way of healing. He told me that his preliminary results showed that after patients in palliative care told an important story of their life, they felt generally better and their pain diminished. My son married a wonderful young lady Natalia from Uruguay. She is an internist. We are now proud grandparents of a beautiful three-year-old granddaughter and a year old grandson. Our younger son Andrew followed an artistic career that took him to New York. He obtained his bachelor's and master's degrees in fine art and has worked as a dancer, choreographer, and theatre director. Some years ago we were proud to attend the performance of his successful play at the Fringe Festival in Toronto. He is also an excellent practitioner of Pilates and Feldenkreis techniques that assist people in improving and maintaining their health.

Nowadays we continue to enjoy art and other events in the city at a more leisurely pace. The choice is broad. Also there are classes that one can take in the community centres in all parts of town, programmes run by the Creative Retirement Manitoba, Manitoba Society of Seniors, and courses on a wide range of subjects offered by the universities. Emilee continued to paint and garden. I listen to music and play the recorder occasionally. I also took lessons in playing clarinet and was able to play some of the beloved compositions of Mozart, although not very well. I took up badminton, a game I enjoy greatly. Although I will never master it, it is a good exercise that must have a salutary influence on my health and I meet many congenial young and older players. I have done some cycling, and in the winter cross-country skiing; the latter a few times in Manitoba provincial parks, of which Spruce Woods was the most beautiful, but mostly in the parks around the city. I have also done some biking and jogging.

About twelve years ago Emilee suggested that we go to a yoga class; she remembered a course she took during our early years in Winnipeg at our community centre. We took classes for a couple of years and I started to practice yoga daily. I then read the book *Full Catastrophe Living* by Dr. Jon Kabat-Zinn, which became my guiding text. It deepened my appreciation of meditation and yoga and led to the evolution of my daily practice that I adhere to regularly. I feel that it is an important part of my life and that it helps me to maintain equilibrium, enjoy life, and deal with its bumps.

I have been very fortunate that I was able to lead a full life in which I met many interesting people and witnessed important events and natural beauty. I was able to start a family and make a modest contribution by my endeavours. About seventy-five percent of my life was spent in Canada, a country that gave countless immigrants an opportunity to live a meaningful and productive life. Over the past half a century or so Canada transformed itself from a state of two founding nations that reluctantly tolerated immigrants and the aboriginal people into a multi-ethnic country of people from practically all over the world living together in peace and relative harmony.

I wondered, as did other survivors of the Holocaust, why did I survive among those few that denied Nazis their desire to annihilate us all? I felt, as did some others, that luck played a large part, but undoubtedly I would not have survived without the members of my family and the Righteous Polish Gentiles, who were an important part of this story. I hope that they will be remembered. I wondered what I would have done if I were the one who saw, from outside, what the Nazis were doing to the Jews. Would I have acted to help the victims or stood silently by, indifferent or fearful for my own safety? I do not know. Humans, when in power, have ways of manipulating others in various ways, apart from threats and torture. At the same time, individuals have personal and group resources that can allow them to resist pressures and thwart the criminals.

Why do people perpetrate heinous crimes on their fellow human beings? The reasons might be inherent in the biological instinct of self-preservation, and probably more importantly, in the distinctly human need for "recognition" as discussed by Francis Fukuyama in his book *The End of History and the Last Man*.[1] This latter need is postulated to be what drives humans to the "fight to the death" for prestige and recognition by others. The pent-up need for recognition in our modern society seems to manifest itself vicariously by identification with sport heroes or teams including violence, both between competitors and between their fans. The European soccer hooligans are a prime example.

That same need for recognition while fraught with dire consequences, however, is likely also the force that leads to creativity and new developments. Over the course of recent history the civilization progressed immensely, including the development of liberal democracy ("the end of history"), a political system that provides its citizens with "recognition" based on the principles of freedom and equality.

Figure 22. From left Emilee, Joel, Andrew, Stefan, Joel's wife Natalia, Winnipeg, 2005.

Yet, freedom and equality are mutually limiting, as my professor of history taught me in the clandestine school in the Warsaw Ghetto.

In the liberal democratic countries of today freedom allows some people to become very successful and much more recognized than others, rendering the society unequal. It seems that there is a caste of powerful or outstanding at the top of the pecking order, including CEO's and sport stars that are paid astronomical salaries and a poor and disenfranchised caste at the bottom. In between the middle class forms a large proportion of the population and contains many grades of "equality". Thus, human history does not seem to have ended. The fine-tuning of the checks and balances of liberal democracies needs to be constantly attended to in order to maintain a necessary balance between freedom and equality.

The rapidity of the progress attained by the human species has been amazing. During a period of time that is miniscule, compared to the time that life has existed on earth, our ancestors spread out throughout the globe. With the beginning of agriculture some ten thousand years ago the growth of the human population accelerated and a hierarchical class system appeared in the societies. The population explosion, which might soon be controlled, and spreading consumerism contributed to the use of large amounts of natural resources. The advent and development of technology and flourishing consumerism seem to lead to a climate change with untoward consequences. I am continually amazed at the amount of the commercial inserts in our daily newspaper, which I chuck into a recycling bin without looking at them. Similarly, I am annoyed by the frequent telephone calls of telemarketers, which disturb us almost daily. At the same time humans ventured into space and landed on the moon.

While medicine conquered a number of diseases and, at least in the developed countries, people live much longer, this is leading to a higher proportion of aging population susceptible to various health problems such as the Alzheimer's disease. Human genetic evolution proceeds at a much slower pace than the scientific progress. For example, overeating and the "epidemic" of obesity that we now witness might be related to the time when our ancestors ate as much as possible when feasting on the meat of a hunted animal to store the nutrients in their bodies, because they had no refrigerators.

The decoding of the Human Genome Project opened a vast field for potential benefits. It should be feasible to conquer a number of diseases and perhaps even modify the human nature. It would indeed be wonderful if in the future humans were "Righteous." That might entail application of empathy to our fellow human beings and accommodation of their need for recognition. Some initial steps in that direction are occurring in the European Union, where nations that warred bitterly for centuries, are co-existing in peace, and where social nets provide security to those that are at the lower end of the social scale brought about by the flux between freedom and equality. This empathy seems to be equivalent of the third part of the motto of the French revolution—Fraternité, which may be necessary to provide the balance to the Liberté and Egalité. Now it is but a hazy dream in a distant future and it might not be feasible or even desirable, if it would entail interference with the innate drive for recognition that fuels human striving and defines what it means to be human. Thus, we might be able to modify human behaviour in addition to achieving it by the use of psychotropic drugs and, for example, alcohol.

In the various future endeavours, humanity must proceed with great caution and put in place a system of strict checks to guard against unintended and deleterious consequences as was suggested by Fukuyama.[2] The world of our children is infinitely more complex than ours was. We wish them and subsequent generations wisdom and success.

APPENDIX 1

"O Lithuania, my fatherland,
Thou art like health; what praise thou shoudst command
Only that man finds who has lost thee quite.
Today I see, and limn, thy beauty bright
In all its splendor, for I yearn for thee.

O holy Virgin, who dost oversee
Bright Czenstochowa and in Wilno shinest
Above the Ostra Gate! Thou who inclinest
To shelter Nowogrodek with its folk
In Faithfulness. When I, in youth, bespoke
Thy help, by miracle thou didst restore
My failing health; when my sad mother bore
Me to thy seat, my deathlike eyes I raised;
Walked to the threshold of thy shrine amazed;
And thanked God for health brought back to me –
So by a miracle thou wilt decree
That we regain our country. Meanwhile bear
To those treed hills my spirit of despair,
To those green meadows, stretching far and wide
By the blue Niemen; to those grain-fields pied
With hues of various harvest, gold with wheat,
Silvered with rye, where mustard-blossoms meet
With buckwheat white as snow; where clover glows
As with a girl's blush; and green turf-strip bows
Engirdle all the earth with ribbons rare,
As quiet pear-trees slumber here and there."

APPENDIX 2

"Many were players of that instrument
But none of them would venture to perform
In Jankiel's presence. (Since that night of storm,
Jankiel had spent the winter none knew where;
But now he suddenly had joined them there
In company with Poland's General Staff.)'"

"Two of his pupils meanwhile gave their aid,
 Knelt by the dulcimer, tuned fresh the strings,
And twanged them as a test of readyings.
Jankiel with half-closed eyes in silence lingers
And holds the hammers sleeping in his fingers.
He lowered them in a triumphal beat,
Then smote the strings again with brisker heat,
As with a shower of rain: all were amazed,
Yet this was but a test that he played;
He stopped, and raised both hammers up aloft.

He played anew; the strings now trembled soft
With motions light as though a fly's faint wing
Sounded a gentle buzz upon the string.
The master gazed intently at the sky
For inspiration; with a haughty eye
He looked down at his silent instrument;
Then raised both hands, dropped them with firm intent
And with both hammers all the strings coerced.

Then all at once from many strings there burst
A sound as though a janissaries' band
With cymbals, bells and drums made glad the land.
The *Polonaise* that marked the Third of May †
Came thundering forth! The rippling notes were gay

---

*   The Polish General Staff arrived with the Polish Legions and Napoleon's army
and temporarily liberated Lithuanian territories in 1811.

†   The constitution of May 3, 1791. By the terms of it the burghers were granted
full equality before the law, the peasantry was placed under the protection of the
government.

And in one's ears they poured a breath of joy;
Girls wished to dance and each impatient boy
Could not stand still-but thoughts of older men
Into the blessed past were borne again,
Those happy years when Deputies and Senate
On that great day saw Liberty's proud tenet
Made perfect in the reconciliation,
That Third of May, between both King and Nation,
"Vivat our King!" then sang the dancing masses,
"Vivat the Diet, people and all classes!"

   The master kept on quickening the time
And ever played with power more sublime;
But suddenly a false note sounded crass-
A snake's hiss or the scratch of steel on glass-
A shudder through the listeners wandered free
And mingled with the general gaiety
An ominous foreboding. All alarmed,
Men wondered if the instrument were harmed
Or if the player's hand had made a blunder.
With such a master lay no cause for wonder!
He purposely kept touching that foul chord
To mar the music with its note abhorred;
Louder and louder still its angry moans
Make plot against the harmony of tones;
At last the Warden understood the master,
Covered his face, in sorrow of disaster,
And cried: "I know those notes too well;
They speak of Targowica*, foul as hell!"

And suddenly the bad string hissed and broke,
The player to the high strings swept his stroke,
Confused the measure, left the treble race,
And hurried with his hammers to the bass.
   A thousand notes ever louder warmed,

---

* A place in the Ukraine where a confederation of Polish-Lithuanian nobility took place that opposed the Polish Constitution of May 3, 1791. Subsequently signed on April 27, 1792 in Saint Petersburg with the backing of Empress Catherine II of Russia.

Of measured marching, war, a city stormed;
One heard reports of guns, and children's groaning,
And mothers in the rape and slaughter moaning,
So well the master all these crimes dissembled
That all the village girls in terror trembled,
Calling to mind, with teardrops not a few,
The massacre of Praga*, which they knew
From song and story; they were glad at last
When the great master from those horrors passed,
Thundering on all the strings a blast of dearth
As if crushed all outcries in the earth.

Scarce had his startled hearers grown estranged
From wonder, when once more the music changed:
First there were only light and gentle hummings,
A few thin strings mourned jointly in their strummings
Like flies that strive to leave the spiders' web.
But more strings mounted upwards from the ebb;
Now scattered tones were blended in the flood,
And legions of rich chords united stood;
Now they advanced with measured steps and strong
In the sad music of that famous song
About the wandering soldier who must travel
Through woods and forests as his days unravel;
He often faints with woe and hunger's need,
And falls at last beside his faithful steed,
Who with his hoof paws out his master's grave-
A poor old song, yet very dear to brave
And wistful Polish troops. The soldiers knew it
And crowded round the master to ensue it;
They hearkened, and remembered that dream season
When by their country's grave they had with reason
Sung that same song and joined the exile's train;
They called to mind long years of wandering pain,
Mid foreign peoples, over sea, and land,

---

* The massacre of the Warsaw suburb of Prague on November 4, 1794, when Russian forces took Warsaw by storm. This marked the end of Tadeusz Kościuszko's insurrection.

Oppressed by winter frost and burning sand,
When by this song they had been comforted,
As thus they thought, they sadly bowed the head!

But raised it straightaway as the master's fire
Blazed out in music that was stronger, higher;
He changed his measure and proclaimed a theme
As different as daylight is from dream.
Once more his eye looked down, the strings to note;
Then suddenly he joined his hands and smote
With both hammers: such skilful blow,
So powerful, that from the loud strings flow
Great brazen trumpet-tones in which is given
A well-known song that mounted to heaven,
A march of triumph: "Poland not yet dead:
March, march Dombrowski, at our legions' head,
To Poland!" And all clapped and cried in chorus:
March, march, Dombrowski, to our land, before us!"

The master seemed amazed at his own song;
He dropped the hammers from his fingers strong
And raised his arms aloft; his fox-skin cap
Was tumbling all unnoticed to his lap;
His beard uplifted waved in majesty;
A flush upon his cheeks glowed strange to see;
His zealous glances showed a youthful blaze.
But when at last the old man turned his gaze
Upon Dombrowski, he made hide his spheres,
And through his fingers gushed a stream of tears.

"My General," said he. "this land we use
Has long awaited you, just as we Jews
Have looked for the Messiah; from of old
Your coming was by prophecies foretold,
Your onset marked by marvels in the sky.
Live then and wage our wars, before we die …"

As the Jew spoke, he sobbed; with honest soul
He'd loved his country as a very Pole!

Dombrowski with a clasp his warm thanks planned,
But Jankiel doffed his cap and kissed his hand.

ENDNOTES

Notes to Chapter I

1 Sachar Abram Leon. A History of the Jews. New York: Knopf, 1948,: 223.

2 Sachar, 223-235.

3 Gutman Yisrael and Shmuel Krakowski. Unequal Victims. New York: Holocaust Library, 1986, : 23

4 Sachar. 378-379.

5 Gutman and Krakowski. 1-26.

6 Paulson Gunnar S. Secret City, The Hidden Jews of Warsaw 1940-1945. New York: Yale University Press, 2002.

7 Patalas Kazimierz ed. Providence Watching; Journeys from Wartorn Poland to the Canadian Prairie,Winnipeg: University of Manitoba Press, 2003, : 158.

8 Potocki S. and Praźmowska T., eds., Polski Słownik Biograficzny (Polish Biographical Dictionary). Polska Akademia Nauk (Polish Academy of Sciences). Wrocław: 1985, Vol. XXVIII/2, part 117,: 342-346, (Polish).

9 Fuks Marian, Hoffman Zygmunt, Horn Maurycy, and Tomaszewski Jerzy, eds., THE POLISH JEWRY: History and Culture. Warsaw: Interpress Publishers, 1982, : 78.

10 Sandal Józef. Murdered Jewish Artists in Poland. Warsaw: 1957, 44-49, (Yiddish)

11 Fuks, Hoffman, Horn, and Tomaszewski, eds.,:70.

12 Fuchs. Muzyka Ocalona, Judaica Polskie, (Saved Music, Polish Judaica). Warsaw: Radio and Television Publications, 1989,: 138, 139 (Polish)

13 Humiński Józef ed. Słownik muzyków Polskich (Dictionary of Polish Musicians). Warsaw: Polskie Wydawnictwo Muzyczne (Polish Musical Publication), 1962: 61, (Polish)

14 Fater Isachar. Jewish Music in Poland Between the Two World Wars. Tel Aviv: World Federation of Polish Jews, 1970: 362, (Yiddish)

15 Fater. The Sacred and Profane in Jewish Music. The conference of Jewish writers, Jerusalem: H. Laivik., 1988, :185 (Yiddish).

16 Fuks. Musical Traditions of Polish Jews. Translated by Maria Piłatowicz.

Polish Music Journal. 6, no. 1, Summer 2003.

17 Mickiewicz Adam. Pan Tadeusz or The Last Foray in Lithuania, Translated by Watson Kirkconnel, New York: University of Toronto Press, 1962.

18 Mickiewicz, 7.

19 Mickiewicz, 362-3.

Notes to Chapter II

1   Roland Charles G. Courage under Siege. New York: Oxford University Press, 1992.

2   Engelking Barbara and Jacek Leociak. Getto Warszawskie, Przewodnik po Nieistniejącym Mieście (The Warsaw Ghetto, A Guide to the Perished City). Warsaw: IfiS Pan, 2001, (Polish).

3   Engelking and Leociak, 668

4   Fuks Marian. Musical Traditions of Polish Jews, translated by Maria Piłatowicz, Polish Music Journal 6, no. 1, Summer 2003.

5   Gutman and Krakowski, 167.

6   Hirshaut Julien. Jewish Martyrs of Pawiak. New York: Holocaust Library, 1982.

7   Paulsson Gunnar S., 165.

Notes to Chapter III

1   Gutman and Krakowski, 365-370.

2   Gutman and Krakowski, 370-374.

3   Arad Yitzak, The Partisan; From the Valley of Death to Mount Zion. New York: Holocaust Library, 1979,: 179.

4   Arad, 190.

Notes to Chapter IV

1   Fine Jonathan. Anti-Semitism in Manitoba in the 1930s and 40s. Manitoba History, 32, (1996): 26-33.

2   Moore Terrence. Quotas' End, Manitoba Medicine, 59, (1989): 29-31.

3   Moore Terrence. Crumbling Foundation: The Medical School and the Depression, Manitoba Medicine, 58, (1988): 139-144.

4   Mitchell Grant. Personal communication.

5   Barsky, Percy. How 'Numerus Clausus' was ended in the Manitoba Medical School. Jewish Historical Society of Canada Journal, 1, no.2, (1977) : 75-81.

6   Rogers Arnold. Essay, unpublished – Archives, Faculty of Medicine, University of Manitoba.

7   Cherniack Saul. Personal communication.

8   Loffman Morris. Justice Triumphs: The Eradication of Racial Discrimination at the University of Manitoba Medical College. Address at the 50th reunion of class of 1954, Faculty of Medicine, University of Manitoba, June 2004.

9   Levi, Charles "There is a definite limitation imposed" (Robin Ross to Claude Bissell, December 4, 1959), The Jewish Quota in the Faculty of Medicine, University of Toronto: Generational Memory Sustained by Documentation,   http;//library.queensu.ca/ojs/index.php/edu_hse-rhe/article/view/477.

10   Moore Terrence. Joe Doupe; Bedside Physiologist. Toronto: Hannah Institute & Dundurn Press, 1989.

Notes to Chapter VI

1   Cousins Norman. Anatomy of an Illness,. New York: Bantam Books, 1979.

2   Kabat-Zinn Jon. Full Catastrophe Living: Using the Wisdom of Your body and Mind to face Stress, Pain and Illness. New York: Bantam Doubleday Dell Publishing Group Inc., 1990.

3   Thompson W. Grant. The Placebo Effect and Health: Combining Science and Compassionate Care. New York: Prometheus Books, 2005.

Notes to Chapter VII

1   Downs Allan. Recruitment and Retention of Canadian Graduates in Canada. Manitoba Medicine, (Fall 2007): 12 -14.

Notes to Chapter VIII

1   The Holocaust Remembered, A Publication of The Holocaust Awareness Committee of the Winnipeg Jewish Community Council, Summer 2002.

2   Stambrook Fred and Bert Friesen eds. A sharing of diversities: Proceedings of the Jewish Mennonite Ukrainian Conference: "Building bridges". Regina: The Canadian Plains Research Center, 1999.

3   Kühl Stefan. The Nazi Connection: Eugenics, American Racism and German National Socialism. New York: Oxford University Press, 1994, 20; quoted in "Medicine Against Society", JAMA 276, no. 20, (1996) 1657-1661.

4   Fukuyama Francis. Our Posthuman Future, Consequences of the Biotechnology Revolution. New York, Farrar, Straus and Giroux, 2002.

5   Chalaskiewicz Stefan, Ukrywałem się w Warszawie (I was hiding in Warsaw). Kraków: Społeczny Instytut Wydawniczy, Znak (Social Publication Institute, Mark), 1988, 51, (Polish).

6   Gutman and Krakowski, 252 – 299.

7   Kunert Andrzej Krzysztof ed. Żegota, The Council for Aid to Jews, 1942-1945. Warsaw: Rada Ochrony Pamięci Walk i Męczeństwa (Council for the Protection of Memory of Struggle and Martyrdom), 2002.

8   Paulsson, 202.

9   Paulsson Gunnar S. Secret City; the Hidden Jews of Warsaw 1840-1945. New Haven: Yale University Press, 2002.

10 Gutman and Krakowski, 58 –142.

11I Laqueur Walter. The Terrible Secret; Suppression of the Truth about Hitler's Final Solution. New York: Henry Holt and Company, 1980.

12 Laqueur Walter and Breitman Richard. Breaking the Silence. New York: Simon and Schuster, 1986.

13 Karski Jan. How One Man Tried to Stop the Holocaust. New York: E. Thomas Wood and Stanisław M. Jankowski, John Wiley & Sons, Inc., 1994.

14 Mendelsohn Shelomo. The Battle of the Warsaw Ghetto. New York: The Yiddish Scientific Institute-YIVO, 1944.

15 Nowak Jan. Courier from Warsaw, Detroit: Wayne State University Press, 1982, 275.

16 Nowak. 274.

17 Gilbert Martin. Auschwitz and the Allies. London: Michael Joseph/Rainbird, 1981.

18 Gilbert. 340-341.

19 Gilbert. 322.

20 Novick Peter. Atrocity's Yardstick. University of Chicago Magazine, 91, nos. 5 & 6, (1999): 17-21.

21 Engelking and Leociak. Getto Warszawskie, Przewodnik po Nieistniejącym Mieście (The Warsaw Ghetto, A Guide to the Perished City), (Warsaw: IfiS Pan, 2001), (Polish).

22 Karski. 255-6.

23 Gruber Ruth. Haven; The unknown story of 1000 World War II refugees. New York: Coward-McCann Inc., 1983.

24 Hilliard Robert. Surviving the Americans, the Continued Struggle of the Jews after Liberation. New York: Seven Stories Press, 1997.

25 CBC Archives, http://archives.cbc.ca/war_conflict/second_world_war/clips/10644

26 Abella Irving and H. Troper, None is Too Many. Toronto: Lester & Orpen Dennys, 1986.

27 Abella and Troper, 284.

28 Smith Frank Dabba. The Greatest Invention of the Leitz Family: The Leica Freedom Train. New York: American Photographic Historical Society, 2002.

29 Stone Daniel. Gentile Heroism during Holocaust. Holocaust Remembered, A Publication of The Holocaust Awareness Committee of the Winnipeg Jewish Community Council, 2, no. 1, (1996) : 2.

30 Thumin Silk Susan. Regret. The Hidden Child, Newsletter of Hidden Child Foundation, XV, (2007): 1-5.

Notes to Chapter IX

1 Shapiro Irene. Revisiting the Shadows. Elk River, MN, DeForest Press, 2004.

2 Bauman Janina. Winter in the Morning. A Young Girl's Life in the Warsaw Ghetto and Beyond 1930-1945. New York: The Free Press, 1986.

Notes to Chapter X

1 Fukuyama Francis. The End of History and the Last Man. New York: The Free Press, A Division of MacMillan, Inc., 1992.

2 Fukuyama Francis. Our Posthuman Future: Consequences of the Biotechnology Revolution. New York: Farrar, Straus and Giroux, 2002.

INDEX OF NAMES